PLATES
of GOLD
The Book of Mormon Comes Forth

ALSO BY MATTHEW B. BROWN:

Symbols in Stone: Symbolism on the Early Temples of the Restoration
(with Paul Thomas Smith)

*The Gate of Heaven: Insights on the Doctrines and
Symbols of the Temple*

All Things Restored: Confirming the Authenticity of LDS Beliefs

The Plan of Salvation: Doctrinal Notes and Commentary

* * * *

available in book
or audio book
from Covenant

PLATES
of GOLD

The Book of Mormon Comes Forth

MATTHEW B. BROWN

Covenant Communications, Inc.

Covenant

Published by Covenant Communications, Inc.
American Fork, Utah

Printed in Canada
First Printing: November 2003

09 08 07 06 05 04 03   10 9 8 7 6 5 4 3 2 1

ISBN 1-59156-370-4

CONTENTS

INTRODUCTION

Most Latter-day Saints are familiar with the general details of the coming forth of the Book of Mormon in the days of Joseph Smith. They know of the visitations of the angel Moroni, the retrieval of the golden plates from the hill called Cumorah, and the extraordinary experience of the Three Witnesses. But there are many fascinating and lesser-known details of the saga that are seldom told and sometimes even forgotten, such as Moroni's announcement in 1823 that the Aaronic and Melchizedek Priesthoods would be restored and accounts of people who were allowed to handle the plates two years before the official Eight Witnesses had their chance to do so.

This book gathers together these scattered and neglected historical fragments and combines them with their more familiar counterparts, allowing readers to study and enjoy a richer and more complete story than has been previously available in one source.

Readers can anticipate that as they follow this book's chronological path, they will be rewarded along the way with numerous insights and an expanded vision of past events. For example, one intriguing detail seldom noted is that the day on which Joseph Smith received the plates of gold was an important Israelite holy day. And on this same day Heber C. Kimball and others saw a vision of a battle taking place in the heavens. The reader will also learn that when David Whitmer and Oliver Cowdery saw the golden plates in their official capacity as witnesses they also saw many other items that they had not anticipated seeing.

In addition to telling an important and engaging story, the material in this book offers a view of the full range of human experience—

from the truly sublime to the truly absurd. On some pages the reader will gain a sense of what it is like to stand in the presence of beings from beyond the veil—to gaze upon their shining countenances; to hear their heaven-sent words; to be overwhelmed by the spiritual force that attends their presence. On other pages will be found the account of how Abner Cole tried to start a fistfight with Joseph Smith because the Prophet wouldn't allow him to illegally reproduce portions of the Book of Mormon.

The four appendices found at the end of this volume have been designed to provide a sharper picture of this segment of Latter-day Saint history. The first examines in detail the objects that Joseph Smith found in the stone box near the top of the Hill Cumorah. The second attempts to explain (through a variety of historical sources) how the Book of Mormon was translated by Joseph Smith. The third is a unique contribution; it is a step-by-step explanation of how the first edition of the Book of Mormon was printed and bound. And the fourth appendix consists of a rebuttal to an 1834 anti-Mormon argument about the origin of the Book of Mormon.

The reader should be made aware that some of the quotations in this book have been standardized to reflect modern spelling, punctuation, capitalization, and grammar. The modifications have been done carefully, however, to ensure that their proper content and context have been preserved.

It is the sincere hope of the author that all those who examine the contents of this volume will gain a better appreciation for how the Book of Mormon came before the world and also find within themselves the motivation to examine and contemplate the Book of Mormon itself. It is "Another Testament of Jesus Christ," the Son of the living God. It contains the word of the Lord and will bless the lives of those who accept it, cherish it, and live by its precepts.

CHAPTER 1

THE VISITATIONS OF MORONI

As the sun slowly disappeared behind the tops of the trees in Palmyra, New York, the townspeople were unaware that on the outskirts of their settlement a new religious dispensation was about to dawn. It was the evening of 21 September 1823, and seventeen-year-old Joseph Smith Jr. made his way up a narrow set of stairs and emerged into the loft of his family's woodland home.

Three years previous to this time Joseph had gone to the Lord in prayer, seeking an answer to the question of which religious denomination he should join. In response to his petition God the Father and His Son Jesus Christ visited young Joseph and informed him that none of the religions of his day had divine sanction. Joseph was expressly forbidden to join himself with any of these sects but was promised that if he remained faithful, the pure gospel of the Savior would eventually be revealed to him.

During the period of time between his First Vision and September 1823, Joseph, like many other young men, was confronted with all kinds of temptations and subsequently "fell into many foolish errors and displayed the weakness of youth." But Joseph realized in his heart that his unwise actions were offensive in the sight of God, and he often felt a sense of condemnation for his imperfections.[1]

Joseph Smith reports that during the evening of 21 September, he meditated upon his past life and the experiences that he had gone through. "I was very conscious that I had not kept the commandments," he said, "and I repented heartily for all my sins and transgression."[2] After humbling himself, Joseph began to petition God in prayer for the forgiveness of all of his sins and follies. In addition to this request, he asked for a divine manifestation whereby he could know of his state and standing before the Lord.[3] "All he desired," said Oliver Cowdery in a rehearsal of the tale, "was to be prepared in heart to commune with some kind messenger who could communicate to him the desired information of his acceptance with God."[4]

Joseph continued to offer up his supplications even after the other members of his family had fallen asleep. A number of hours passed by as he focused his mind on the object of his petition and poured out the desires of his soul. It might have been 11:00 P.M., midnight, or even later,[5] but he was still "awake, and in solemn prayer."[6]

MORONI'S FIRST VISITATION

Joseph recalled that a bright, pure, and glorious light suddenly burst into the room. It "was as though the house was filled with consuming and unquenchable fire. This sudden appearance of a light so bright . . . occasioned a shock or sensation, visible to the extremities of the body. It was, however, followed with a calmness and serenity of mind, and an overwhelming rapture of joy that surpassed understanding."[7] The light, said Joseph, "continued to increase until the room was lighter than at noon-day."[8]

In a moment, a personage appeared,[9] standing in the air.[10] And "notwithstanding the room was previously filled with light above the brightness of the sun," says Oliver Cowdery, "yet there seemed to be an additional glory surrounding or accompanying this personage, which shone with an increased degree of brilliancy, of which he was in the midst."[11] The personage "was a little above the common size of men in this age"[12] and wore an exceedingly white, seamless robe that was evidently tied at the waist with a sash.[13] Joseph said that the personage was not only "clothed with purity inexpressible,"[14] but, interestingly, even his hands and feet were pure and white.[15] Indeed, said Joseph, "his whole person was glorious beyond description."[16] Oliver recounts that "though his countenance was as lightning, yet it was of a pleasing, innocent and glorious appearance."[17]

Introduction and Announcements

"When I first looked upon him I was afraid," said Joseph, "but the fear soon left me."[18] One late but intriguing secondhand source claims that the personage spoke with "a voice sweeter than music."[19] From the Prophet's own account we learn that he called Joseph by name,[20] identified himself by the name Moroni,[21] and indicated his origin, saying, "I am a messenger sent from God."[22]

The first message delivered by this angel was an answer to Joseph Smith's prayer. According to Oliver Cowdery the messenger proceeded to inform the young man that "his own sins were forgiven, and his former transgressions to be remembered against him no more, if he then continued to walk before the Lord according to His holy commandments." This heaven-sent declaration reportedly filled Joseph's heart with a feeling of indescribable joy.[23]

Moroni then began to give a multitude of instructions to his earthbound student. He informed Joseph that God had a work for him to do,[24] and he had been "chosen to be an instrument in the hands of God to bring about some of His purposes in this glorious dispensation."[25] Because of the work that he had been selected to carry out, said the angel, Joseph's name was destined to be "had for good and evil, among all nations, kindreds, and tongues; or that it should be both good and evil spoken of among all people."[26]

Moroni is said in one source to have explained the nature of God's work by telling Joseph "of the corruptions of Christendom,"[27] evidently meaning that he told him about the Great Apostasy. A similar idea is put forward by Katherine Smith, the Prophet's sister. She claims the angel said that the gospel Joseph was familiar with "had been adulterated," and therefore "there was no true Church on earth."[28] But, explained Moroni, "the covenant which God made with ancient Israel was at hand to be fulfilled, that the preparatory work for the second coming of the Messiah was speedily to commence." Therefore, "the time was at hand for the gospel, in all its fullness, to be preached in power unto all nations that a people might be prepared for the Millennial reign."[29] In connection with the preceding concepts Moroni then told Joseph about a small group of Israelites that came to the Americas "from Jerusalem by the direct guidance of the Almighty, some six centuries before Christ; [and] that in a vessel, which they built by the command of God, they came round by the Gulf of Arabia [and] crossed the great Pacific Ocean."[30] These were, according to Oliver Cowdery's version of the angel's words, "an enlightened and intelligent people" who possessed "a correct knowledge of the gospel, and the plan of restoration and redemption."[31]

Book of Mormon Plates

After being given "a brief sketch of their origin, progress, civilization, laws, governments, of their righteousness and iniquity, and the blessings of God being finally withdrawn from them as a people,"[32] Joseph Smith said he was informed that they had created "a sacred record which was written on plates of gold."[33] This record was "an abridgement of the records of the ancient prophets that had existed on this continent,"[34] and Moroni "said that the fullness of the everlasting gospel was contained in it, as delivered by the Savior to the ancient inhabitants" of the Americas.[35]

These plates had been "deposited [in the earth] by the commandments of God and kept by the power thereof" for centuries.[36] "While he was conversing with me about the plates," said Joseph, "the vision was opened to my mind [so] that I could see the place where the plates were deposited . . . clearly and distinctly."[37] Moroni reportedly told young Joseph that it would be his "privilege, if obedient to the commandments of the Lord, to obtain, and translate" the plates.[38] He also mentioned "that there were two stones in silver bows [deposited with the plates], and these stones fastened to a breastplate constituted what is called the Urim and Thummim, . . . and the possession and use of these stones was what constituted 'seers' in ancient or former times, and that God had prepared them for the purpose of translating the book."[39]

The Prophet's mother, Lucy Mack Smith, relates that her son Joseph was told by the angel that the purpose of the golden plates was "to bring forth that light and intelligence which [had] been long lost in the earth,"[40] and from Oliver Cowdery we learn he was expressly informed that bringing this record before the world "must be done with an eye single to the glory of God; if this consideration did not wholly characterize all his proceedings in relation to it, the adversary of truth would overcome him, or at least prevent his making that proficiency in this glorious work which he otherwise would."[41]

Joseph was further informed by his heavenly visitor that "a part of the book was sealed, and was not to be opened yet. The sealed part, said [the angel], contains the same revelation which was given to John [the Apostle] upon the isle of Patmos, and when the people of the Lord are prepared, and found worthy, then it will be unfolded unto them."[42]

Not all of the angel's words were of a pleasant or uplifting nature. It is recorded that he also issued a dire warning. The angel "told me," said Joseph, "that when I got those plates of which he had spoken (for the time that they should be obtained was not yet fulfilled) I should not show them to any person, neither the breastplate with the Urim and Thummim, only to those to whom I should be commanded to show them, [and] if I did *I should be destroyed.*"[43]

Instructions from Biblical Texts

The next portion of Moroni's conversation consisted of the recitation of various prophecies found in the Bible. Not only did the angel quote these ancient predictions but he also offered many explanations concerning them.[44]

From Wilford Woodruff we learn that Joseph's angelic visitor referred to the second chapter of the book of Daniel and also to Matthew 24:14. In a public address, he said,

> When the angel of God delivered this message to Joseph Smith he told him the heavens were full of judgments; that the Lord Almighty had set His hand to establish the kingdom that Daniel saw and prophesied about, as recorded in the second chapter of [the book of] Daniel; and that the gospel had to be preached to all nations under heaven as a witness to them before the end should come and that, too, in fulfillment of the revelation of God, as given here in the Old and New Testaments.[45]

Joseph Smith published a list of several of the other scriptures that the angel Moroni cited to him on that memorable September evening. They are as follows:

Malachi 3. This was only a partial quote (possibly of verses 1–4).
Malachi 4:1–6. These verses were given with "a little variation." Verse 1 was changed to say, "*they* that cometh shall burn them." Verse 5 was rendered, "Behold, I will reveal unto you the Priesthood by the hand of Elijah." Verse 6 was quoted as saying that Elijah would "plant in the hearts of the children the promises made to the fathers."
Isaiah 11:1–16. The angel stated that these verses were about to be fulfilled.
Acts 3:22–23 [see Deut. 18:15, 19]. These verses were given precisely as they read in the New Testament, clarifying that the prophet was Jesus Christ and that soon the day would come that those who would not hear His voice would be cut off.
Joel 2:28–32. These verses were soon to be fulfilled.
Romans 11:25. The angel "stated the fullness of the Gentiles was soon to come in."[46]

Joseph Smith stated that in addition to this biblical material, Moroni "quoted many other passages of scripture."[47] Fortunately, Oliver Cowdery preserved a list of the other scriptures and the teachings associated with them. He interviewed Joseph in regard to the angelic visitation and published what he learned in an early Church periodical. He noted that even though he would not necessarily provide the precise words used by the angel, he would strictly confine himself to the facts in substance. According to Cowdery, the heavenly messenger also quoted or alluded to the following scriptures and themes:

Scriptures
1 Corinthians 1:27–29. "God has chosen the foolish things of the world to confound the things which are mighty."
Isaiah 29:14. "I will proceed to do a marvelous work among this people, even a marvelous work and a wonder."
John 10:16. The house of Israel must come to a knowledge of the gospel and own the Messiah whom their fathers rejected. When this occurs they and the Gentiles will "rejoice in one fold under one Shepherd."

Isaiah 28:21. The Lord chose Joseph Smith to "bring to light that which shall perform His act, His strange act"—meaning the Book of Mormon.

Isaiah 29:13. In relation to this particular scripture the angel reportedly said, "Wherever the sound [of this work] shall go it shall cause the ears of men to tingle, and wherever it shall be proclaimed, the pure in heart shall rejoice, while those who draw near to God with their mouths, and honor Him with their lips, while their hearts are far from Him, will seek its overthrow, and the destruction of those by whose hands it is carried. Therefore, marvel not if your name is made a derision, and had as a by-word among such, if you are the instrument in bringing it, by the gift of God, to the knowledge of the people."

Isaiah 29:11. The angel said that "the scripture must be fulfilled before [the Book of Mormon] is translated, which says that the words of a book, which were sealed, were presented to the learned; for thus has God determined to leave men without excuse, and show to the meek that His arm is not shortened that it cannot save."

Themes

The themes encapsulated in the remaining scriptures that Cowdery said were cited by the angel follow a logical and chronological sequence. They run as follows:

1. The house of Israel has been dispersed among all the nations of the earth because of iniquity.

2. In the last days the house of Israel will be gathered from the four corners of the earth. They will be gathered by missionaries who bring them a message of peace and joy.

3. The gathering of Israel will be to Zion. The Lord's house (or temple) will be found there.

4. The Lord will establish a new covenant with the house of Israel.

5. "[W]hat is to be fulfilled in the last days, is not only for the benefit of Israel, but the Gentiles, if they will repent and embrace the gospel, for they are to be remembered also in the same

covenant, and are to be fellow heirs with the seed of Abraham, inasmuch as they are so by faith for God is no respecter of persons [Acts 10:34]. . . . In consequence of the transgression of the Jews at the coming of the Lord [in the meridian of time], the Gentiles were called into the kingdom, and for this obedience, [they] are to be favored with the gospel in its fullness first, in the last days; for it is written, 'The first shall be last, and the last first' [Mark 10:31; Luke 13:30]. Therefore, when the fullness of the gospel as was preached by the righteous upon this land [i.e., the ancient American continent] shall come forth, it shall be declared to the Gentiles first, and whoso will repent shall be delivered, for they shall understand the plan of salvation and restoration for Israel, as the Lord manifested to the ancients. They shall be baptized with water and with the Spirit."

6. "[A]s the time draws near when the sun is to be darkened, the moon turn[ed] to blood, and the stars fall from heaven [Joel 2:31; Matt. 24:29], the Lord will bring to the knowledge of His people His commandments and statutes, that they may be prepared to stand when the earth shall reel to and fro as a drunken man [Isa. 24:20], earthquakes cause the nations to tremble, and the destroying angel goes forth to waste the inhabitants at noon day [Ps. 91:6]: for so great are to be the calamities which are to come upon the inhabitants of the earth, before the coming of the Son of Man the second time, that whoso is not prepared cannot abide."[48]

When the angel Moroni had finished providing Joseph Smith with all of the information that he had been sent forth to bestow, he departed back into heaven. "After this communication I saw the light in the room begin to gather immediately around the person of him who had been speaking to me," said the Prophet, "and it continued to do so until the room was again left dark except just around him, when instantly I saw as it were a conduit open right up into heaven, and he ascended up till he entirely disappeared and the room was left as it had been before this heavenly light had made its appearance."[49] After the angel's dramatic departure Joseph is reported as saying that he felt a sense of tranquility; he was left with "a calmness and peace of soul past the language of man to paint."[50]

MORONI'S SECOND VISITATION

Joseph's state of serenity did not last very long because the whole episode was repeated after only a short space of time had elapsed. The Prophet states in his published recitation of the event, "I lay musing on the singularity of the scene and marveling greatly at what had been told me by this extraordinary messenger, when in the midst of my meditation I suddenly discovered that my room was again beginning to get lighted, and in an instant, as it were, the same heavenly messenger was again by my bedside. He commenced and again related the very same things which he had done at his first visit without the least variation."

But this was not all. After Moroni had finished delivering his message the second time he informed Joseph of "great judgments which were coming upon the earth, with great desolations by famine, sword, and pestilence, and that these grievous judgments would come on the earth in this generation. Having related these things he again ascended as he had done before."[51]

MORONI'S THIRD VISITATION

At this point Joseph lay on his bed overwhelmed in astonishment. But his unsettled state of mind was soon interrupted. He was surprised when the same angelic messenger appeared at his bedside and rehearsed the very same message for a third time. On this occasion, however, the angel added a cautionary note, telling Joseph that Satan would try to tempt him to alleviate his family's poverty by obtaining the golden plates for the purpose of getting rich. The angel expressly forbade Joseph from doing this and told him that he "must have no other object in view in getting the plates but to glorify God, and must not be influenced by any other motive but that of building His kingdom."[52] Oliver Cowdery's notes on this episode indicate that Joseph was to remember that this work was designed "to fulfill certain promises previously made to a branch of the house of Israel, of the tribe of Joseph" and was intended to bring about "the welfare and restoration of the house of Israel." If these were not his only motivations, said the angel, he would only receive "disappointment and reproof."[53]

After the third visitation had ended, the heavenly visitor once again ascended out of sight and into heaven. And once again Joseph was left to himself to "ponder on the strangeness" of what he had just experienced.[54]

MORONI'S FOURTH VISITATION

Almost immediately after the angel's third ascension a rooster crowed out in the Smiths' farmyard, signaling the imminent approach of sunrise. Joseph reports that he arose from his bed shortly thereafter and went about his usual daily chores.[55] Eventually he made his way out into the field to harvest crops with his brothers, but they noticed that something was different about him. He stopped working and for some time seemed to be in deep thought. Alvin hurried him, saying that they wouldn't finish their assigned task unless they kept on performing their labor. Joseph resumed reaping but then stopped again as before. According to Lucy Mack Smith, Alvin noticed that he looked very pale and told him that he should go to the house and tell his mother that he was sick.[56]

Joseph took his brother's advice and headed off toward the family dwelling, but he only made it as far as an apple tree that was planted near the farm's fence-line. "[I]n attempting to cross the fence out of the field where we were," said the Prophet, "my strength entirely failed me and I fell helpless on the ground and for a time was quite unconscious of anything. The first thing that I can recollect was a voice speaking unto me, calling me by name. I looked up and beheld the same messenger standing over my head surrounded by light as before. He then again related unto me all that he had related to me the previous night."[57] In addition to these familiar instructions the angel also evidently told Joseph "to go immediately and view those things of which he had been informed, with a promise that he should obtain them if he followed the directions and went with an eye single to the glory of God."[58] At the same time the angel also commanded Joseph to go to his father and tell him of the vision and commandments that he had received.[59] Lucy Mack Smith provides an interesting insight into this matter. She relates that her son had initially decided not to tell his father about the angel's visits the night before because he was afraid that his father would not believe him. But the angel assured Joseph that his father would believe every word that he told him.[60]

Joseph continued on toward the house and after awhile he summoned the members of his family to his side. William Smith, the Prophet's brother, remembered that it was their mother who came out into the field where the men were working and said that they were all requested to come into the house, that Joseph had something that he wanted to tell them.[61] His father's response to the recital of events was that "it was of God," and he directed his son to "go and do as commanded by the messenger."[62]

As Joseph made the journey to the hill, which stood about three miles south of Palmyra, a mighty struggle began to take place in his mind. On the one hand, says Oliver Cowdery, he thought about the bright heavenly messenger and the important errand that he had been assigned to accomplish for the glory of God; on the other hand he began to think that such a treasure as the golden plates would surely raise his family above the poverty, abuse, and misery that they had suffered throughout their lives.[63]

With these competing thoughts still unresolved, Joseph soon arrived at the hill. He records in his published history that he came to "the place where the messenger had told [him] the plates were deposited; and owing to the distinctness of the vision which [he] had had concerning it, [he] knew the place the instant that [he] arrived there."[64]

MORONI'S FIFTH VISITATION

The hill where the golden plates of the Book of Mormon were buried was a drumlin, a long mound created from glacial deposits. Edward Partridge, who served as the first Presiding Bishop of the restored Church, recorded in his journal that it was "perhaps 100 feet high, running from a trifle west of north to a little east of south, the north end breaks off very square, and when from a distance we view it the sides appear steep like the roof of a house."[65] At the time that Joseph Smith first went to this spot "there were several trees standing: enough to cause a shade in summer, but not so much as to prevent the surface being covered with grass."[66]

Joseph Smith reports what happened once he had arrived at his destination. He says, "On the west side of this hill not far from the top, under a stone of considerable size, lay the plates deposited in a stone box: this stone was thick and rounding in the middle on the upper side, and thinner towards the edges, so that the middle part of it was visible above the ground, but the edge all round was covered with earth. Having removed the earth and obtained a lever which I got fixed under the edge of the stone and with a little exertion raised it up, I looked in and there indeed did I behold the plates, the Urim and Thummim and the breastplate."[67] (A detailed description of these objects is found in appendix 1 of this book.) Oliver Cowdery expands our understanding of what happened at this point. He relates in a published article:

> No sooner did he behold this sacred treasure than his hopes were renewed, and he supposed his success certain; and without first attempting to take it from its long place of deposit, he thought, perhaps, there might be something more equally as valuable, and to take only the plates might give others an opportunity of obtaining the remainder which, could he secure, would still add to his store of wealth. These, in short, were his reflections, without once thinking of the solemn instruction of the heavenly messenger, that all must be done with an express view of glorifying God.
>
> On attempting to take possession of the record a shock was produced upon his system by an invisible power which deprived him, in a measure, of his natural strength. He desisted for an instant, and then made another attempt, but was more sensibly shocked than before. What was the occasion of this he knew not—there was the pure unsullied record, as had been described. He had heard of the power of enchantment, and a thousand like stories, which held the hidden treasures of the earth, and supposed that physical exertion and personal strength was only necessary to enable him to yet obtain the object of his wish. He therefore made the third attempt with an increased exertion,

when his strength failed him more than at either of the former times, and without premeditating he exclaimed, "Why can I not obtain this book?" "Because you have not kept the commandments of the Lord," answered a voice, within a seeming short distance. He looked, and to his astonishment, there stood the angel who had previously given him the directions concerning this matter. In an instant, all the former instructions—the great intelligence concerning Israel and the last days—were brought to his mind: he thought of the time when his heart was fervently engaged in prayer to the Lord, when his spirit was contrite, and when this holy messenger from the skies unfolded the wonderful things connected with this record. He had come, to be sure, and found the word of the angel fulfilled concerning the reality of the record, but he had failed to remember the great end for which they had been kept, and in consequence could not have power to take them into his possession and bear them away.[68]

At this point the Prophet turned to the Lord in prayer. As he focused his thoughts on communing with his Heavenly Father, darkness began to "disperse from his mind," and he was "filled with the Holy Spirit." The heavens were then opened, and the glory of the Lord shone around him. As Joseph gazed in admiration upon this marvelous sight, the angel said, "Look!" The scene then changed drastically. "He beheld the prince of darkness, surrounded by his innumerable train of associates. All this passed before him, and the heavenly messenger said, 'All this is shown, the good and the evil, the holy and impure, the glory of God and the power of darkness, that you may know hereafter the two powers and never be influenced or overcome by that wicked one.'"[69] After discoursing briefly upon the nature of good and evil, Moroni apparently then said to the young Prophet in effect:

You now see why you could not obtain this record; that the commandment was strict, and that if ever these sacred things are obtained they must be by prayer and faithfulness in obeying the Lord. They are not deposited here for the sake of accumulating gain and wealth for the glory of this world: they were sealed by the prayer of faith, and because of the knowledge which they contain they are of no worth among the children of men, only for their knowledge. On them is contained the fullness of the gospel of Jesus Christ, as it was given to His people on this land.[70]

The angel Moroni then gave Joseph a sign whereby he would know that the Lord was God, that He would fulfill His purposes, and that the knowledge contained on the record would go to every nation, kindred, tongue, and people. "This is the sign," said the angel. "[W]hen it is known that the Lord has shown you these things, the workers of iniquity will seek your overthrow: they will circulate falsehoods to destroy your reputation, and also will seek to take your life; but remember this, if you are faithful, and shall hereafter continue to keep the commandments of the Lord, you shall be preserved to bring these things forth; for in due time He will again give you a commandment to come and take them." Moroni also told Joseph something that is seldom noticed by Latter-day Saints. He said that when the plates had been interpreted the Lord would restore the priesthood to the earth. When this took place persecution would rage even more as wicked individuals tried to overthrow the restored Church. But it would only increase the more it was opposed, and spread farther and farther. "Now, go thy way," said the angel, "remembering what the Lord has done for thee, and be diligent in keeping His commandments, and He will deliver thee from temptations and all the arts and devices of the wicked one. Forget not to pray, that thy mind may become strong, that when he shall manifest unto thee, thou mayest have power to escape the evil, and obtain these precious things."[71]

According to the statements of Katherine Smith and Joseph Knight Sr., the angel directed Joseph to return to the hill where the golden plates were buried on 22 September the following year. And in a most curious turn, the angel reportedly instructed Joseph to bring his oldest brother, Alvin Smith, along with him.[72]

NOTES TO CHAPTER 1

1. *Times and Seasons,* vol. 3, no. 11, 1 April 1842, 749. Joseph Smith's sister Katherine relates that on the night of 21 September 1823 the Prophet "lay in bed . . . studying what he had seen" in the First Vision (*Kansas City Times,* 11 April 1895).

2. Dean C. Jessee, ed., *The Personal Writings of Joseph Smith,* rev. ed. (Salt Lake City: Deseret Book, 2002), 105.

3. See *Times and Seasons,* vol. 3, no. 11, 1 April 1842, 749. The Prophet reports in this same source, "I had full confidence in obtaining a divine manifestation as I had previously had one" (i.e., the First Vision).

4. *Messenger and Advocate,* vol. 1, no. 5, February 1835, 78.

5. See ibid., 79. It is possible that the response to Joseph Smith's prayer occurred sometime after midnight. If so, the angel Moroni would have made his first appearance to the Prophet on 22 September 1823—the fall equinox.

6. Ibid., vol. 1, no. 10, July 1835, 156.

7. Ibid., vol. 1, no. 5, February 1835, 79. The description of this event in *Times and Seasons,* vol. 3, no. 9, 1 March 1842, 707, is very similar.

8. *Times and Seasons,* vol. 3, no. 12, 15 April 1842, 753. "[T]he room was illuminated above the brightness of the sun" (Jessee, ed., *The Personal Writings of Joseph Smith,* 105). William Smith, in recounting the "story of the angel . . . as told by [his] brother," said that "a bright cloud like that of fire appeared before him and in that cloud he saw" the angel (*Zion's Ensign,* vol. 3, no. 35, 27 August 1892).

9. "[I]n a moment a personage stood before him" (*Messenger and Advocate,* vol. 1, no. 5, February 1835, 79); "in a moment a personage stood before me" (*Times and Seasons,* vol. 3, no. 9, 1 March 1842, 707); "when immediately a personage appeared at my bedside" (ibid., vol. 3, no. 12, 15 April 1842, 753). It must be stressed that this experience "was not a dream," it was "an open vision" (*Messenger and Advocate,* vol. 1, no. 10, July 1835, 156).

10. See *Times and Seasons,* vol. 3, no. 12, 15 April 1842, 753; he "stood between the floors of the room" (Jessee, ed., *The Personal Writings of Joseph Smith,* 105). Katherine Smith reports that the personage "did not touch the floor, but he stood in the air" (*Kansas City Times,* 11 April 1895).

11. *Messenger and Advocate,* vol. 1, no. 5, February 1835, 79. Joseph Smith said that this "personage . . . [was] surrounded with a glory yet greater than that with which I was already surrounded" (*Times and Seasons,* vol. 3, no. 9, 1 March

1842, 707). "The room was exceedingly light, but not so very bright as immediately around his person" (ibid., vol. 3, no. 12, 15 April 1842, 753).

12. *Messenger and Advocate,* vol. 1, no. 5, February 1835, 79.

13. The personage "had on a loose robe of most exquisite whiteness. It was a whiteness beyond anything earthly I had ever seen; . . . exceedingly white and brilliant" (*Times and Seasons,* vol. 3, no. 12, 15 April 1842, 753); Oliver Cowdery said, "his garment was perfectly white, and had the appearance of being without seam" (*Messenger and Advocate,* vol. 1, no. 5, February 1835, 79). Katherine Smith said that the personage "was dressed in white raiment, of whiteness beyond anything Joseph had ever seen in his life, and had a girdle about his waist" (*Kansas City Times,* 11 April 1895).

14. Jessee, ed., *The Personal Writings of Joseph Smith,* 105.

15. The personage's "hands and feet were . . . pure and white" (ibid.). Katherine Smith repeats this information. She says, "his hands and wrists . . . were pure and white" (*Kansas City Times,* 11 April 1895). Joseph could see that his visitor's "hands . . . and his arms . . . a little above the wrist . . . [and] his feet . . . [and] his legs a little above the ankles [were bare]. His head and neck were also bare" (*Times and Seasons,* vol. 3, no. 12, 15 April 1842, 753).

16. Ibid.

17. *Messenger and Advocate,* vol. 1, no. 5, February 1835, 79.

18. *Times and Seasons,* vol. 3, no. 12, 15 April 1842, 753. Joseph Smith told his brother William that the angel said to him, "fear not" (*Zion's Ensign,* vol. 3, no. 35, 27 August 1892; cf. Gen. 15:1; 21:17; 26:24; Josh. 8:8; Isa. 41:13; Matt. 28:5; Luke 1:13; 2:10; Rev. 1:17).

19. *Times and Seasons,* vol. 1, no. 10, August 1840, 152.

20. See ibid., vol. 3, no. 12, 15 April 1842, 753.

21. The Lord identified the messenger as "Moroni" in an 1830 revelation (D&C 27:5). Oliver Cowdery identified the personage in 1835 as "the angel Moroni" (*Messenger and Advocate,* vol. 1, no. 7, April 1835, 112). In 1838 Joseph Smith identified the personage who appeared to him as "Moroni" (*Elders' Journal,* vol. 1, no. 3, July 1838, 42). Doctrine and Covenants 128:20, which was written by Joseph Smith in 1844, also makes this identification. Katherine Smith likewise says, "He said that he was Moroni" (*Kansas City Times,* 11 April 1895). Given all of this published evidence, it seems clear that the information printed in *Times and Seasons,* vol. 3, no. 12, 15 April 1842, 753, which identifies the angel as Nephi, is an inadvertent error.

22. Jessee, ed., *The Personal Writings of Joseph Smith,* 105. "He . . . said unto me that he was a messenger sent from the presence of God to me" (*Times and Seasons,* vol. 3, no. 12, 15 April 1842, 753). The angel "declare[d] himself to be a messenger sent by commandment of the Lord, to deliver a special message" (*Messenger and Advocate,* vol. 1, no. 5, February 1835, 79). "This messenger proclaimed himself to be an angel of God" (*Times and Seasons,* vol. 3, no. 9, 1 March 1842, 707).

23. *Messenger and Advocate,* vol. 1, no. 10, July 1835, 156. Moroni admonished Joseph to "be faithful and keep [God's] commandments in all things" (Jessee, ed., *The Personal Writings of Joseph Smith,* 105).

24. See *Times and Seasons,* vol. 3, no. 12, 15 April 1842, 753.

25. Ibid., vol. 3, no. 9, 1 March 1842, 707.

26. Ibid., vol. 3, no. 12, 15 April 1842, 753.

27. Ibid., vol. 1, no. 10, August 1840, 152.

28. *Kansas City Times,* 11 April 1895.

29. *Times and Seasons,* vol. 3, no. 9, 1 March 1842, 707.

30. George D. Watt, comp., *Journal of Discourses,* 26 vols. (London: F. D. and S. W. Richards and Sons, 1854–1886), 17:280. In this same source Elder Orson Pratt says that these were, "in substance," the things that "were taught by the angel of God who administered to Joseph Smith in September, 1823." Pratt included in conjunction with this information the idea that Lehi's group "landed on the western coast of South America." Near the end of their history, says Pratt, "the Lamanites of South America drove the Nephites from the Isthmus" of Darien, or Panama, in Central America.

This particular conception of Book of Mormon geography was taught by LDS missionaries at a very early stage of Church history. In 1830 either Oliver Cowdery, Parley P. Pratt, Peter Whitmer Jr., or Ziba Peterson (or all of them) taught a gathering of people in northern Ohio that Lehi's colony "landed on the coast of Chil[e] 600 years before the coming of Christ" (*Observer and Telegraph,* vol. 1, no. 38, 18 November 1830). Alexander Campbell had somehow heard by 1831 that the situations taking place near the beginning of the Book of Mormon occurred "at the Isthmus of Darien" (*Millennial Harbinger,* vol. 2, no. 2, 7 February 1831, 94). In March 1832 "a couple of young men styling themselves Mormonites" taught a large group in Franklin, Pennsylvania, that Lehi and his associates "landed on the coast of South America, where they increased very fast, and the Lord raised up a great many prophets among them." Furthermore, said these "Mormonites," the "first battle" between Nephites and Lamanites "was fought nigh to the straits of Darien," or the Isthmus of Panama, in Central America (*Fredonia Censor*, vol. 11, no. 50, 7 March 1832). Just one month after this statement was made Orson Pratt and Lyman Johnson were teaching in Cincinnati, Ohio, that "six hundred years before Christ a certain prophet called Lehi went out to declare and promulgate the prophecies to come; he came across the water into South America. . . . The last battle that was fought among these parties was on the very ground where the plates were found, but *it had been a running battle,* for they commenced at the Isthmus of Darien and ended at Manchester," New York (*Catholic Telegraph*, vol. 1, no. 26, 14 April 1832; emphasis added). By February 1833 the Saints saw the "discovery of ancient ruins in Central America" as "good testimony in favor of the Book of Mormon" (*Evening and Morning Star*, vol. 1, no. 9, February 1833, 71). A note written by Frederick G. Williams (possibly in the School of the Prophets, where, as a member of the First Presidency, he taught between 1834 and 1836) says that Lehi's party "sailed in a southeast direction and landed on the continent of South America in Chile thirty degrees south latitude" (Frederick G. Williams Papers, Historical Department Archives, The Church of Jesus Christ of Latter-day Saints, Salt Lake City, Utah).

Many of the preceding ideas were mentioned by Elder Orson Pratt in an 1840 publication called *An Interesting Account of Several Remarkable Visions* (Edinburgh, Scotland: Ballantyne and Hughes, 1840). In this source, Elder Pratt claimed that Lehi's group "landed upon the western coast of South America" (p. 16); the Nephites then "emigrated towards the northern parts of South America" (ibid.); the Nephites eventually "multiplied and spread forth to the east, and west, and north" (17); "in the process of time, the Nephites began to build ships near the Isthmus of Darien, and launch them forth into the western ocean, in which great numbers sailed a great distance to the north-ward, and began to colonize North America" (18); the Nephites saw Jesus Christ—after His Resurrection—at "their temple in the northern parts of South America" (20); the last great battle between the Nephites and Lamanites "commenced at the Isthmus of Darien. . . . At length, the Nephites were driven before their enemies, a great distance to the north, and north-east; and having gathered their whole nation together, both men, women, and children, they encamped on, and round about the hill Cumorah, where the records [of the Book of Mormon] were found, which is in the state of New York" (21).

Church periodicals that were printed during Joseph Smith's lifetime continued to point to the newly discovered antiquities of Central America as evidence for the authenticity of the Book of Mormon (see *Millennial Star,* vol. 1, no. 5, September 1840, 118; *Times and Seasons,* vol. 2, no. 16, 15 June 1841, 440; *Millennial Star,* vol. 2, no. 5, September 1841, 83; ibid., vol. 2, no. 11, March 1842, 161–65; *Times and Seasons,* vol. 3, no. 18, 15 July 1842, 858–60; ibid., vol. 4, no. 12, 1 May 1843, 185–86; ibid., vol. 4, no. 22, 1 October 1843, 346–47; ibid., vol. 5, no. 1, 1 January 1844, 390). Two articles published in September 1842 are of particular interest because they say that "Lehi . . . landed a little south of the Isthmus of Darien" (*Times and Seasons,* vol. 3, no. 22, 15 September 1842, 922), and "the Nephites in the Book of Mormon . . . lived about the narrow neck of land, which now embraces Central America, with all the cities that can be found" (ibid., 915). For LDS sources after the death of Joseph Smith that equated Central American ruins with the cities of the Book of Mormon, see *Times and Seasons,* vol. 6, no. 4, 1 March 1845, 830–31; ibid., vol. 6, no. 6, 1 April 1845, 855; *Millennial Star,* vol. 10, no. 22, 15 November 1848, 347. In 1852 Parley P. Pratt wrote that Lehi's group "landed on the western coast of America, within the bounds of what is now called 'Chil[e]'" (*Millennial Star,* vol. 14, no. 30, 18 September 1852, 469), and in 1855 he repeated this view, stating that they "landed in safety on the coast of what is now called Chil[e], in South America" (Parley P. Pratt, *Key to the Science of Theology* [Liverpool: F. D. Richards, 1855; reprint, Salt Lake City: Deseret Book, 2002], 15). In 1866 Orson Pratt taught that the land Bountiful was in the "north-western portions of South America" near the "Isthmus of Darien" (*Millennial Star,* vol. 28, no. 24, 16 June 1866, 370). In 1868 Orson Pratt once again said that "the Nephite colony . . . landed on the western coast of South America, in the country we call Chil[e]" (*Journal of Discourses,* 12:342).

It is not clear how much of the information in the above statements might be based upon revelation from God or the angel Moroni, intellectual reasoning after examination of textual evidence, guesswork, or some combination of each. It seems, however, from one source that the "Chile" landing site for Lehi's group may be a belief based upon textual interpretation (see Orson Pratt's comments in *Journal of Discourses,* 14:325; *Millennial Star,* vol. 38, no. 44, 30 October 1876, 692; and footnote *k* to 1 Nephi 18:23 in the 1879 edition of the Book of Mormon. Notice Pratt's statement in *Journal of Discourses,* 19:208, that his view on the location of the Jaredite landing spot is based upon textual interpretation).

31. *Messenger and Advocate,* vol. 1, no. 5, February 1835, 79–80.

32. *Times and Seasons,* vol. 3, no. 9, 1 March 1842, 707–708.

33. Jessee, ed., *The Personal Writings of Joseph Smith,* 105.

34. *Times and Seasons,* vol. 3, no. 9, 1 March 1842, 707.

35. Ibid., vol. 3, no. 12, 15 April 1842, 753. According to Katherine Smith, Moroni told Joseph that the record contained "the pure gospel of Jesus Christ, and would be preached in these last days" (*Kansas City Times,* 11 April 1895). About six hundred years before the mortal ministry of Jesus Christ, an angel told the prophet Nephi that the Apostles of the Lamb would write down His teachings, those writings would be gathered into a book (the Bible), and over time many of the "plain and most precious" parts of that book would be altered or lost. In order to ensure that the recipients of this book did not continue to stumble blindly because of its imperfections, the Lord commanded that another record of His gospel be prepared, one that would be brought before the world in a different manner than the Bible had been and therefore not subjected to the same process of alteration (see 1 Ne. 13:24–29, 32–34, 39–41).

36. Jessee, ed., *The Personal Writings of Joseph Smith,* 12.

37. *Times and Seasons,* vol. 3, no. 12, 15 April 1842, 753. "I saw in the vision the place where they were deposited" (Jessee, ed., *The Personal Writings of Joseph Smith,* 105). "While describing the place where the record was deposited, he gave a minute relation of it, and the vision of his mind being opened at the same time, he was permitted to view it critically" (*Messenger and Advocate,* vol. 1, no. 5, February 1835, 80). Katherine Smith: "He also opened the vision and showed him the hill [Cumorah] where the records laid" (*Kansas City Times,* 11 April 1895).

    Oliver Cowdery was evidently informed by Joseph Smith that Moroni referred to the place where the plates were hidden as "Cumorah" (Scot F. Proctor and Maurine J. Proctor, eds., *Autobiography of Parley P. Pratt,* rev. ed. [Salt Lake City: Deseret Book, 2000], 64). David Whitmer reports that while he was moving Joseph Smith and Oliver Cowdery to Fayette, New York, in order to complete the translation of the Book of Mormon, they unexpectedly met a white-haired man who had been assigned the task of transporting the golden plates during the journey. When this person was asked if he wanted to ride in the wagon he replied, "No, I am going to Cumorah" and then "instantly disappeared." David, in repeating this incident to Joseph F. Smith and Orson Pratt, said, "This was something new to me, I did not know what

Cumorah meant" (Joseph F. Smith Diary, 7–8 September 1878, Historical Department Archives, The Church of Jesus Christ of Latter-day Saints, Salt Lake City, Utah).

38. *Messenger and Advocate*, vol. 1, no. 5, February 1835, 80.

39. *Times and Seasons*, vol. 3, no. 12, 15 April 1842, 753. "[H]e told me . . . that the Urim and Thummim, was hid up with the record, and that God would give me power to translate it, with the assistance of this instrument" (Jessee, ed., *The Personal Writings of Joseph Smith*, 105).

40. Lavina F. Anderson, ed., *Lucy's Book: A Critical Edition of Lucy Mack Smith's Family Memoir* (Salt Lake City: Signature Books, 2001), 336.

41. *Messenger and Advocate*, vol. 1, no. 5, February 1835, 80.

42. Ibid. For further reading on the contents of the sealed portion of the Book of Mormon, see Valentin Arts, "A Third Jaredite Record: The Sealed Portion of the Gold Plates," *Journal of Book of Mormon Studies* 11, no. 1 (2002): 50–59.

43. *Times and Seasons*, vol. 3, no. 12, 15 April 1842, 753; emphasis added.

44. See ibid. The Prophet says, "he explained many of the [biblical] prophesies to me" (Jessee, ed., *The Personal Writings of Joseph Smith*, 105). Also, said Joseph, "he revealed unto me many things concerning the inhabitants of the earth which since [July–November 1832] have been revealed in commandments and revelations" (ibid., 12–13). In addition, says Katherine Smith, he "told [Joseph] what was coming upon the earth. . . . He told him the prophecies of Isaiah were being fulfilled and would come true" (*Kansas City Times*, 11 April 1895).

45. *Journal of Discourses*, 24:241.

46. This information is gleaned from *Times and Seasons*, vol. 3, no. 12, 15 April 1842, 753.

47. Ibid.

48. The information in this section has been gathered from *Messenger and Advocate*, vol. 1, no. 5, February 1835, 79–80; ibid., vol. 1, no. 7, April 1835, 109–12.

49. *Times and Seasons*, vol. 3, no. 12, 15 April 1842, 754.

50. *Messenger and Advocate*, vol. 1, no. 10, July 1835, 156.

51. *Times and Seasons*, vol. 3, no. 12, 15 April 1842, 754.

52. Ibid.

53. *Messenger and Advocate*, vol. 1, no. 10, July 1835, 157.

54. *Times and Seasons*, vol. 3, no. 12, 15 April 1842, 754.

55. See ibid.

56. See Anderson, ed., *Lucy's Book*, 339; William Smith says that he, Alvin, Hyrum, and Samuel were all "at work in [an] adjoining field near the house" (*Zion's Ensign*, vol. 3, no. 35, 27 August 1892). Joseph Smith states that his father was also laboring alongside of him, and it was he who told the Prophet to go home (see *Times and Seasons*, vol. 3, no. 12, 15 April 1842, 754).

57. Ibid., vol. 3, no. 12, 15 April 1842, 754.

58. *Messenger and Advocate*, vol. 1, no. 10, July 1835, 156.

59. See *Times and Seasons*, vol. 3, no. 12, 15 April 1842, 754.

60. See Anderson, ed., *Lucy's Book*, 340.

61. See *Zion's Ensign*, vol. 3, no. 35, 27 August 1892. "They came to the house and sat and talked quite a spell," said Katherine Smith. "I wondered at it. I was young, and I didn't know what they were talking about [and] I [knew] they were so busy with their harvesting" (*Kansas City Times*, 11 April 1895). William Smith recalled what was said during this important family meeting. "After we were all gathered, [Joseph] arose and told us how the angel appeared to him. . . . He continued talking to us sometime. The whole family were melted to tears, and believed all he said. Knowing that he was very young, that he had not enjoyed the advantages of a common education; and knowing too, his whole character and disposition, they were convinced that he was totally incapable of arising before his aged parents, his brothers and sisters, and so solemnly giving utterance to anything but the truth. All of us, therefore, believed him and anxiously awaited the result of his visit to the hill Cumorah, in search of the plates containing the record of which the angel told him" (William B. Smith, *William Smith on Mormonism* [Lamoni, Iowa: Herald Steam Book and Job Office, 1883], 9–10).

62. *Times and Seasons*, vol. 3, no. 13, 2 May 1842, 771.

63. See *Messenger and Advocate*, vol. 1, no. 10, July 1835, 157.

64. *Times and Seasons*, vol. 3, no. 13, 2 May 1842, 771. Oliver Cowdery states that it was still in the "morning" when Joseph Smith arrived at the hill where the plates were deposited (*Messenger and Advocate*, vol. 2, no. 1, October 1835, 197).

65. Edward Partridge Journal, 23, Historical Department Archives, The Church of Jesus Christ of Latter-day Saints, Salt Lake City, Utah.

66. *Messenger and Advocate*, vol. 2, no. 1, October 1835, 196.

67. *Times and Seasons*, vol. 3, no. 13, 2 May 1842, 771.

68. *Messenger and Advocate*, vol. 2, no. 1, October 1835, 197–98. On one occasion Joseph Smith testified under oath "that when he dug into the earth, and reached the plates, that he was kicked out of the hole he had dug and lifted

into the air by some 'unseen power'" (James A. Briggs, letter, 19 January 1884, in *Cleveland Leader,* vol. 37, January 1884). Katherine Smith also refers to a repelling phenomenon: "He reached forth his hands to take it and he felt a pressure pushing him away. He tried the second time, and the third time he fell to the earth with the pressure" (*Kansas City Times,* 11 April 1895). Lucy Mack Smith reports that Joseph was "hurled back to the ground" during this incident (Anderson, ed., *Lucy's Book,* 347).

69. *Messenger and Advocate,* vol. 2, no. 1, October 1835, 198.

70. Ibid.

71. Ibid., 199. Oliver Cowdery makes note of the wisdom of God in allowing Joseph Smith to have this experience at the hill. This was a time of instruction, given so that the Prophet's mind would go through a maturing process. Oliver says, "two invisible powers were operating upon the mind of [Joseph Smith] while going to Cumorah. In this, then, I discover wisdom in the dealings of the Lord: it was impossible for any man to translate the Book of Mormon by the gift of God and endure the afflictions and temptations and devices of Satan without being overthrown, unless he had been previously benefited with a certain round of experience. And had our brother obtained the record the first time, not knowing how to detect the works of darkness, he might have been deprived of the blessing of sending forth the word of truth to this generation. Therefore, God knowing that Satan would thus lead his mind astray began at that early hour, that when the full time should arrive, He might have a servant prepared to fulfill His purpose. So, however afflicting to his feelings this repulse might have been, he had reason to rejoice before the Lord and be thankful for the favors and mercies shown; that whatever other instruction was necessary to the accomplishing [of] this great work, he had learned by experience how to discern between the Spirit of Christ and the spirit of the devil" (ibid., 199–200).

72. Joseph Knight Sr. reports that after this failure to obtain the Nephite record, Joseph asked the angel, "'When can I have it?' The answer was the 22nd day of September next [year] if you bring the right person with you. Joseph [asked], 'Who is the right person?' The answer was, 'Your oldest brother,'" meaning Alvin (Dean C. Jessee, "Joseph Knight's Recollection of Early Mormon History," *BYU Studies* 17, no. 1 [fall 1976]: 31). Katherine Smith reports the same instruction, but she says the Prophet asked the angel "What shall I do?" The angel replied, "Come here the next year at this time and bring your oldest brother with you, and you can receive the records" (*Kansas City Times,* 11 April 1895).

CHAPTER 2

PREPARATION OF A PROPHET

William Smith relates that when his brother Joseph returned home from his trip to the hill where the golden plates had been concealed, he told his family that "in consequence of his not obeying strictly the commandments which the angel had given him, he could not obtain the record until four years from that time."[1] The Smith family, reports Lucy Mack Smith, sat up very late that night and listened attentively to all that Joseph had to say regarding his unusual experiences.[2] Then Alvin, seeing that his brother was exhausted, suggested that the family work through the next day and then continue their conversation in the evening.

After the workday had come to a close on 23 September 1823, Joseph began the conversation in a curious way by charging his family not to speak outside of their home about what he would tell them. His mother remembered his words as follows: "The angel of the Lord says that we must be careful not to proclaim these things or to mention them abroad for we do not any of us know the wickedness of the world which is so sinful." Joseph warned his parents and siblings that if they let other people know of these things their reputations would be slandered and some people would even attempt to take their lives for the sake of the gold. He then told his attentive family members more about "the obtaining of the plates," the goodness, knowledge and power of God, and "the great salvation that lay before the faithful."[3]

These evening discussions continued in the Smith home for some time. Joseph's mother conveys some of what was said during these gatherings. She says, "In the course of our evening conversations Joseph would give us some of the most amusing recitals which could be imagined. He would describe the ancient inhabitants of this continent; their dress, their manner of traveling, the animals which they rode, the cities that were built by them, the structure of their buildings, with every particular of their mode of warfare [and] their religious worship—as particularly as though he had spent his life with them."[4]

THE 1824 AND 1825 VISITS TO THE HILL

Only a short while after Joseph Smith had seen the golden plates for the first time a terrible tragedy struck his family. Alvin, Joseph's twenty-five-year-old brother, died on 19 November 1823. A few days before, on the fifteenth, Alvin had come down with a case of bilious colic. He requested that his father summon a doctor to take care of him, but the regular family physician was not available and so another was found, farther away. This doctor administered—against the will of the patient—a heavy dose of calomel. This overdose of medicine lodged in Alvin's intestines and could not be removed by five additional doctors who were called to the house. Alvin fully understood that he was going to die from his condition. As he had always shown a great deal of zeal and anxiety in regard to the Book of Mormon plates, before he passed away he admonished Joseph with these words: "I want you to . . . do everything that lays in your power to obtain the records. Be faithful in receiving instruction and keeping every commandment that is given you." Lucy Mack Smith reports that for a length of time after Alvin died, the family could not endure to hear Joseph speak about the plates because it reminded them of Alvin and gave them fresh feelings of grief.[5]

This was not just a tragedy for the Smith family, it was a very personal tragedy for young Joseph. The angel had told him that he must bring Alvin to the hill on 22 September 1824 and now that was entirely impossible. Katherine Smith relates that when the day for her brother's annual visit to the hill arrived, "Joseph went to the place and inquired of the angel what he should do now. The angel said: 'You must bring some person with you.' And Joseph said: 'Who shall I bring? My oldest brother is gone.' The angel said: 'You will know her when you see her.'"[6] According to Joseph Knight Sr., this angelic instruction was taken by the young seer in the most literal way. Joseph Smith had evidently possessed a personal seerstone for some years previous to this time and upon looking into it he found that the girl referred to by the angel was Emma Hale of Harmony, Pennsylvania—someone Joseph had seen before while he was visiting that vicinity of the country with Mr. Knight.[7]

While Emma would indeed accompany him on his final trip to the hill in 1827, Joseph recorded little about the intervening yearly visits with Moroni. He did say, however, that at each interview he "received instruction and intelligence . . . respecting what the Lord was going to do and how and in what manner His kingdom was to be conducted in the last days."[8] These words would apply to each of the visits made on 22 September, including the one in 1825. Katherine Smith may cast further light on Joseph's yearly meetings with Moroni. She says, "I well remember the trials my brother had, before he obtained the records. After he had the vision, he went frequently to the hill, and upon returning would tell us, 'I have seen the records, also the brass plates and the sword of Laban with the breastplate and interpreters.'"[9] Joseph himself states in his official history that the golden plates, the breastplate, and the interpreters were kept inside the stone box on the hill, but he never did say that the brass plates and sword of Laban were kept there as well.[10] This evidence may indicate that during Joseph's yearly tutorials he was shown several ancient Nephite relics that were kept in a separate location—objects that would also be shown to the Three Witnesses when an angel showed them the golden plates in June 1829.

THE SILVER MINE EXPEDITION

Joseph Smith reports that in October 1825 he was hired to work in a mining operation by Josiah Stowell of South Bainbridge, New York. When Josiah had heard about an old abandoned Spanish silver mine in Harmony, Pennsylvania, his interest was piqued. He had been excavating the earth in an attempt to find the mine but had so far been unsuccessful.[11] Josiah wanted to hire Joseph because he had heard that the young man "possessed certain keys, by which he could discern things invisible to the natural eye."[12]

Joseph stayed at Josiah's house while the search for the lost silver mine was taking place, and he worked with several other people who had been hired for the job. This company of men made excavations for nearly one month, but they were unsuccessful in their venture. Joseph says in his history, "Finally I prevailed with the old gentleman to cease digging after it."[13] Martin Harris provides an interesting insight into why Joseph was eager to abandon this project even though he was being paid for his efforts.[14] According to Martin, "Joseph said the angel told him he must quit the company of the money-diggers. That there were wicked men among them. He must have no more to do with them."[15] In fact, at a later time, some of the men from this group would accuse Joseph of being a traitor because he would not share the golden plates with them.[16]

A PERIOD OF VEXATION

Around the time of Joseph's return from the Spanish mine project (he probably returned about 20 November 1825), the Smiths learned that a new land agent named John Greenwood was overseeing the property on which their new home was being built. Several gentlemen in the state of Pennsylvania had made known their desire to purchase some flour from the Smith farm, and a bargain was struck so that the Smiths could obtain the money needed to make the last payment on their property and thus acquire the deed. Father Smith sent his son Hyrum to meet with the new land agent and inform him that the last payment would be made on 25 December 1825. The agent, after being informed of the Smiths' intentions, gave his approval to their plan.[17]

However, the Smiths' plan would soon meet opposition. On 2 November 1825 a man known as Squire Stoddard had purchased 150 acres of land immediately to the south of the Smith family farm.[18] Russell Stoddard, the squire's brother, had been the principal carpenter on the two-storied frame house that the Smiths were building on their property. He had offered the Smiths $1,500 for the house when it was completed, but they had declined his offer. It does not seem, however, that Stoddard would take no for an answer. While Father Smith and Joseph were away on business, Stoddard and some other men went to see the new land agent and falsely reported that the father and son had fled and that Hyrum was destroying the premises. Once the land agent believed that he would never receive the final payment on the farm, he sold the deed to Stoddard. Russell and two other men then went to the Smith farm and ordered the family off of the property.

When the land agent was finally told the truth of the matter by the Smiths, he became enraged and sent for the men who had deceived him. But they flatly refused to come and so the agent threatened that if they didn't appear immediately he would obtain a warrant. The prospect of legal action seems to have motivated these men to reconsider their stance, and they made their way to the agent's office, arriving on a Thursday. Mr. Greenwood tried to reason with them about giving the deed back, but according to Mother Smith they tauntingly replied, "We've got the land, sir, and we've got the deed, so just let Smith help himself. Oh, no matter about Smith. He has gold plates, gold money, and gold Bibles. He's rich, he don't want [for] anything." After more discussion Stoddard and his cronies finally agreed that if they were paid $1,000 by Saturday they would relinquish the deed.

After Father Smith and Joseph returned from their trip, the whole family began a frantic and seemingly unrealistic search for sufficient funds to pay for their farm.[19] Finally, on Saturday, they found a buyer in Lemuel Durfee, a high sheriff. Lemuel agreed to the purchase but stipulated that Samuel Smith, the Prophet's brother, must work for him for the period of six months. Lemuel also said that if the Smiths kept up the property in good condition for one year, they could remain on it indefinitely as tenant farmers.

When it came time for the Smiths to redeem their farm their persecutors did not give in easily; they claimed that the appointed time for redemption had actually expired. But their argument was overpowered by those who were present, and they ended up handing over the deed.[20] Lemuel Durfee's records indicate that this transaction took place by 20 December 1825.[21]

The persecution of the Prophet did not let up but continued on in accordance with the angel's prophecy spoken in 1823. In March 1826, Peter G. Bridgeman—a nephew of Josiah Stowell's wife—filed charges against Joseph Smith as a disorderly person. Bridgeman didn't like the fact that Joseph claimed to have the gift of seership. But at the pretrial hearing Josiah Stowell took the stand himself and boldly testified that Joseph had demonstrated to him, beyond any doubt, that he did indeed possess such a marvelous gift. The official Church newspaper reports that after these proceedings had taken place the Prophet was honorably acquitted of the charges that had been brought against him.[22]

FURTHER INSTRUCTIONS

Oliver Cowdery indicates in an early Church periodical that between the time of the March 1826 legal entanglement and his yearly visit to the hill south of Palmyra, Joseph "continued to receive instructions concerning the coming forth of the fullness of the gospel, from the mouth of the heavenly messenger."[23] It appears that Moroni was not the only angel visiting the future President of the restored Church. Joseph states that between the time that he first saw the plates and the day he received them into his custody, he "received many visits from the angels of God unfolding the majesty, and glory of the events that should transpire in the last days."[24] Who were these visitors from the upper realm? John Taylor provides at least a partial answer. He says that "when Joseph Smith was raised up as a prophet of God, Mormon, Moroni, Nephi and others of the ancient prophets who formerly lived on this continent . . . came to him and communicated to him certain principles pertaining to the gospel of the Son of God."[25]

On 22 September 1826 it was time once again for Joseph to walk south of Palmyra and ascend the hill where the golden plates were concealed. Here he once again had a conversation with the last Nephite historian to write upon the golden plates. Knowledge of their conversation is sparse, but it can be said with certainty that Moroni instructed Joseph Smith concerning the Lord's work in the last days.[26]

EMPLOYMENT AND MARRIAGE

After Joseph had his annual meeting with Moroni at the hill, he went back to Josiah Stowell's house in southern New York in order to work—possibly on Josiah's 800 acres of farmland or at one of his sawmills. This would have been in late September or perhaps even October 1826. But this employment situation was not ideal. Cash was scarce, and one source states that Mr. Stowell "could not pay him money for his work very well."[27]

By November Joseph had left Josiah's homestead and started working at Joseph Knight Sr.'s farm. Knight owned property on the south side of the Susquehanna River in Colesville, New York, where he had built a gristmill. He also owned a carding mill on the river with two carding machines. Mr. Knight later purchased three other farms in the vicinity and hired many hands to work for him, including the young Joseph Smith. According to Joseph Knight's son, his father said that

> Joseph was the best hand he ever hired, we found him a boy of truth, he was about 21 years of age. I think it was in November [that] he made known to my father and I that he had seen a vision, that a personage had appeared to him and told him where there was a gold book of ancient date buried and if he would follow the directions of the angel he would get it. We were told it in secret; . . . [M]y two elder brothers [Nahum and Newell] did not believe in such things; my Father and I believed what he told us.[28]

While Joseph Smith was working at this location, Mr. Knight supplied him with a horse and cutter (a light sleigh) so he could pay visits to Emma Hale in Harmony, Pennsylvania.[29] Joseph eventually asked Isaac Hale, Emma's father, for the hand of his daughter in marriage, but Isaac refused on the grounds that Joseph was a stranger and had been involved with a business that he did not approve of.[30] Because of this opposition Joseph and Emma decided that it would be necessary for them to elope, and on 18 January 1827 they were married by Squire Zachariah Tarbell at his home in South Bainbridge,

New York.[31] After the wedding Josiah Stowell moved Joseph and Emma to the Smith family farm back in Palmyra, New York,[32] and here Joseph farmed with his father for a season.[33]

ADMONITION AND PRECAUTION

Soon after Joseph and Emma began their life together as husband and wife in Palmyra, Father Smith sent Joseph to the town of Manchester on a matter of business. Joseph was expected to come back to the house by six o'clock in the evening, but he did not arrive by that time. In fact, he did not return until three hours later, and when he did he looked pale and exhausted. Father Smith asked him if everything was all right, and the response, as reported by his mother, was, "I have had the severest chastisement that I ever had in my life." Indignant, Father Smith inquired as to the identity of the person who had taken his son to task for so long. Joseph replied that on his way home he was met by the angel of the Lord. "He says I have been negligent," declared the Prophet, "that the time has now come when the record should be brought forth, and that I must be up and doing, that I must set myself about the things which God has commanded me to do. But father, give yourself no uneasiness as to this reprimand, for I know what course I am to pursue, and all will be well." It was evidently signified to Joseph during his lengthy interview with the angelic instructor that he should make another attempt to obtain the golden plates on 22 September of that year, but Joseph did not make that fact known to his parents during their conversation.[34]

It is interesting to note that in June 1827, Father Smith told the story of his son, the angel, and the golden plates to a Methodist class leader and furniture-maker named Willard Chase.[35] This is a significant piece of information because in the forepart of September 1827 Joseph Smith himself went to Willard Chase and placed an order for a chest in which he could lock up his "gold book." Willard, however, refused to make the chest—on not one but two separate occasions.[36] It appears that Willard's refusal is yet another example of the prejudice the Prophet encountered throughout his lifetime on account of his divine calling to bring forth the Book of Mormon.

RETRIEVAL OF THE GOLDEN PLATES

Joseph Smith anticipated that trouble might arise as the time for the retrieval of the golden plates drew near. Right before nightfall on 21 September 1827, he asked his father to go over to the house of Samuel Lawrence and check to see if he was making preparations to go to the hill where the plates were buried. Lawrence had somehow heard about the golden plates and had previously been to the hill in an effort to locate them. If Father Smith found out that Lawrence was preparing to interfere with the proceedings of the night, he was to warn him that Joseph would "thrash the stumps with him." Fortunately for Lawrence, Father Smith saw no such signs of activity.[37]

On this night the Prophet's mother was up very late attending to some pressing business. About midnight Joseph asked her if she had a chest with a lock and key. She replied that she did not, since all of the locks had been broken during the family's prior move. She was alarmed at the situation, but Joseph told her to be calm since he could do very well without it for the time being. But Mother Smith felt a sense of anxiety about these circumstances, remembering the Prophet's first failure to obtain the plates from the angel. Joseph soon left the house with his wife Emma, and Mother Smith spent the night in prayer.

Josiah Stowell and Joseph Knight were both visiting the Smith family home at this time, and once Joseph and Emma got outside of the house they hitched up Joseph Knight's horse to his wagon and drove three miles south to the hill where the Book of Mormon plates were concealed.[38] When they arrived at their destination, Joseph stopped the wagon beside the road, walked by himself about thirty or forty rods from the road to the hill, and then began to climb towards the top.[39] Katherine Smith recalled that the Prophet's appointment with the angel was for 2:00 A.M.[40] In the meantime, Emma stayed with the horse and wagon and knelt down and offered up a prayer.[41]

By the time the angel Moroni made his appearance near the top of the hill, it was 22 September 1827. Joseph may not have been aware that this was one of the high holy days of the ancient Israelite calendar. It was Rosh ha-Shanah, or the Feast of Trumpets, a day when God remembered His covenants with the Israelites to "bring them back from exile" and when "ritual trumpet blasts signify the issuance of revelation and a call for Israel to gather for God's word of redemption."[42]

The Prophet reports that on this morning the angel Moroni finally delivered the Book of Mormon plates into his hands.[43] Two secondhand accounts, related by Wilford Woodruff and Joseph's mother, convey the words of the angel to Joseph Smith on this important occasion. Wilford Woodruff states that as the transfer of the custody of the plates took place,

> the vision of [Joseph's] mind was opened, and the angel showed unto him the condition of the nations of the earth, and said, "This record which I now commit unto your hand contains the words of life—the gospel of Jesus Christ—and the Lord is now about to establish His kingdom upon the earth. The world [is] in darkness; the Gentiles have departed from the gospel of Jesus Christ; they have forsaken the light, the glory, and the power of the Priesthood of the Son of God which was given to and enjoyed by the Gentile nations when Israel was cut off."[44]

According to Lucy Mack Smith, the angel also declared,

> Now you have got the record into your own hands, and you are but a man, therefore you will have to be watchful and faithful to your trust, or you will be overpowered by wicked men, for they will lay every plan and scheme that is possible to get them away from you. And if you do not take heed continually, they will succeed. While they were in my hands I could keep them, and no man had power to take them away, but now I give them up to you. Beware, and look well to your ways.[45]

When his conversation with the angel had ended, Joseph descended the hill with the plates and hid them in a hollow log somewhere between the hill and his house.[46] The Prophet's mother explains, "The record . . . he had deposited in a cavity [of] a birch log three miles distant [from the house] and covered it with the bark of the same."[47]

This was an exceptional day not only for Joseph and his family but also for others who would later believe and embrace the Book of Mormon, as evidenced by a little-known incident connected with the day's events. In the early morning hours of the twenty-second, an extraordinary sight was witnessed in the sky. The first to see it was John P. Green, who woke Heber C. Kimball; both men would later convert to the restored gospel. Heber relates,

> September 22, 1827, while living in the town of Mendon, I having retired to bed, John P. Greene, a traveling reformed Methodist preacher, [woke] me up calling upon me to behold the scenery in the heavens. I called my wife and Sister Fanny Young (sister of Brigham Young) who was living with me. It was so clear that you could see to pick up a pin. We looked to the eastern horizon and beheld a white smoke arise towards the heavens, and as it ascended it formed itself into a belt and made a noise like the rustling of a mighty wind, and continued southwest, forming a regular bow dipping in the western horizon. After the bow had formed it began to widen out and grow clear and transparent, of a bluish cast; it grew wide enough to contain twelve men abreast.
>
> In this bow an army moved, commencing from the east and marching to the west. They moved in platoons, and walked so close [that] the rear ranks trod in the steps of their file leaders, until the whole bow was literally crowded with soldiers. We could see distinctly the muskets, bayonets, and knapsacks of the men—who wore caps and feathers like those used by the American soldiers in the last war with Britain. [We] also [saw] their officers with their swords and equipage, and heard the clashing and jingling of their instruments of war and could discover the form and features of the

men. The most profound order existed throughout the entire army. When the foremost man stepped, every man stepped at the same time: I could hear the step. When the front rank reached the western horizon a battle ensued, as we could distinctly hear the report of the arms and the rush.

No man could judge of my feelings when I beheld that army of men, as plainly as I ever saw armies of men in the flesh. It seemed as though every hair of my head was alive. This scenery we gazed upon for hours, until it began to disappear.

Subsequently I learned this took place the same evening that Joseph Smith received the records of the Book of Mormon from the angel Moroni. John Young, Sr., and John P. Green's wife, Rhoda, were also witnesses of this scenery. My wife, Vilate, being frightened at what she saw, said, "Father Young, what does all this mean?" He replied in a lively, pleased manner, "Why, its one of the signs of the coming of the Son of Man." The next night similar scenery was beheld in the west, by the neighbors, representing armies of men who were engaged in battle.[48]

And indeed a battle had begun, a battle for the souls of men. A battle that would not be fought with powder and ball, nor with sword and bayonet, but with the words of a long-buried book.

NOTES TO CHAPTER 2

1.   William B. Smith, *William Smith on Mormonism* (Lamoni, Iowa: Herald Steam Book and Job Office, 1883), 10.
2.   See Lavina F. Anderson, ed., *Lucy's Book: A Critical Edition of Lucy Mack Smith's Family Memoir* (Salt Lake City: Signature Books, 2001), 341–42.
3.   Ibid., 343.
4.   Ibid., 345.

5. Ibid., 350–52, 356.

6. *Kansas City Times,* 11 April 1895. An affidavit by one of Joseph Smith's neighbors claims that the Prophet told him after obtaining the plates that an angel "told him he could not get the plates until he was married" (Henry Harris, affidavit, cited in Francis W. Kirkham, *A New Witness for Christ in America* [Independence, Mo.: Zion's Printing and Publishing, 1942], 1:133).

7. See Dean C. Jessee, "Joseph Knight's Recollection of Early Mormon History," *BYU Studies* 17, no. 1 (fall 1976): 31.

8. *Times and Seasons,* vol. 3, no. 13, 2 May 1842, 771.

9. *Saints' Herald,* vol. 33, 1 May 1886, 260.

10. Joseph Smith describes the objects as follows: "I looked in [the stone box] and there indeed did I behold the plates, the Urim and Thummim and the breastplate" (*Times and Seasons,* vol. 3, no. 13, 2 May 1842, 771). No mention is made of any other items.

11. See ibid., 772.

12. Anderson, ed., *Lucy's Book,* 389. It appears that it was Joseph Knight Sr. who gave Josiah Stowell this information (see ibid., 359–60).

13. *Times and Seasons,* vol. 3, no. 13, 2 May 1842, 772. In this same source Joseph notes that it was his participation in this project that earned him a lifelong reputation as a "money digger." An affidavit from Isaac Hale (Emma Hale's father) indicates that the search for the Spanish mine stopped about 17 November 1825, meaning that the operation would have commenced about mid-October 1825 (see *Susquehanna Register,* vol. 9, 1 May 1834).

14. "Was not Jo Smith a money digger? Answer. Yes, but it was never a very profitable job to him, as he only got fourteen dollars a month for it" (*Elders' Journal,* vol. 1, no. 3, July 1838, 43).

15. *Tiffany's Monthly,* vol. 5, no. 4, August 1859, 169.

16. See ibid., 167.

17. See Anderson, ed., *Lucy's Book,* 361–62.

18. See Donald L. Enders, "The Joseph Smith, Sr., Family: Farmers of the Genesee," in Susan Easton Black and Charles D. Tate Jr., eds., *Joseph Smith: The Prophet, The Man* (Provo, Utah: BYU Religious Studies Center, 1993), 216.

19. Anderson, ed., *Lucy's Book,* 359–61, 365–69.

20. See ibid., 369–72.

21. See Richard L. Anderson, "The Reliability of the Early History of Lucy and Joseph Smith," *Dialogue* 4, no. 2 (summer 1969): 26.

22. For further reading see Marvin S. Hill, "Joseph Smith and the 1826 Trial: New Evidence and New Difficulties," *BYU Studies* 12, no. 2 (winter 1972): 223–33; Gordon A. Madsen, "Joseph Smith's 1826 Trial: The Legal Setting," *BYU Studies* 30, no. 2 (spring 1990): 91–107.

23. *Messenger and Advocate,* vol. 2, no. 1, October 1835, 201.

24. *Times and Seasons,* vol. 3, no. 9, 1 March 1842, 707.

25. George D. Watt, comp., *Journal of Discourses,* 26 vols. (London: F. D. and S. W. Richards and Sons, 1854–1886), 17:374.

26. See *Times and Seasons,* vol. 3, no. 13, 2 May 1842, 771.

27. Jessee, "Joseph Knight's Recollection of Early Mormon History," 32.

28. Biographical Sketch of Joseph Knight Sr. by Joseph Knight Jr., 16 August 1862, Historical Department Archives, The Church of Jesus Christ of Latter-day Saints, Salt Lake City, Utah. The year that these events took place, 1826, is established in Larry C. Porter, "The Colesville Branch and the Coming Forth of the Book of Mormon," *BYU Studies* 10, no. 3 (spring 1970): 369.

29. See Jessee, "Joseph Knight's Recollection of Early Mormon History," 32.

30. See *Susquehanna Register,* vol. 9, 1 May 1834.

31. See Milton V. Backman Jr., *Eyewitness Accounts of the Restoration* (Orem, Utah: Grandin Book, 1983), 54.

32. See Jessee, "Joseph Knight's Recollection of Early Mormon History," 32.

33. See *Times and Seasons,* vol. 3, no. 13, 2 May 1842, 772.

34. Anderson, ed., *Lucy's Book,* 373–75.

35. Story cited in Kirkham, *A New Witness for Christ in America,* 1:133–34.

36. Ibid., 1:134.

37. Jessee, "Joseph Knight's Recollection of Early Mormon History," 32–33.

38. Anderson, ed., *Lucy's Book,* 376.

39. See Willard Chase's report of Joseph Smith's statement in Eber D. Howe, *Mormonism Unvailed* (Painesville, Ohio: Telegraph Press, 1834), 245–46.

40. "[H]e was commanded to go on the 22[n]d day of September 1827 at 2 o'clock" (*Saints' Herald,* vol. 33, 1 May 1886, 260).

41. See *Tiffany's Monthly,* vol. 5, no. 4, August 1859, 164–65.

42. Lenet H. Read, "Joseph Smith's Receipt of the Plates and the Israelite Feast of Trumpets," *Journal of Book of Mormon Studies* 2, no. 2 (fall 1993): 110.

43. See *Times and Seasons,* vol. 3, no. 9, 1 March 1842, 707.

44. *Journal of Discourses,* 7:99.

45. Anderson, ed., *Lucy's Book,* 388.

46. See *Kansas City Times,* 11 April 1895.

47. Anderson, ed., *Lucy's Book,* 385.

48. *Millennial Star,* vol. 26, no. 30, 23 July 1864, 472; ibid., vol. 26, no. 31, 30 July 1864, 487.

CHAPTER 3

OPPOSITION IN PALMYRA

In the early morning hours of 22 September 1827, Lucy Mack Smith went about the business of preparing breakfast for her family and their guests. She expected every moment that Joseph and Emma would return home and, with the dreadful thought in her mind that her son might once again fail to obtain the golden plates, her heart fluttered each time she heard the sound of footsteps.

When the men of the house sat down to eat their breakfast, Joseph's father inquired as to his son's whereabouts, insisting that he should come to the table and share the meal. But Lucy, not wanting to mention the reason for Joseph's conspicuous absence, replied that she would serve him and his new wife their breakfast together and told Father Smith that he should not worry about it.

Everything was fine until Joseph Knight Sr. came into the house and announced that he couldn't find his horse anywhere. Lucy told Mr. Knight not to worry; she would send her son William out onto the property to search for the beast. With this assurance Mr. Knight was satisfied, but shortly thereafter he noticed that his wagon was gone too! He concluded that some rogue must have stolen them both during the night. Lucy tried to calm Mr. Knight down, saying that all would be taken care of and then she sent him outside to talk with Father Smith.

While Mr. Knight was outside the residence, Joseph and Emma returned from their excursion to the hill. Lucy was so worried that Joseph had failed in his task once again that she had to leave the room to hide her emotions. Joseph followed her and said reassuringly, "Do not be uneasy, all is right." Lucy reports that he then handed her the Urim and Thummim covered by a handkerchief. After she had handled and examined this ancient object for a short time, Joseph took it from her and left without saying a single word about the record.[1]

After eating his breakfast Joseph called Mr. Knight to come and see him in the other room. The Prophet did not tell Knight where he had been, but he did say, "It is ten times better than I expected." Joseph then "went on to tell the length and width and thickness of the plates" and said that they appeared to be made of gold. "But he seemed to think more of the glasses or the Urim and Thummim than he did of the plates," said Joseph Knight. The younger Joseph told him, "I can see anything; they are marvelous." He also mentioned that he desired to get the characters on the plates translated.[2]

DANGER TO THE PLATES

Before the translation could commence, the Prophet needed to provide for the protection of the Book of Mormon plates, and so he went to his mother and asked her about obtaining a chest to put them in. Lucy directed him to go and see the man who was making furniture for her daughter, and she instructed Joseph to tell him that if he would construct a suitable chest he would be paid half in cash and half in produce. Joseph replied that he would go and talk to this man, but he didn't have any idea where he would come up with the money that would be needed for the payment—there wasn't even a shilling in the house.[3]

The very next day, 23 September 1827, a man named Mr. Warner came from the town of Macedon—about three miles west of Palmyra—and told Joseph Smith that a widow from his town, who had never met a member of the Smith family before, asked that he be sent to her home in order to remove the wall of a well. She promised that she would pay young Joseph for the labor that he performed. The Smiths felt that this was "a provision of Providence" because the money that would be gained from doing this job would enable Joseph to pay for the chest that would be used to secure the Book of Mormon plates.[4]

Joseph had been away on his job in Macedon only a little while when one of the Smiths' neighbors started to ask Father Smith many questions about the golden plates. Soon after this unusual interrogation, Father Smith was informed that about a dozen men, led by Willard Chase, had sent about twenty miles north for a conjuror[5] to come and "divine . . . by magic art" where the plates had been concealed. Father and Mother Smith did not know where Joseph had hidden the Book of Mormon plates and were afraid they might be discovered by this group. The morning after learning of this plan, Father Smith went over the hill on the eastern side of his property to see what intelligence he could gather among the neighbors.

Samuel Lawrence's house was the first residence that the Prophet's father came to, and here he found the group of conspirators with Willard Chase and the "conjuror." Father Smith entered through the front door, and sitting near the back door with a newspaper in hand, he listened in on the conversation that was taking place out back. These men were scheming to find "Joe Smith's gold Bible," but they were talking so loudly that Mrs. Lawrence stepped out back and warned them in a hushed, but vehement, tone that their conversation could be overheard. When he was given this warning the conjuror reportedly roared, "I am not afraid of anybody. We will have the plates in spite of Joe Smith or all the devils in hell!" When Lawrence's wife went back into the house Father Smith excused himself and left the premises.[6]

After arriving back at his residence Father Smith found Lucy, and together they went to find Joseph's wife, Emma. They found her busily weaving, according to one source,[7] and asked her if she knew where the plates were hidden; she answered that she did not know. Father Smith then told her about the neighbors' scheme, and she decided that it would be best to go to Macedon and tell her husband what was happening. Father Smith told his son William to go and fetch a stray horse that had been on their property for the past two days, and within fifteen minutes Emma was galloping westward along the roadway.

The Prophet had taken the interpreters, or Urim and Thummim, with him to Macedon. While he was working inside the well, he looked into the instrument and saw Emma approaching. By the time

Emma arrived, Joseph was above ground to greet her. She told him of the conspiracy to find the plates, but Joseph assured her that they were perfectly safe for the moment. Nevertheless, he decided that he would return home with her.

Widow Wells was none too pleased at Joseph's announcement that he would need to leave and take care of some pressing business, but he promised her that he would return and finish his job as agreed. After a horse was fetched for Joseph, he and Emma then rode home through the streets of Palmyra. When they came within about one mile of the Smith family farm, they found Father Smith pacing anxiously back and forth, but Joseph assured him that there was no danger to the golden plates.

Once they all arrived at the house, Joseph sent his younger brother Don Carlos to Hyrum Smith's home with the request that Hyrum come and see Joseph. When Hyrum arrived Joseph asked him to have a chest with a good lock and key at the house by the time that he returned.[8]

RUNNING THE GAUNTLET

According to Lucy Mack Smith's history, Joseph traveled about three miles to the birch log where he had hidden the golden plates, and once he had removed them from their place of concealment, he wrapped them up in his linen work smock and headed for his house.[9]

He walked along the road for a short distance but then decided that it would be safer for him to travel through the woods. He had not traveled far through the forest when he came upon a clearing of fallen trees and jumped over one of the logs. A man suddenly sprang up, grabbed for the plates, and demanded that they be given to him.[10] When Joseph refused to relent, the man struck him hard with a gun. Joseph reciprocated by knocking down his assailant, and then he ran at the top of his speed for half a mile. But instead of being free of his problem, Joseph unexpectedly ran into another man. He knocked this individual down also and began to run again. The Prophet then encountered a third individual who gave him a severe stroke with a gun. This time Joseph hit his attacker so hard that he dislocated his thumb.[11] But this injury did not prevent him from sprinting once again toward his house.

When Joseph finally crossed over the fence that ran along his father's field, he threw himself down in the crevice created by the meeting of the wooden beams and tried desperately to catch his breath. He then noticed the serious problem with his hand. Joseph summoned all of his remaining strength and made a final dash for his house. He arrived both frightened and exhausted. His sister Katherine reports that Joseph burst through the front door, carrying the golden plates in his smock. She "took the plates from him and laid them on the table, temporarily, and helped revive him until he got breathing properly."[12]

Joseph asked his mother to send his brother Don Carlos to go find his father, Joseph Knight Sr., and Josiah Stowell in order to form a search party and look for his assailants. Don Carlos was then to go and inform Hyrum that it was time to bring his chest to the family house.

When Don Carlos entered into Hyrum's home, he found that his brother was entertaining guests. Don Carlos touched Hyrum on the shoulder and the older sibling suddenly remembered his assignment. Without warning he dropped his drinking cup, unceremoniously dumped the contents of a wooden lap desk out, and hurried through the doorway with it perched on his shoulder. His houseguests were a bit perplexed by this singular behavior and told his wife that he was positively crazy. But she just laughed and told them that he was fine; he had just remembered a neglected duty.

When Hyrum's lap desk arrived at the Smith family house, the Prophet placed the plates inside of it and threw himself down on the bed for some much needed rest. After he had recovered a little of his strength, Father Smith and Joseph Knight returned from looking for his pursuers, but they had not had any luck in locating them. Joseph then told them about his harrowing adventure and asked his father to reset his thumb because it had become very painful. After the procedure was finished, Joseph told Knight and Stowell "the whole history of the record . . . up to the time when he took [it] out of the stone box." This recital of events "interested them very much," and it is said that they "believed all that was told them."[13]

THE FIRST WITNESSES

It appears that Josiah Stowell and Joseph Knight had good reason to believe Joseph Smith's story—he allowed them to handle the golden plates while they were in his house. William Smith recounted the activity of that remarkable day. He says in two separate, but complementary, sources, "When the plates were brought [into the house] they were wrapped in a tow frock [or a long linen work shirt]. My father then put them into a pillow case. Father said, 'What, Joseph, can we not see them?'"[14] "Joseph, putting his hand on them said, 'No, I am instructed not to show them to anyone. If I do, I will transgress and lose them again.'"[15] "'I was disobedient the first time, but I intend to be faithful this time; for I was forbidden to show them until they are translated, but you can feel them.'" William says, "We handled them and could tell what they were. . . . [We] could raise the leaves this way (raising a few leaves of the Bible before him). One could easily tell that they were not a stone, hewn out to deceive, or even a block of wood."[16] William admits, "I did not see them uncovered, but I handled them and hefted them while wrapped in a tow frock. . . . I could tell they were plates of some kind and that they were fastened together by rings running through the back."[17]

Others also handled the plates. Katherine Smith recounted to her grandson that on this day in 1827 "Joseph allowed her to 'heft' the package but not to see the gold plates, as the angel had forbidden him to show them at that period. She said they were very heavy."[18] Lucy Mack Smith was interviewed about her experience with the plates by a woman named Sally Parker. Sally said of their conversation, "I asked her if she saw the plates. She said no, it was not for her to see them, but she hefted and handled them."[19] In a dictated letter sent to Joseph Smith in 1843, Josiah Stowell said that he "never staggered at the foundation of the work, for he knew too much concerning it. If I understand him right," said the person taking the dictation, "he was the first person that took the plates out of your hands the morning you brought them in, and he observed, 'Blessed is he that sees and believeth, and more blessed is he that believeth without seeing'"[20] (see John 20:29).

Because of the experience that those in the Smith homestead had with the plates in the fall of 1827 they qualify as the first latter-day witnesses to the physical reality of the Book of Mormon plates. At this point in time they all knew beyond any doubt that young Joseph possessed an object that upon tactile scrutiny seemed to confirm the story he had been telling them all along.

THE NEIGHBORS COME KNOCKING

Lucy Mack Smith reports that during the fall of 1827, Joseph "commenced work with his father on the farm in order to be near the treasure that was committed to his care."[21] But the tranquility of the Smiths' pastoral farming life was soon interrupted. Knowledge that their family possessed a golden book soon began to spread throughout the countryside. Martin Harris remembered that it "was about the first of October, 1827" that his brother, Preserved Harris, first told him about Joseph Smith's "Golden Bible." Preserved said that he had heard about this unusual volume while visiting Palmyra, New York. Martin took a trip to Palmyra the very next day and spoke with other people who had heard the same thing. These other people said that they had heard the tale directly from the Prophet's father. It is both significant and insightful that the people who talked to Martin Harris on this day believed that Joseph Smith was a liar and should be tarred and feathered—and in turn Martin thought that they were "of the devil's kingdom."[22]

It was sometime in the fall of 1827 that Martin Harris passed on his knowledge of the Book of Mormon plates and the interpreters to a man by the name of John H. Gilbert. This person would later play a key role in the coming forth of the ancient record. Beginning in the late summer of 1829, Gilbert would act not only as the editor but also as the typesetter and primary pressman for the first edition of the Book of Mormon.[23]

Joseph Knight recalled what happened once word had gotten out that the Smiths were storing a gleaming set of tablets in their home. He writes, "Now it soon got about that Joseph Smith had found the plates and people came in to see them but he told them that they could not for he must not show them. But many insisted and offered

[him] money and property to see them." Joseph remained resolute, however, and because he kept the plates from the gaze of the people his family began to be persecuted and abused.[24]

Katherine Smith recalled that the problems caused by the neighbors who had knowledge of the plates did not stop at verbal animosity. She states that from the time the plates were brought into the house, the Smiths' premises were searched all around on a regular basis. Mobs of people even looked through the farm's field and its standing wheat stacks in the hopes of finding the rumored treasure.[25]

One day Joseph Smith came running up to his family's home and asked if a company of men had been there yet. When he was informed that nobody had arrived, Joseph said that a mob of people would be there by nighttime, if not before, in order to search for the Book of Mormon plates. They determined that they should hide the Nephite record. Alva Beman, a man from the neighboring village of Livonia, helped the Smiths take their brick hearth partially apart, hide the plates in the cavity underneath, and then rebuild the structure. The hearth had scarcely been relaid when an armed group of men came rushing toward the house. Joseph's mother relates that in response to the attack, the Prophet threw open the door of the dwelling and shouted as if he were giving military orders. At the same time, the males inside the building rushed out headlong toward the mob. This action caught the company of bandits completely by surprise, and they "thought it best to give leg bail while they were able" and fled back into the woods.[26]

Even though the Smiths had successfully repelled the attackers their troubles had barely begun. Around the time of this episode Samuel Lawrence and an unidentified "rodsman" (believed by some historians to be Luman Walter and possibly also the previously mentioned conjurer) showed up at the Smith home and announced that they wanted to talk to Joseph. The young Prophet took the two men into the west room of the house where the fireplace was located, and once they were there the two visitors "proposed to go shares with him and tried every way to bargain with him, but could not. Then [Walter] took out his [divining] rods and held them up and they pointed down to the hearth where [the plates] were hid. 'There,' [said Walter], 'it is under that hearth.'" The available historical records do not record what happened next, but it is documented that after this unnerving incident took place, the Smiths had to continually guard their residence.[27]

It was only a short time after the Smiths had scared the armed mob away from their farm that Joseph received an intimation that another mob was on the way.[28] This time Joseph removed the golden plates from their hiding place inside the hearth and took them across the road to his father's cooperage, or barrel-making shop. It is reported that he took them out of the box where they were secured, wrapped them carefully in some cloth, and then hid them inside a quantity of flax that was stowed in the shop's loft. Next, Joseph renailed the now empty box that had held the plates, tore up some of the planks in the building's floor, and buried the box. As soon as darkness fell, the mob arrived and ransacked the workshop. They split the box that had contained the plates into pieces, but when they didn't find what they were looking for they went away. A few days after this act of vandalism occurred, the Smiths learned that the sister of Willard Chase had led the mob to the barrel-making shop after looking through a piece of green glass and seeing the place where the Prophet had hidden the "Gold Bible." It is said that even after their failure to find the plates this mob still followed Chase's sister around to other places in a vain attempt to locate them.[29]

PREPARING FOR THE TRANSLATION

Soon after the incident in the cooper shop, it became necessary for the Prophet Joseph Smith to "take some measures to accomplish the translation of the record into English." Joseph was instructed to make a facsimile of some of the reformed-Egyptian characters found on the Book of Mormon plates (see Morm. 9:32) and then "send them to all the learned men that he could find and ask them for the translation of the same." Joseph's mother says that he was very solicitous about getting this work accomplished, but up to that point in time "no means had come into his hands [for] accomplishing it."[30] According to Martin Harris, the Prophet said that the angel Moroni told him to go and look into the interpreters (or "spectacles" as they were sometimes called), and he would be shown the man who would assist him in his work. Upon looking into the ancient instrument, Joseph saw Martin Harris standing plainly before him.[31]

The Prophet asked his mother if she would go to the Harrises' home in Palmyra and request Martin to come and see him. Lucy didn't like the idea of going there; she was reluctant to proceed because Martin's wife—also named Lucy—had a jealous and suspicious temperament. Joseph's mother asked her son for permission to talk to Mrs. Harris about the purpose of her trip before she approached Martin. With Joseph's approval she then set off for the Harris farm on 6 October 1827.[32]

When Joseph's mother arrived at her destination she told Lucy Harris how her son obtained the gold plates in as much detail as necessity demanded. Mrs. Harris seemed enthusiastic about what she heard and immediately volunteered money for the accomplishment of the Prophet's work. Joseph's mother politely declined the offer and asked to see Martin. But Mrs. Harris insisted on rendering financial assistance to the project. Upon another refusal to accept the donation Mother Smith was finally taken to see Martin.

Mr. Harris had just finished a large amount of work on his house and farm. He planned on hiring a person to take care of his property while he traveled for one full year. After Lucy Smith delivered the request for Martin to pay Joseph a visit, Mr. Harris agreed to go see him in a few days. Martin's wife announced, apparently without any consultation, that she would accompany her husband on this trip.

The Harrises arrived at the Smith family farm on a Tuesday afternoon, probably 9 October 1827. And Mrs. Harris wasted no time in confronting Joseph about the golden plates. She asked the Prophet if he was telling the truth, at the same time claiming that if he did indeed possess such objects she would surely see them. Joseph told her in reply that this was simply not possible since "he was not permitted to exhibit [the plates] to anyone except those whom the Lord [would] appoint to testify of them." Mrs. Harris then stated that if she could get a witness that Joseph Smith was indeed telling the truth about the ancient record then she would surely provide financial support for its translation.

Mrs. Harris retired to sleep at the Smith home that evening, and during the night she is said to have had a rather peculiar experience.

The Prophet's mother recalled that in the morning she told them about "a very remarkable dream. She said that a personage had appeared to her the night before and said to her that inasmuch as she had disputed the servant of the Lord, and said that his word was not to be believed, and asked him many improper questions, that she had done that which was not right in the sight of God. 'Now,' said [he], 'behold, here are the plates. Look upon them and believe.'" Mother Smith recalled that "she then described the record minutely" and again offered the Prophet some money. Joseph, it is reported, finally agreed to her proposition but only "in order to get rid of her importunities."[33]

Martin Harris likewise told the Prophet that if he could get a witness from God that this was His work he would support the publication of the Book of Mormon financially. Martin then went to his home and asked God in prayer to show him whether this was His work. He also covenanted that if he received such a witness he would put forth his best ability to bring the translation of the plates before the world. Martin testified that the "still small voice" then spoke to him, confirming that this was indeed the Lord's work, "and that it was designed to bring in the fullness of His gospel to the Gentiles to fulfill His word."[34]

With conviction in his heart, Mr. Harris was now willing to assist in pushing the Lord's work forward. When he ran into Joseph Smith at a public house in Palmyra, he took a bag from his pocket and gave it to the Prophet. Inside the pouch was fifty dollars in silver coins. He said, "Here, Mr. Smith, is fifty dollars. I give it to you to do the Lord's work with. No, . . . I give it to the Lord for His own work." Joseph protested and said that he would prefer to sign a note for the money, but Martin called upon all of the strangers present to witness that he gave it freely and did not demand any compensation or return. The money was for the purpose of doing the work of the Lord.[35] Martin received a wonderful blessing for his act of charity, one that would have a direct impact on the work of bringing the ancient Nephite record before the world. Joseph Smith records in his history that "because of [Martin Harris's] faith and *this* righteous deed, the Lord appeared unto him in a vision and showed unto him His marvelous work which He was about to do." But there was more. Martin also

informed Joseph that "the Lord had shown him that he must go to
New York City with some of the characters" from the Book of
Mormon plates.[36] Thus the stage was set for the fulfillment of a
biblical prophecy that the angel Moroni had quoted to Joseph Smith
in September 1823.

NOTES TO CHAPTER 3

1. Lavina F. Anderson, ed., *Lucy's Book: A Critical Edition of Lucy Mack Smith's Family Memoir* (Salt Lake City: Signature Books, 2001), 376–79.
2. Dean C. Jessee, "Joseph Knight's Recollection of Early Mormon History," *BYU Studies* 17, no. 1 (fall 1976): 33.
3. See Anderson, ed., *Lucy's Book*, 379.
4. Ibid., 380.
5. This man is believed by some historians to be Luman Walter of Pultneyville, New York. Katherine Smith says that her father heard about the "conjuror" a "few days" after Joseph had hidden the plates in the log (*Kansas City Times*, 11 April 1895). Brigham Young was acquainted with this person and said that he was a "fortune-teller, a necromancer, an astrologer, a soothsayer, and possessed as much talent as any man that walked on the American soil, and was one of the wickedest men I ever saw." During the same season that Joseph Smith obtained the golden plates, this man evidently traveled to Palmyra, New York, on three different occasions in an attempt to get the plates for himself. Brigham declared, "Those spirits driven from heaven were with him and with others who tried to prevent Joseph's getting the plates" (George D. Watt, comp., *Journal of Discourses*, 26 vols. [London: F. D. and S. W. Richards and Sons, 1854–1886], 5:55).
6. Anderson, ed., *Lucy's Book*, 381–82.
7. See *Kansas City Times*, 11 April 1895.
8. Anderson, ed., *Lucy's Book*, 382–85.
9. See ibid., 385.
10. Katherine Smith (Salisbury) says that Joseph told her that the first attack came when he jumped over a rail fence; the assailant grabbed for the plates but Joseph knocked him down with his right fist and then ran the gauntlet with several other assailants (see H. S. Salisbury, grandson of Katherine Smith (Salisbury), interview by I. B. Ball, 31 August 1854, p. 2, Historical

Department Archives, The Church of Jesus Christ of Latter-day Saints, Salt Lake City, Utah). Martin Harris said that the first attacker demanded the plates from Joseph and struck him so hard with a club that his side turned black and blue (see *Tiffany's Monthly*, vol. 5, no. 4, August 1859, 166).

11. Katherine Smith (Salisbury) states that she examined Joseph's hand and treated it for bruises on the knuckles (see H. S. Salisbury, interview, 31 August 1854, 2). In another source Katherine says that "he had his thumb put out of place and his arm was very lame" (*Kansas City Times*, 11 April 1895). According to Elder Parley P. Pratt, the Prophet's attackers pursued him until he got near his father's house, at which point they fled the other way for fear of being detected (see Parley P. Pratt, *A Voice of Warning* [New York: W. Sandford, 1837; reprint, Salt Lake City: Deseret Book, 2002], 65).

12. H. S. Salisbury, interview, 31 August 1854, 2.

13. Anderson, ed., *Lucy's Book*, 386–88.

14. *Saints' Herald*, vol. 31, no. 40, 4 October 1884, 643–44.

15. *Zion's Ensign*, vol. 5, no. 3, 13 January 1894, 6. Katherine Smith said of this incident, "We had supposed that when [Joseph] should bring [the plates] home, the whole family would be allowed to see them, but he said it was forbidden of the Lord. They could be seen only by those who were chosen to bear their testimony to the world. We had, therefore, to be content until they were translated and we could have the book to read" (*Saints' Herald*, vol. 33, 1 May 1886, 260). The commandment not to show the plates to anybody but chosen witnesses is also verified in Joseph Knight's history. He says that the Prophet "was commanded not to let [any]one see those things but a few for witness at a given time" (Jessee, "Joseph Knight's Recollection of Early Mormon History," 33); Martin Harris likewise relates, "the Lord had forbid Joseph exhibiting them openly" (Edward Stevenson Journal, 4 September 1870, Historical Department Archives, The Church of Jesus Christ of Latter-day Saints, Salt Lake City, Utah).

16. *Saints' Herald*, vol. 31, no. 40, 4 October 1884, 643–44.

17. *Zion's Ensign*, vol. 5, no. 3, 13 January 1894, 6. William Smith stated that his father, Samuel, Hyrum, "and other members of the family" saw the plates as he did "while in the frock" on the day they were brought into the house—probably indicating that they all handled the plates in the same manner that he did (ibid.).

18. Herbert S. Salisbury, "Things the Prophet's Sister Told Me," signed transcript, 30 June 1945, cited in Richard L. Anderson, *Investigating the Book of Mormon*

Witnesses (Salt Lake City: Deseret Book, 1981), 26. Herbert was the grandson of Katherine Smith (Salisbury).

19. Sally Parker to Francis Tufts, 26 August 1838, Sunbury, Ohio, document in private possession, cited in Anderson, *Investigating the Book of Mormon Witnesses,* 25. Herbert was the grandson of Katherine Smith (Salisbury).

20. Dictated letter, Josiah Stowell to Joseph Smith, 19 December 1843, Historical Department Archives, The Church of Jesus Christ of Latter-day Saints, Salt Lake City, Utah.

21. Anderson, ed., *Lucy's Book,* 389.

22. *Tiffany's Monthly,* vol. 5, no. 4, August 1859, 167–68.

23. See John H. Gilbert, "Memorandum," 8 September 1892, Palmyra, New York, 4, cited in Royal Skousen, "John Gilbert's 1892 Account of the 1830 Printing of the Book of Mormon," in Stephen D. Ricks, Donald W. Parry, and Andrew H. Hedges, eds., *The Disciple as Witness: Essays on Latter-day Saint History and Doctrine in Honor of Richard Lloyd Anderson* (Provo, Utah: FARMS, 2000), 383–405.

24. Jessee, "Joseph Knight's Recollection of Early Mormon History," 33.

25. See *Kansas City Times,* 11 April 1895.

26. Anderson, ed., *Lucy's Book,* 390–92.

27. Jessee, "Joseph Knight's Recollection of Early Mormon History," 33–34.

28. According to Martin Harris, the Prophet hid the plates in the loft of his father's barrel-making shop after he had been "warned by an angel" (*Tiffany's Monthly,* vol. 5, no. 4, August 1859, 167).

29. Anderson, ed., *Lucy's Book,* 392–93.

30. Ibid., 393.

31. *Tiffany's Monthly,* vol. 5, no. 4, August 1859, 169.

32. This date is determined with the help of the following evidence. On 8 October 1845 Lucy Mack Smith "addressed the congregation about an hour, speaking of the history of herself and family in bringing forth the Book of Mormon. She said it was eighteen years ago last Monday [i.e., 6 October 1827] since she commenced preaching the gospel being called upon by Joseph to go and tell Martin Harris and family that he had got the plates and he wanted him to take an alphabet of the characters and carry them to the learned men to decipher" (Norton Jacob, autobiography, L. Tom Perry Special Collections Library, Harold B. Lee Library, Brigham Young University, Provo, Utah, 16).

33. Anderson, ed., *Lucy's Book,* 394–400.

34. *Tiffany's Monthly,* vol. 5, no. 4, August 1859, 169–70.

35. Anderson, ed., *Lucy's Book,* 400.

36. Dean C. Jessee, ed., *The Papers of Joseph Smith* (Salt Lake City: Deseret Book, 1989), 1:9; emphasis added.

CHAPTER 4

THE MOVE TO HARMONY

The excitement in Palmyra, New York, on the subject of the golden plates eventually rose to such a high pitch that some people "threatened to mob Joseph [Smith], and also to tar and feather him" unless he exhibited the ancient artifacts. Since it had become so dangerous for the Prophet to remain at his current residence, it was determined that he should move to Harmony, Pennsylvania, and stay with his wife's family instead (there was a reconciliation after Joseph and Emma's elopement). Alva Hale, Joseph's brother-in-law, was summoned by letter to come up to Palmyra and assist in the move south.[1]

But as soon as a few outsiders ascertained that Joseph was contemplating a move to a new location, they gathered together a mob of about fifty men. These ruffians decided to "follow Joe Smith and take his Gold Bible away from him." They tried to recruit a man known as Dr. McIntyre to take command of the enterprise, but the good doctor "told them they must be a pack of devilish fools and bid them go home and mind their own business." A quarrel then ensued about who should be in charge of the operation, and the disagreement got so heated that the mob ultimately broke up.[2]

The safety of the Nephite relics was prominent in the Prophet's mind, and so he devised a clever plan for their safe transport to his new residence. First, the "breastplate and record . . . were securely nailed up in a box and the box put into a strong cask [or barrel] made for the purpose [of concealment]. The cask was then filled with beans" and sealed shut.[3] Second, the itinerary of the trip was changed. It had originally been decided that the group would depart on a Monday, but they began their journey on a Saturday instead. And third, in case of an emergency Martin Harris advised Joseph and Alva to each cut themselves "a good cudgel and put [them] into the wagon with them, which they did."[4]

The extra preparations for the journey turned out to be well warranted. Parley P. Pratt relates that before the Prophet and his companions had traveled very far along the road, they were

> overtaken by an officer with a search warrant, who flattered himself with the idea that he should surely obtain the plates; [but] after searching very diligently, he was sadly disappointed at not finding them. [Joseph] Smith then drove on; but before he got to his journey's end he was again overtaken by an officer on the same business and, after ransacking the wagon very carefully, he went his way—as much chagrined as the first at not being able to discover the object of his search. Without any further molestation [Joseph] pursued his journey until he came into the northern part of Pennsylvania, near the Susquehanna river, in which part his father-in-law resided.[5]

Joseph, Emma, and Alva arrived in Harmony, Pennsylvania, sometime in the month of December 1827.[6] Even though Joseph was not on the best of terms with his in-laws, he was fortunate in that they were opposed to all mobs. They were, therefore, willing to allow the Prophet "to continue the work of translation without interruption" and promised him protection from "all unlawful proceedings" as far as it was in their power.[7] This does not mean, however, that there was no friction between the two families. Isaac Hale (Emma's father) was told that Joseph had brought the golden plates with him from New York, and he was even allowed at one point to hold them as they lay enclosed in a box. But he, like everyone else, was not allowed to look upon the ancient Nephite tablets. This set of circumstances did not sit well with Isaac. He informed Joseph that he was determined to see the golden plates, and that if he was not allowed to view them for himself, then they would simply have to be removed from his house. Isaac reports that after he issued this ultimatum, he heard that the plates were hidden out in the woods.[8]

THE FULFILLMENT OF ISAIAH'S PROPHECY

Before Joseph Smith had departed from Palmyra, New York, he and Martin Harris agreed that the latter would come down to Pennsylvania as soon as the Prophet had been given sufficient time to transcribe some of the reformed-Egyptian hieroglyphics that covered the golden plates. Martin would then take these characters "to the East and through the country in every direction to all who were professed linguists [in order] to give them an opportunity of showing their talents" at deciphering them.[9] The angel Moroni had informed Joseph during his first visitation in 1823 that before the translation of the plates took place "the scripture must be fulfilled . . . which says that the words of a book, which were sealed, were presented to the learned [Isa. 29:11–12]; for thus has God determined to leave men without excuse, and show to the meek that His arm is not shortened that it cannot save."[10]

By February 1828, Joseph Smith had not only "copied a considerable number" of the Book of Mormon characters from the plates, but "by means of the Urim and Thummim" he had also "translated *some* of them."[11] Meanwhile, Martin Harris's wife had discovered that her husband planned to go throughout the eastern part of the country on a trip, and she declared her intention to accompany him. Martin did not believe that this would be a good idea, so he unexpectedly slipped away and headed off for Harmony, Pennsylvania. When Mrs. Harris found out what her husband had done, she became "highly enraged" and "determined to have satisfaction in some way for the slight which she had received."[12]

Martin arrived at Joseph Smith's residence sometime in the month of February, and after gathering the materials that had been prepared by the Prophet, he headed off toward New York City.[13] William W. Phelps wrote in an 1831 letter that when Martin Harris was on his way to New York City, he took the transcript of the Book of Mormon characters to Utica and Albany.[14] Harris's son adds that his father also took the transcript to the city of Geneva. Martin is said to have presented the writings to "many . . . learned men at the different schools of learning" in these locations.[15] Two separate historical sources state that when Harris stopped in Albany he showed the transcript and partial translation to Luther Bradish, a man who was known to be a student of ancient languages and had also been to several near eastern countries.[16]

When Martin arrived in New York City he paid visits to at least two well-known scholars there. The first he visited was Dr. Samuel L. Mitchill—a scientist, professor, and vice-president of Rutgers Medical College.[17] He was a member of dozens of scholarly and scientific societies, had written many books and articles on a variety of subjects, and was described by some people as a living encyclopedia. A newspaper article from 1831 relates that Mitchill examined Martin's transcript of Book of Mormon symbols and "thought them very curious, but admitted that he could not decipher them." It is then asserted that he said, "Mr. Harris you had better go to the celebrated Doct[or] [Anthon] and show them to him. He is very learned in these ancient languages, and I have no doubt [he] will be able to give you some satisfaction." "Where does he live[?]" asked Harris. He was told, and off he posted with the engravings from the golden plates.[18]

Martin Harris recalled that when he went to Charles Anthon's house he found him there alone in his office.[19] Harris, according to one report, was received very politely by Professor Anthon,[20] and we are told by Anthon himself that Harris handed over a letter of introduction that had been given to him earlier by Doctor Mitchill. This letter requested Anthon to decipher, if at all possible, the hieroglyphics on the paper that Harris would hand to him.[21] Harris relates that he then

> presented the characters which had been translated, with the translation thereof, to Professor [Anthon, who] . . . stated that the translation was correct, more so than any he had before seen translated from the Egyptian. [Martin] then showed him those which were not yet translated, and he said that they were Egyptian, Chaldeac, Assyriac, and

Arabic, and he said that they were true characters. He gave [Mr. Harris] a certificate certifying to the people of Palmyra that they were true characters, and that the translation of such of them as had been translated was also correct.[22]

"I took the certificate and put it into my pocket, and was just leaving the house," said Martin, "when Mr. [Anthon] called me back, and asked me how the young man found out that there were gold plates in the place where he found them. I answered that an angel of God had revealed it unto him."[23] Various secondhand records of Harris's statements can be connected together to reveal what happened next. He evidently related that "Professor Anthon then said, 'Let me see the certificate!'—upon which I took it from my waistcoat pocket and unsuspectingly gave it to him,"[24] "thinking he was going to add something to it."[25] "He then tore it up in anger"[26] and "consigned it to the wastebasket,"[27] "saying there was no such thing as angels now—it was all a hoax."[28] He also announced, recalled Harris, that "if I would bring the plates to him, he would translate them. I informed him that a part of the plates were sealed, and that I was forbidden to bring them."[29] Orson Pratt claims that upon hearing this comment Professor Anthon "very sarcastically remarked that he could not read a sealed book."[30] "Thus," Martin is represented as saying, "the prophecy of Isaiah was fulfilled which will be found in the 29th chapter and 11 verse." But Martin "did not know that [he] was fulfilling it at the time."[31] It is because of Charles Anthon's involvement in this episode that the document filled with hieroglyphics is commonly referred to today as the "Anthon Transcript."

RETURN AND DELAY

It seems that Martin Harris returned from his trip to the eastern cities completely satisfied that Joseph Smith had told him the truth.[32] Orson Pratt provides a lesser-known detail about what happened next. He said before a gathering of Saints in the Rocky Mountains that "after Martin Harris returned to Joseph Smith and told him the conversation that had taken place, how that Professor Anthon could not decipher the records, Joseph inquired of the Lord, and the Lord commanded him that he should translate the records, and that he should do it through the medium of the Urim and Thummim."[33] Thus we learn that even the Lord's earthly representative did not take the prerogative upon himself to proceed but sought direction at the hand of his Master. Martin Harris indicated in one of several interviews that took place later in his life that he offered to act as the Prophet's scribe during the translation process, and the Prophet gladly accepted the offer,[34] because as David Whitmer pointed out, "Joseph Smith was a man of limited education and could hardly write legibly."[35]

The Prophet's mother reports in her history that when Martin Harris returned to his home in Palmyra, New York, he found that all was not well there. His wife had prepared a separate bedroom for him, and she refused to enter it. Mrs. Harris was so upset by Martin's leaving without her that she had approached a young man by the name of Flanders Dykes—who was interested in her oldest daughter but of whom she did not approve—and promised him that if he could secretly get the Anthon Transcript from her husband, make an accurate copy of it, and deliver it to her, then he could marry her daughter. Flanders reportedly succeeded in his clandestine mission and delivered the copy to Mrs. Harris.

Martin, in the meantime, made preparations to go to Harmony, Pennsylvania, where he would write for Joseph during the translation of the plates. His wife again insisted on going with him, but Martin proposed that she stay only "a week or two on a visit," and then he would take her home and return to Pennsylvania to write for Joseph. Mrs. Harris agreed to the arrangement, and they headed out for Harmony.

The Harrises made several stops along the way to Joseph's house, and the first time Martin displayed the Anthon Transcript to someone, his wife pulled out her ill-gotten copy and boasted that "Joe Smith was not the only one that was in possession of this great curiosity." She claimed that her set of characters were every bit as genuine as those displayed by her husband and continued this kind of behavior all during their long journey. One can only imagine Martin's reaction to his wife's odd behavior.

When the Harrises finally arrived at the Smith home in Harmony, Mrs. Harris announced that she had come to see the golden plates and wouldn't leave until she did. "The next day Joseph was compelled to take them out of the house and bury both the breastplate and the record," says Lucy Smith, because Mrs. Harris began ransacking the premises in an attempt to find them.

The following day Martin's wife reportedly went outside to hunt for the plates and kept up her search until two o'clock in the afternoon. While she was looking in the woods she came upon a place where she believed the plates must be buried. She stooped down to scrape away the snow and leaves from the ground when a huge black snake stuck its head up and started hissing at her. Badly frightened, she ran as fast as she could back to the house and was in a "very ill-natured" mood upon her arrival there. She was so perplexed and disappointed at her inability to find the Book of Mormon plates that she left the Smith residence and took up her lodgings at the nearest tavern. Her subsequent behavior provides a glimpse into her way of thinking and helps explain some of her future actions. She went through the neighborhood telling the residents that Joseph Smith was a "grand imposter" and was using all his deceptive efforts to defraud her husband of his property.

After Mrs. Harris's two weeks in Harmony finally expired and the Harrises returned to Palmyra, Mrs. Harris tried to dissuade her husband from having anything more to do with the translation and transcription of the Book of Mormon. But Martin "paid but little attention to her" and headed back to Pennsylvania to write for Joseph. As soon as Martin left his house, however, Lucy went through her own neighborhood, calling Joseph Smith a fraud and claiming that the Prophet was going to take away all of her possessions. And to prevent such a thing from occurring, Mrs. Harris is said to have deposited all of her movable belongings in the houses of her friends.[36]

THE BOOK OF LEHI

Around 12 April 1828, Joseph Smith and Martin Harris began to translate and transcribe the material found on the Book of Mormon plates. (A possible explanation of how the translation might have been accomplished can be found in appendix 2 of this book.) The section of text that they worked with was called the book of Lehi, and when it was fully written down it filled 116 pages of foolscap paper. Unfortunately, not much detail is recorded in historical sources about the work that these men accomplished, but it is known that their labors lasted until 14 June 1828.[37]

While the translation was still in progress, Martin requested that Joseph allow him to carry the writings that he had produced to his home in Palmyra in order to display them to other people. He also asked the Prophet to inquire of the Lord to see if this privilege might be granted. Joseph reports that he did inquire of the Lord through the Urim and Thummim, but the answer came back that he must not do such a thing. But Martin was dissatisfied with the response, and sometime later he asked the Prophet to inquire again. The answer came back the same as before.[38] Lucy Mack Smith tells a very interesting, and seldom discussed, part of this episode in her dictated history. She says that when it came time for Martin to return home he "requested Joseph to permit him to look upon the plates for he desired a further witness of their work that he might be better able to give a reason for the hope that was within him [see 1 Pet. 3:15] of seeing great things come to pass in the last days." Because of their friendship Joseph felt a great desire "to gratify the man's feelings," but the Lord had strictly forbidden such a thing to take place and Martin's request was denied.[39] "This discouraged Mr. Harris from saying much more about the plates," said Lucy, "but he insisted upon taking that which he had written home with him that he might show his family what he had been employed in during his absence from them. He also hoped that it might have a salutary effect upon his wife's feelings." Furthermore, Martin hoped that the manuscript "might be the means of carrying the truth home to [the] hearts" of his family members and thus bring about a "union of sentiment" among them. He was anxious in his desires and animated in his pleas. "Joseph for a long time resisted every entreaty of this kind,"[40] but as the Prophet reports in his own recollection of events,

> After much solicitation I again inquired of the Lord, and
> permission was granted him to have the writings on certain

conditions, which were that he show them only to his brother Preserved Harris, his own wife, his father, and his mother, and a Mrs. Cobb—a sister to his wife. In accordance with this last answer I required of him that he should bind himself in a covenant to me in the most solemn manner, that he would not do otherwise than [he] had been directed. He did so. He bound himself as I required of him, took the writings and went his way.[41]

On the day after Martin's departure, 15 June 1828, Emma Smith gave birth to a son in her and Joseph's home, but sadly, the baby died the same day. This was the couple's first child, and the loss must have been heart-wrenching. For the next two weeks Emma's own fate was uncertain, and Joseph had a great deal of trouble sleeping. Emma eventually began to improve, but Martin had not written or sent word regarding the manuscript since he had left, and his silence became a source of anxiety for both the Prophet and his wife. Joseph decided that as soon as Emma had gained strength, he would go to New York and check on Martin and his circumstances.[42]

In the meantime, Martin had arrived at his home in Palmyra and quickly exhibited the 116 pages of the book of Lehi to his wife and family. Mrs. Harris seemed highly pleased with the things that she heard and was so amiable toward the manuscript that she allowed her husband to lock it up in a set of drawers that he had never before been permitted to look into.

The Harrises then took a trip to visit a relative who lived several miles away. When Martin proposed to return home, his wife declined to accompany him so he went by himself. While he was at his home he was visited by a friend who after being told the story of the Nephite record, became anxious to view the manuscript that was in Martin's possession. Even though it was contrary to his obligation to the Prophet, Martin was anxious to gratify his friend's curiosity, so he headed for his wife's bureau. But Mr. Harris couldn't find the key that opened the drawer where the manuscript was being kept. He decided to pick the lock and open it anyway. In the process of circumventing the security of the drawer, Martin did something that would have a direct, and unfortunate, impact on the events of Church history; he badly marred his wife's bureau. He then put the manuscript in his own set of drawers and started showing it to any good friend who happened to stop by at his house.

Trouble was waiting just around the corner. When Mrs. Harris returned from her relative's residence and saw that her bureau had been damaged, she lost her temper and her ensuing tirade knew no bounds. Her indignation simmered for a very long time.[43]

Back at the Prophet's house in Pennsylvania, Joseph prepared to go in search of Martin and the manuscript. He left his wife in the care of her mother and booked passage on a stagecoach headed for New York. There was only one other passenger onboard the stage (a non-talkative gentleman), so the Prophet had ample time to think about his current situation. From what is recorded by his mother in her recollections, we know that during the trip Joseph thought about the great and expansive calling that God had given to him. He also reflected on the fact that he no longer felt the sense of assurance and favor before the Almighty that he had once enjoyed, and he feared the dire consequences that would surely befall him should the Book of Mormon manuscript not be safe. In this state of mind he neither ate nor slept during the journey.

When the stagecoach finally pulled into its drop-off point, the Prophet still had twenty miles to travel in order to get to his parents' house. The other passenger in the coach, upon learning that Joseph was about to walk this distance at night, objected to his traveling alone. After being told the Prophet's circumstances, the man offered to accompany him, lest in his degraded mental and physical state he should meet with some kind of misfortune.

The two men walked along the roads and through the forest all night long, and on the last four miles of their journey the benevolent stranger had to lead Joseph by the arm because he was falling asleep on his feet every few minutes.

The weary companions arrived at the Smith family farm just before daybreak. Upon their entering the house, Joseph requested that his parents send for Martin Harris with all possible speed (he only lived three miles from the Smith home). The kind stranger was served breakfast then went on his way without revealing his identity.

It is reported that by six in the morning, Martin had not yet arrived. He usually made a quick appearance when called for. Neither did he arrive at eight, nine, ten, or eleven that morning. It was not until 12:30 in the afternoon that the Smiths finally saw Martin Harris walking slowly towards their house with his eyes cast down toward the ground. He did not enter through the gate but instead sat on the fence and covered his eyes with his hat. When he finally entered the house, he seated himself at the table but was unable to eat. Instead, he

> pressed his hands upon his temples and cried out in a tone of anguish, "Oh! I have lost my soul. I have lost my soul."

> Joseph, who had smothered his fears till now, sprang from the table exclaiming, "Oh! Martin, have you lost that manuscript? Have you broken your oath and brought down condemnation upon my head as well as your own?"

> "Yes," replied Martin, "it is gone and I know not where."

> "Oh! my God, my God," said Joseph, clenching his hands together. "All is lost, is lost. What shall I do? I have sinned. It is me that tempted the wrath of God by asking Him for that which I had no right to ask, as I was differently instructed by the angel." And he wept and groaned, walking the floor continually.

Joseph insisted that Martin return home and look for the manuscript again but Mr. Harris said that he knew it was not there. He had searched everywhere in vain—even ripping open the beds and pillows that were in the dwelling.[44]

Martin explained that "when Joseph sent for him he went immediately to his drawer, but the manuscript was gone. He asked his wife where it was [but] she solemnly averred that she did not know anything about it whatever."[45] She evidently told a different story to other people, however. One person who knew her quite well states that she admitted to burning the manuscript of the book of Lehi.[46]

Lucy Mack Smith hints that Martin Harris incurred divine wrath and paid a heavy price for the part that he played in this unnecessary tragedy. She says he "lost his spiritual blessing [and] a great temporal blessing also—for there was a heavy fog which swept over his fields and blighted all his wheat while that on the opposite [side] of the road remained untouched by the mildew which spoiled his grain."[47]

REPENTANCE AND REDEMPTION

The morning after Joseph Smith learned of the loss of the book of Lehi manuscript, he returned to his Harmony, Pennsylvania, home with a heavy heart.[48] His sister reports that he fasted for several days,[49] and his mother says that he humbled himself in mighty prayer. Pouring out his soul, he asked the Lord that if it were possible to obtain mercy at His hands he desired to be forgiven for all that he had done which was contrary to divine will. While Joseph was offering up this supplication, says Mother Smith, an angel appeared before him and spoke. The heavenly messenger told Joseph that he had sinned in that he had "delivered the manuscript into the hands of a wicked man." And since Joseph had ventured to become responsible for Martin's faithfulness, he "would of necessity suffer the consequences of his indiscretion." The angel then informed Joseph that he must give back the golden plates[50] and also the interpreters, or Urim and Thummim.[51] The angel did not leave Joseph without hope, however. He said that if the Prophet were "sufficiently humble and penitent" then he would receive the Nephite relics again on 22 September.[52]

According to Lucy Mack Smith, the Prophet received Doctrine and Covenants section 3 soon after this visitation took place. The Lord evidently wanted to speak directly to the Prophet about what had just happened. Joseph relates the circumstances under which he received this divine message. He states, "I was walking out a little distance [from my home in Pennsylvania when the same] heavenly messenger appeared and handed to me the Urim and Thummim. . . . I inquired of the Lord through them" and thus the revelation was given.[53]

In section 3, which is dated as being received in July 1828, the Lord warned Joseph Smith that even though he was "chosen to do the work of the Lord" (v. 9) and given "sight and power to translate" (v. 12) it was still possible for him to "fall" because of transgression (v. 9). The Lord also rebuked the Prophet, saying that he "should not have feared man more than God" (v. 7) and he "should have been faithful" (v. 8). Martin Harris, the revelation says, had "set at naught the counsels of God," had "broken the most sacred promises which were made before God," had "boasted in his own wisdom" and had "depended upon his own judgment" (v. 13). Because of these things the Lord considered Martin to be "a wicked man" (v. 12). And because of the action that the Prophet had taken he was informed that he had "lost [his] privileges for a season" (v. 14). Nevertheless, the Prophet was admonished to repent for acting contrary to the Lord's commandment. A choice was laid out clearly before him. If he would repent he would still be chosen to carry out the work that had been assigned to him (v. 10), but if not, he would lose his gift and become like other men (v. 11).

"After I had obtained the above revelation," says Joseph, "the Urim and Thummim were taken from me again." The angel—who had also brought the golden plates along with him—then disappeared with the ancient objects.[54] The Prophet's mother recalled that her son then "continued . . . [his] supplications to God without cessation that His mercy might again be exercised towards" him.[55] And according to the Prophet the angel eventually visited him again and once more handed him the Urim and Thummim. Joseph then inquired of the Lord through that instrument and received the revelation that is known today as section 10 of the Doctrine and Covenants.[56]

In this revelation Joseph Smith was reminded that he had lost the gift to translate because he turned the 116 pages of the book of Lehi over to Martin Harris and they were then lost (D&C 10:1–2). Nevertheless, his gift to translate had now been restored (v. 3). He was to continue on and finish the remainder of the translation but was not to labor beyond his strength and means (vv. 3–4). Verse 8 indicates that wicked men had taken the 116 pages of the book of Lehi, and verses 10–13 say that Satan had put it into their hearts to alter those writings so that if a retranslation of the material occurred they could claim that the two sets of writings were different and that the translation was a fraud. Therefore, said the Lord, the lost portion was not to be retranslated (v. 30).[57] The Prophet was to "translate the engravings which [were] on the plates of Nephi" instead since they covered the same material but contained more detail. In this way the Lord would confound those who had altered His words (vv. 39, 41–42). The

Prophet was also instructed not to let the world know of the Lord's counterplan until the translation had been completed (v. 34).

Lucy Mack Smith records in her reminiscences that Joseph received the golden plates back into his custody on 22 September 1828 and this event gave him "joy and satisfaction." She says that when the angel returned the Nephite records back into the keeping of their earthly guardian, he rejoiced and said that he was pleased with the Prophet's "faithfulness and humility" and that God loved him because of his "penitence and diligence in prayer."[58]

BEGINNING ANEW

At this point Joseph took to heart the directives that were given to him in the tenth section of the Doctrine and Covenants. He "did not . . . go immediately to translating, but went to laboring with [his] hands upon a small farm which [he] had purchased [from his] wife's father, in order to provide for [his] family."[59] But even with these careful preparations, the Prophet eventually found himself in need of the necessities of life. At the beginning of the winter he and his wife went to the home of Joseph Knight Sr. in the hope of obtaining some supplies—since his in-laws were not willing to help them out. Bur Mr. Knight was not in easy circumstances himself, and his family members were not very disposed to assist in Joseph's cause. Nevertheless, Joseph Knight was a charitable man and he gave Joseph a few provisions, three dollars in currency, and a pair of shoes from his store.[60]

There was yet another problem that pressed in upon Joseph during this period of time. After Martin Harris lost the first 116 pages of the Book of Mormon, he "was never permitted to write for the Prophet anymore."[61] This was a serious obstacle, but the angel had promised Joseph Smith that if he were successful in receiving the golden plates again, the Lord would send somebody to write for him, and the Prophet trusted that it would indeed be so.[62] In the meantime, Joseph employed his wife as a scribe whenever he could. Lucy Mack Smith indicates that the translation went slowly during these days. She explains this by saying that the Prophet was "hurried with business," and "Emma had so much of her time taken up with her work that she could write but little for him."[63]

And thus the Book of Mormon, which had begun to come forth with a respectable amount of momentum, almost stalled in its progress. Joseph made the best of the circumstances in which he was placed, but he looked forward to the time when the Lord would provide him with a new scribe and the work could go forward more rapidly.

NOTES TO CHAPTER 4

1. *Tiffany's Monthly,* vol. 5, no. 4, August 1859, 170.
2. Lavina F. Anderson, ed., *Lucy's Book: A Critical Edition of Lucy Mack Smith's Family Memoir* (Salt Lake City: Signature Books, 2001), 401–402.
3. Ibid., 401.
4. *Tiffany's Monthly,* vol. 5, no. 4, August 1859, 170.
5. Parley P. Pratt, *A Voice of Warning* (New York: W. Sandford, 1837; reprint, Salt Lake City: Deseret Book, 2002), 65.
6. See Brigham H. Roberts, ed., *History of the Church,* rev. ed., 7 vols. (Salt Lake City: The Church of Jesus Christ of Latter-day Saints, 1932–1951), 1:19. Lucy Mack Smith also notes in her history that "Joseph started [in] December for Pennsylvania" (Anderson, ed., *Lucy's Book,* 402).
7. *History of the Church,* 1:44.
8. See *Susquehanna Register,* vol. 9, 1 May 1834. Joseph Smith eventually decided that it was best to move out of his father-in-law's house, so he "bought a piece of land [from Emma's] father with a house and barn on it. Here the people began to tease him to see the book and to offer him money and property and they crowded so hard that he had to hide it in the mountain" (Dean C. Jessee, "Joseph Knight's Recollection of Early Mormon History," *BYU Studies* 17, no. 1 [fall 1976]: 34).
9. Anderson, ed., *Lucy's Book,* 402.
10. *Messenger and Advocate,* vol. 1, no. 5, February 1835, 80. For a much expanded version of this prophecy, see 2 Nephi 27:6–22. In this text it is made known that the Lord would tell the person to whom he would deliver the Book of Mormon (Joseph Smith) to take some of "the words of the book" from its unsealed portion (Anthon Transcript) and give them to another person (Martin Harris) who would in turn take them to the "learned" (Charles Anthon).

11. *History of the Church,* 1:19; emphasis added.

12. Anderson, ed., *Lucy's Book,* 402–403.

13. See *History of the Church,* 1:19. Martin Harris told Thomas Godfrey that on this trip he "drove a team from western New York to New York City" (Thomas Godfrey, affidavit, 2 July 1933, L. Tom Perry Special Collections Library, Harold B. Lee Library, Brigham Young University, Provo, Utah).

14. See the letter written by William W. Phelps to Eber D. Howe, 15 January 1831, in Eber D. Howe, *Mormonism Unvailed* (Painesville, Ohio: Telegraph Press, 1834), 273.

15. "Martin Harris, Jr. Reports Death and Testimony of His Father," *Adventure,* vol. 1, no. 4., n.d., cited in Milton V. Backman Jr. and Keith W. Perkins, *Testimonies of the Book of Mormon Witnesses* (n.p., n.d.,), 468.

16. See Pomeroy Tucker, *Origin, Rise, and Progress of Mormonism* (New York: D. Appleton and Co., 1867), 42; John H. Gilbert, "Memorandum," 8 September 1892, Palmyra, New York, 5, cited in Royal Skousen, "John Gilbert's 1892 Account of the 1830 Printing of the Book of Mormon," in Stephen D. Ricks, Donald W. Parry, and Andrew H. Hedges, eds., *The Disciple as Witness: Essays on Latter-day Saint History and Doctrine in Honor of Richard Lloyd Anderson* (Provo, Utah: FARMS, 2000), 383–405.

17. It appears that some historical documents incorrectly state that Martin Harris visited Samuel Mitchill after going to see Charles Anthon. Such an idea is discounted by the fact that Anthon said Harris "called upon [him] with a note from Doctor Mitch[i]ll" asking him to decipher the Book of Mormon characters if possible (Charles Anthon to Eber D. Howe, 17 February 1834, in Howe, *Mormonism Unvailed,* 270). Another early source confirms this sequence of events. William W. Phelps, who was personally acquainted with Martin Harris, related that "the characters . . . were shown to Dr. Mitch[i]ll, and he referred [Harris] to professor Anthon" (William W. Phelps to Eber D. Howe, 15 January 1831, in Howe, *Mormonism Unvailed,* 273).

    There are alternate spellings for the name Mitchill. This spelling has been determined to be the most accurate.

18. *Morning Courier: New York Enquirer,* vol. 7, no. 563, 1 September 1831. Charles Anthon confirms this point when he says that in Dr. Mitchill's letter of introduction he "confessed he had been unable to understand" the hieroglyphics on the paper that Harris showed him (Charles Anthon to Eber D. Howe, 17 February 1834, in Howe, *Mormonism Unvailed,* 270).

19. *Millennial Star,* vol. 21, no. 34, 20 August 1859, 545–46.

20. See *Morning Courier: New York Enquirer,* vol. 7, no. 563, 1 September 1831.

21. See the letter written by Charles Anthon to Eber D. Howe, 17 February 1834, in Howe, *Mormonism Unvailed,* 270.

22. *Times and Seasons,* vol. 3, no. 13, 2 May 1842, 773. There is some evidence that Charles Anthon came to the conclusion that these were "true characters" by comparing them with current literature. According to an account by James G. Bennett, Professor Anthon "made a learned dissertation on them— compared them with the hieroglyphics discovered by Champollion in Egypt— and set them down as the language of a people formerly in existence in the East, but now no more" (*Morning Courier: New York Enquirer,* vol. 7, no. 563, 1 September 1831). David Whitmer claimed that "Prof[essor]s Anthon and Mitch[i]ll both admitted they were ancient characters, resembling the reformed Egyptian and Hebrew characters" (*St. Louis Republican,* 16 July 1884). Martin Harris said that "the Professor pronounced them correct Egyptian characters, but somewhat changed" (*Millennial Star,* vol. 48, no. 27, 5 July 1886, 421). "Oliver Cowdery . . . [observed that] none among the most learned in the United States could read and interpret the handwriting (save one, and he could decipher but a few lines correctly)" (*Observer and Telegraph,* vol. 1, no. 38, 18 November 1830). A man named James Murdock of New Haven, Connecticut, was told the following by "a minister of the Mormons" who is identified as a member of the Smith family: Joseph Smith "made a facsimile of some parts of the inscription, and sent it to professor Anthon of New York City. The professor pronounced the characters to be ancient Hebrew corrupted, and the language to be degenerate Hebrew, with a mixture of Egyptian. He could decipher only one entire word" (*Peoria Register and North-Western Gazetteer,* vol. 5, no. 23, 3 September 1841).

23. *Times and Seasons,* vol. 3, no. 13, 2 May 1842, 773.

24. *Millennial Star,* vol. 21, no. 34, 20 August 1859, 545–46.

25. Thomas Godfrey, affidavit, 2 July 1933, L. Tom Perry Special Collections Library, Harold B. Lee Library, Brigham Young University, Provo, Utah.

26. *Millennial Star,* vol. 21, no. 34, 20 August 1859, 545–46.

27. Ibid., vol. 44, no. 5, 30 January 1882, 79.

28. Ibid., vol. 21, no. 34, 20 August 1859, 546.

29. *Times and Seasons,* vol. 3, no. 13, 2 May 1842, 773.

30. George D. Watt, comp., *Journal of Discourses,* 26 vols. (London: F. D. and S. W. Richards and Sons, 1854–1886), 18:157.

31. William Pilkington, statement sworn before Joseph W. Peterson, 3 April 1934,

L. Tom Perry Special Collections Library, Harold B. Lee Library, Brigham Young University, Provo, Utah. Joseph Smith notes in his 1832 history that after Martin Harris had taken "some of the characters . . . to the learned," and they had professed that they could not read the writing, he returned and "gave them to [Joseph] to translate, [but the Prophet] said, 'I cannot for I am not learned.' But the Lord had prepared spectacles for to read the book therefore [Joseph] commenced translating the characters and thus the prophecy of Isaiah was fulfilled which is written in the 29th chapter concerning the book" (Dean C. Jessee, ed., *The Personal Writings of Joseph Smith*, rev. ed. [Salt Lake City: Deseret Book, 2002], 13–14).

32. "Martin Harris said he then went home satisfied that it was the truth" (Thomas Godfrey, affidavit, 2 July 1933). John H. Gilbert adds that "Martin [Harris] returned from his trip east satisfied that 'Joseph' was a 'little smarter than Prof[essor] Anthon'" (Gilbert, "Memorandum," 5).

33. *Journal of Discourses,* 14:143.

34. See William Pilkington, statement, 3 April 1934.

35. M. J. Hubble, interview, 13 November 1886, Missouri State Historical Society, Columbia, Missouri. Elder Orson Pratt said, "being a poor writer [the Prophet] was under the necessity of employing a scribe, to write the translation as it came from his mouth" (Orson Pratt, *An Interesting Account of Several Remarkable Visions* [Edinburgh, Scotland: Ballantyne and Hughes, 1840], 14).

36. Anderson, ed., *Lucy's Book,* 403–407.

37. See *Times and Seasons,* vol. 3, no. 14, 16 May 1842, 785. David Whitmer: "When Joseph [Smith] first received the plates he translated 116 pages of the book of 'Lehi,' with Martin Harris as scribe" (*Kansas City Journal,* 5 June 1881; see also the preface of the 1830 edition of the Book of Mormon, where these writings are identified as the book of Lehi).

38. See *Times and Seasons,* vol. 3, no. 14, 16 May 1842, 785.

39. Anderson, ed., *Lucy's Book,* 408.

40. Ibid., 410–11.

41. *Times and Seasons,* vol. 3, no. 14, 16 May 1842, 785.

42. See Anderson, ed., *Lucy's Book,* 412–13.

43. See ibid., 420–22.

44. Ibid., 413–18. David Whitmer said of Martin Harris, "Upon retiring at night he locked up the precious pages in a bureau drawer, along with his money and other valuables. In the morning he was shocked to find that they had been stolen, while his money had been left untouched" (*Chicago Inter-Ocean,* 17 October 1886).

45. Anderson, ed., *Lucy's Book,* 422.

46. Lorenzo Saunders (a critic of Joseph Smith) claimed, "Martin Harris's wife . . . burned up those papers. I heard her say she burned the papers. . . . [S]he says she burned them up. And there was no mistake, but she did. . . . [A]nd she never denied of burning the papers" (Dan Vogel, ed., *Early Mormon Documents* [Salt Lake City: Signature Books, 1998], 2:149). Another person (who was unfriendly to the Saints) relates: "Harris' wife became exceedingly annoyed and disgusted with what she called her husband's 'craziness.' She foresaw, as she thought, that if he incurred the printing liability, as he had avowed to her his purpose of doing, the event would be the ruin of himself and family. Thus exercised she contrived, in her husband's sleep, to steal from him the particular source of her disturbance, and burned the manuscript to ashes. For years she kept this incendiarism a profound secret to herself, even until after the book was published. Smith and Harris held her accountable for the theft, but supposed she had handed the manuscript to some 'evil-designing persons' to be used somehow in injuring their cause" (Pomeroy Tucker, *Origin, Rise, and Progress of Mormonism* [New York City: D. Appleton and Co., 1867], 45–46). Martin Harris "said he believed his wife burned it up, as she was very bitter against him having anything to do with Joseph Smith" (William Pilkington, statement, 3 April 1934).

47. Anderson, ed., *Lucy's Book,* 423.

48. See ibid., 419.

49. See *Kansas City Times,* 11 April 1895.

50. Anderson, ed., *Lucy's Book,* 424–25.

51. In the Prophet's published history he recalled, "the Urim and Thummim . . . had been taken from me in consequence of my having wearied the Lord in asking for the privilege of letting Martin Harris take the writings which he lost" (*Times and Seasons,* vol. 3, no. 14, 16 May 1842, 786).

52. Anderson, ed., *Lucy's Book,* 425.

53. *Times and Seasons,* vol. 3, no. 14, 16 May 1842, 786.

54. Ibid., vol. 3, no. 15, 1 June 1842, 801.

55. Anderson, ed., *Lucy's Book,* 428.

56. See *Times and Seasons,* vol. 3, no. 15, 1 June 1842, 801. For important information on the dating of section 10 of the Doctrine and Covenants, see Max H. Parkin, "A Preliminary Analysis of the Dating of Section 10," in *Sidney B. Sperry Symposium: Doctrine and Covenants* (Provo, Utah: BYU Religious Instruction Dept., 1979), 68–84.

57. Katherine Smith asserts that when the plates were returned to the Prophet, he was told "not to translate that [which] was lost, but to begin where he had left off" (*Kansas City Times*, 11 April 1895).

58. Anderson, ed., *Lucy's Book*, 428.

59. *Times and Seasons*, vol. 3, no. 16, 15 June 1842, 817.

60. See Jessee, "Joseph Knight's Recollection of Early Mormon History," 35–36.

61. It is reported that Martin Harris revealed this fact in the William Pilkington, statement sworn before Joseph W. Peterson, 3 April 1934, L. Tom Perry Special Collections Library, Harold B. Lee Library, Brigham Young University, Provo, Utah.

62. See Anderson, ed., *Lucy's Book*, 428.

63. Ibid., 438. Later in her life, Emma reminisced about the days when she helped to bring forth the fullness of the gospel in the latter-day dispensation. Her description of the plates is a significant testimony of their reality. She said, "The plates often lay on the table without any attempt at concealment, wrapped in a small linen table cloth, which I had given [Joseph] to fold them in. I once felt of the plates as they thus lay on the table, tracing their outline and shape. They seemed to be pliable like thick paper, and would rustle with a metallic sound when the edges were moved by the thumb, as one does sometimes thumb the edges of a book. . . . I moved them from place to place on the table, as it was necessary in doing my work" (*Saints' Herald*, vol. 26, no. 19, 1 October 1879, 290).

CHAPTER 5

THE PROPHET'S NEW SCRIBE

In the fall of 1828, Joseph Smith's parents took in a twenty-two-year-old boarder by the name of Oliver Cowdery. He had been accepted as a schoolteacher in the Palmyra district and had asked Father Smith to put him up at his house, at least until he could get acquainted with his patrons.

It did not take long for Oliver to hear rumors from the townspeople about the connection between the golden plates of the Book of Mormon and the people he was living with. He tried for a long time to get Father Smith to talk to him about the stories he had heard, but the patriarch of the family was reticent to discuss the matter. Eventually, however, Oliver gained the trust of his host and prevailed in obtaining a sketch of facts that related to the plates.

One day Oliver came home from school in a lively mood and told Father Smith that it had been put into his heart that he would have the privilege of acting as a scribe for his son. He had determined in his own mind that as soon as the school term ended in the spring, he would go down to Harmony, Pennsylvania, and pay Joseph a visit.

The following day there was a torrential downpour of rain, and even though the weather had almost rendered the roads impassable, Oliver made his way from the schoolhouse to the Smith family farm. When he arrived at his destination Oliver informed the Smiths that he could not get the thought of being Joseph's scribe out of his head. Then Oliver announced, "I have made it a subject of prayer, and I firmly believe that it is the will of the Lord that I should go and that there is a work for me to do in this thing. And I am determined, if there is, to attend to it."[1]

Joseph Smith records a little-known incident in his writings that helps to explain why Oliver Cowdery had such a staunch determination to serve as his scribe. The Prophet relates that the "Lord appeared unto a young man by the name of Oliver Cowdery and showed unto him the plates in a vision and also the truth of the work and what the Lord was about to do through me, His unworthy servant. Therefore he was desirous to come and write for me."[2] Interestingly, the other divinely assigned scribe, Martin Harris, had also been granted a vision of the Lord and informed of His divine plan prior to the commencement of his duties.

VISITORS FROM THE NORTH

In January 1829 Father Smith and his son Samuel decided to pay the Prophet a visit and see how the work of translation was progressing. When they got as far south as Colesville, New York, they stopped off at the house of Joseph Knight. Mr. Knight was busy drawing lumber when they arrived, but he said that the two men had traveled far enough and he would take them in his sleigh the next day to see the Prophet down in Harmony, Pennsylvania.

When the small group of travelers completed their journey of about thirty miles, they were warmly welcomed by their hosts and together they conversed about many things. Mr. Knight eventually decided that it would be best if he returned to his home the next morning, but before he departed he gave Joseph Smith a little money so that he could buy paper for the Book of Mormon's transcription.[3]

Martin Harris also paid the Prophet a visit during the winter of 1829, arriving sometime in the month of March. In his conversations with the Prophet, Martin made an unusual request. He said that he wanted to receive a divine witness that Joseph really and truly had possession of the golden plates. Joseph showed extraordinary kindness toward the man who had caused him so much personal anguish, and he petitioned the Lord on his behalf.

The answer he received is now found in section 5 of the Doctrine and Covenants. In this heaven-sent communication, Martin learned that the Lord had required Joseph to enter into a covenant with Him not to show the plates to anyone except those to whom he would be commanded (see v. 3). The Lord also told Martin that even if unbelievers were allowed to see the plates they would still not believe the divine words that were written upon them (see v. 7). Nevertheless, the Lord promised that in "a little while" (v. 17) three witnesses, whom He would "call and ordain," would not only be shown the plates by Him, but they would also be given a sure testimony that the writings upon them were true—the Lord Himself would declare it from the heavens (vv. 11–12). These three special witnesses would then give their testimony before the world that the writings on the plates were indeed true (v. 15). Martin Harris was promised by the Lord that if he would humble himself in mighty prayer and sincere faith he would be granted the privilege of seeing the plates (vv. 23–25). In the latter part of this revelation the Lord spoke directly to Joseph Smith and told him that after he had translated a few more pages of the Book of Mormon he was to stop and await the command to begin again (v. 30). The Lord then assured His prophet, seer, and revelator that he would be provided with the means necessary to accomplish all that he had been commanded to do (v. 34).

THE NEW SCRIBE

At the beginning of the month of April, Joseph Smith decided to lay hold on the previous promise of the Lord's angel that he would have another scribe to assist him in his labors. The Prophet offered up a prayer to God and was answered that his new assistant would be arriving within a few days.[4] At the same time of the month, Oliver Cowdery and Samuel Smith left Palmyra, New York, and headed south on the long journey to Harmony, Pennsylvania. The two young men had to travel through inclement weather and along difficult roadways,[5] but they arrived at their destination on 5 April.[6] Lucy Mack Smith relates what happened next.

> Soon after Oliver was introduced to [Joseph] he said, "Mr. Smith, I have come for the purpose of writing for you."
> This was not at all unexpected to Joseph, for although he

had never seen Mr. Cowdery before he knew that the Lord
was able to perform and that He had been faithful to fulfill
all His promises.

They then sat down and conversed together until late . . .
and Joseph told Oliver his entire history as far as it was
necessary for his information in those things which
concerned him.[7]

Joseph Smith—with Oliver Cowdery as his new scribe—
commenced to translate the Book of Mormon again on 7 April 1829.[8]
They continued their work for some time, and then the Lord Jesus
Christ sent a message to Oliver through His earthly revelator.[9] This
message, known today as section 6 of the Doctrine and Covenants,
was received in the month of April and was issued in response to
inquiries that Oliver had made. In this revelation the Lord admonished Oliver to give heed unto His words (D&C 6:2) and assist to
bring forth His work (v. 9). In addition, the Lord offered an assurance
to the new scribe by stating, "the words or the work which thou hast
been writing are true. Therefore be diligent, stand by my servant
Joseph, faithfully, in whatsoever difficult circumstances he may be for
the word's sake" (vv. 17–18). The Savior then reminded Oliver that
he had already received a divine witness of the truth of the work at a
time when he had requested such at the hand of God (see vv. 22–23).
After saying these words the Lord bestowed an especially precious gift
upon Joseph's assistant, giving him the "keys" to actually translate the
Nephite record (vv. 25–28).[10] According to the Lord, the objective in
granting such a blessing was to fulfill the divine law of witnesses,
which states that the truth is to be established in the mouth of two or
three individuals (see v. 28).

It is evident from Doctrine and Covenants section 8 that Oliver
Cowdery asked the Lord how he was to go about exercising his
wonderful new gift. In verses 1 through 4 and verse 11, the Savior
names the prerequisites for the enjoyment of this blessing and also
gives a brief explanation of what Oliver will experience once his gift
has been activated. He says,

[Y]ou [shall] receive a knowledge of whatsoever things you shall ask in faith, with an honest heart, believing that you shall receive a knowledge concerning the engravings of old records, which are ancient, which contain those parts of my scripture of which has been spoken by the manifestation of my Spirit.

Yea, behold, I will tell you in your mind and in your heart, by the Holy Ghost, which shall come upon you and which shall dwell in your heart.

Now, behold, this is the spirit of revelation. . . .

[T]his is thy gift; apply unto it. . . .

Ask that you may know the mysteries of God, and that you may translate and receive knowledge from all those ancient records which have been hid up, that are sacred; and according to your faith shall it be done unto you.

It is apparent from the information found in section 9 of the Doctrine and Covenants that Oliver Cowdery went forward and actually began the translation process on part of the ancient Nephite record (see v. 5) but then quickly decided to go back to acting in the capacity of a scribe (see v. 1). It appears from the text of this revelation that Oliver's failure in translating occurred because of his fear (v. 11) and also his lack of understanding about how he was to proceed. He evidently thought that all he had to do was ask the Lord to reveal the appropriate translation to him (v. 7), when in fact he was required to study the translation out in his own mind and then ask the Lord for a mental and physical confirmation concerning his conclusion (vv. 8–9). After Oliver had given up on his undertaking the Lord said that it was not expedient for him to translate the Book of Mormon text (vv. 3, 10), but he was to continue on acting in the capacity of a scribe (vv. 1, 4). When that particular project was finished, said the Lord, then Oliver would be allowed to assist in the translation of "other records" that He planned to bring before the world (v. 2).

PRIESTHOOD RESTORATION

As the translation of the Book of Mormon text pressed forward, Joseph and Oliver had questions concerning the doctrine they were learning about in the book. On 15 May 1829, they "went into the woods to pray and inquire of the Lord respecting baptism for the remission of sins, as [they] found mentioned in the translation of the plates"[11] (see 3 Ne. 11:21–28).[12] Oliver recounts that while they were thus engaged in prayer they heard the voice of the Redeemer speak peace unto them from the midst of eternity as the veil of the heavens parted.[13] From Joseph's retelling of the incident we learn that "a messenger from heaven descended in a cloud of light." This glorious being, who identified himself as John the Baptist, ordained the two men to the Aaronic Priesthood by the laying on of hands and told them that the authority he bestowed held "the keys of . . . baptism by immersion, for the remission of sins." He informed them, however, that the Aaronic Priesthood did not hold the power to lay on hands for the gift of the Holy Ghost. Nevertheless, this particular power was promised to Joseph and Oliver at a future time. Indeed, the angel specified that they would receive the Melchizedek Priesthood. With these instructions given, the angel commanded the Prophet and his scribe to go and baptize each other (Joseph performing the rite for Oliver first) and then confer the Aaronic Priesthood upon each other by the laying on of hands (in the same order).[14]

Some Latter-day Saint scholars believe that the restoration of the Melchizedek Priesthood most likely occurred within the next sixteen days.[15] This ordination, said Joseph Smith, took place on the banks of the Susquehanna River between Colesville, New York, and Harmony, Pennsylvania.[16] Here Peter, James, and John—the Savior's chief Old World Apostles—made their appearance. They declared that they possessed "the keys of the kingdom, and of the dispensation of the fullness of times" (D&C 128:20) and proceeded to ordain Joseph and Oliver to the holy apostleship (D&C 27:12).[17] Addison Everett recalled hearing Joseph Smith, while living in Nauvoo, Illinois, say that the three angels made their appearance just at daybreak after he and Oliver had spent a harrowing night fleeing from a mob that had attempted to charge them in court with being false prophets.[18]

CONVERSION, DIRECTION, NEEDS, AND BLESSINGS

One of the benefits of Joseph's and Oliver's baptisms was that they were endowed with the spirit of prophecy and thereby given knowledge about the rising Church and the generation in which they lived. With their minds thus enlightened, they began to have the true meaning of the more mysterious passages of scripture revealed to their understanding. In turn, they felt that it was their duty to use the scriptures to reason with their friends and acquaintances and try to persuade them "concerning the gospel of Jesus Christ which was now about to be revealed in its fullness." When Joseph's brother Samuel came to visit them they informed him of the Lord's imminent work, showed him the part of the translation that they had thus far prepared, and reasoned with him out of the Bible. But Samuel was not easily persuaded. He decided—after asking many questions—that it was best to rely upon the Lord with respect to these things, and he would thereby be enabled to make a proper judgment. Samuel's wise course of action was amply rewarded. In a secluded place he fervently petitioned the Almighty and "obtained revelations for himself sufficient to convince him of the truth" of what he had heard. He was then led by Oliver Cowdery into the waters of baptism and returned to his Palmyra home "greatly glorifying and praising God."[19]

Not many days after Samuel's conversion Hyrum Smith—another of Joseph's brothers—came to Harmony, to learn more concerning these things. He earnestly requested his sibling to inquire of the Lord on his behalf, and upon doing so, through the Urim and Thummim, Joseph received section 11 of the Doctrine and Covenants. The Lord told Hyrum in this divine communication to cleave with all his heart to Jesus Christ, the Son of God, so that he could assist in bringing to light the translation of the Book of Mormon (v. 19). Furthermore, Hyrum was admonished to study the word of the Lord that was found in the Bible and also in the translation of the golden plates (v. 22). In this way Hyrum would be able to build upon the Lord's rock, which is His gospel (v. 24).

It was particularly difficult for Joseph to engage in the work of translation and at the same time provide for those who resided under his roof. At some point in the month of May supplies began to run low in Joseph's household, and he had no money to buy anything else. Joseph decided that it would be best to take Oliver with him and see if Joseph Knight could help them out of their predicament. But Mr. Knight wasn't home when they got there; he was off conducting some out-of-town business. The only thing that the two men could do was leave word of their need and then head back over the Pennsylvania state border.

When Mr. Knight finally returned from his trip, he learned of Joseph and Oliver's visit but was scheduled to leave town again the very next day. He left on his appointed trip, but while he was gone he decided to gather a few supplies for the Smiths and their houseguests. Upon the second return to his New York residence, he thought it would be best to pull together even more provisions for them. By the time Mr. Knight was finished gathering goods, he had one barrel of fish, six bushels of potatoes, ten bushels of grain, a small amount of beverage, and lined writing paper. He loaded all of these items into his wagon, climbed aboard, and headed off for Harmony. Mr. Knight states that he didn't find Joseph and Oliver at home when he arrived because they were out hunting for temporary employment. But when they returned from their unsuccessful search, they were happy to see their friend with his much-needed supplies.[20]

The Prophet was always grateful for the assistance rendered by Joseph Knight during this trying and crucial time in his life. In the published history of the Church, he made honorable mention of his benefactor and said that the old gentleman

> very kindly and considerately brought us a quantity of provisions, in order that we might not be interrupted in the work of translation, by want of such necess[it]ies of life; and I would just mention here (as in duty bound) that he several times brought us supplies (a distance of at least thirty miles) which enabled us to continue the work which otherwise we must have relinquished for a season.[21]

For the moment, life seemed to be in proper order. The Prophet had provisions for his household, he and his scribe were making good progress in bringing forth the Book of Mormon, and the Lord was graciously blessing them with revelations, power, and authority. But as with any work that bears the stamp of heavenly approval, it was about to grind against the forces of opposition.

NOTES TO CHAPTER 5

1. Lavina, F. Anderson, ed., *Lucy's Book: A Critical Edition of Lucy Mack Smith's Family Memoir* (Salt Lake City: Signature Books, 2001), 431–33.

2. Dean C. Jessee, ed., *The Personal Writings of Joseph Smith,* rev. ed. (Salt Lake City: Deseret Book, 2002), 14.

3. See Dean C. Jessee, "Joseph Knight's Recollection of Early Mormon History," *BYU Studies* 17, no. 1 (fall 1976): 36.

4. See Anderson, ed., *Lucy's Book,* 438.

5. See ibid., 437.

6. See *Messenger and Advocate,* vol. 1, no. 1, October 1834, 14.

7. Anderson, ed., *Lucy's Book,* 438–39.

8. See *Messenger and Advocate,* vol. 1, no. 1, October 1834, 14.

9. The Prophet notes in his published history, right before a recital of this revelation, that during the month of April "Oliver Cowdery became exceedingly anxious to have the power to translate bestowed upon him" (*Times and Seasons,* vol. 3, no. 18, 15 July 1842, 853).

10. As far as is known, the restriction on displaying the golden plates and the interpreters was *not* lifted by the Lord when Oliver Cowdery was given the chance to translate. It may be, therefore, that Joseph gave Oliver the Anthon Transcript to use in his attempt at translation (this document was kept by Cowdery until he died). Notice that the method of translation granted to Oliver (see D&C 9:8–9) differs markedly from the method granted to Joseph (see appendix 2).

11. *Times and Seasons,* vol. 3, no. 19, 1 August 1842, 865.

12. Oliver Cowdery identifies "the account given of the Savior's ministry to the remnant of the seed of Jacob, upon this continent" as the text which prodded him and Joseph to ask the Lord for proper priesthood authority. More specifically, he points to the translation and transcription of "the directions given to the Nephites, from the mouth of the Savior, of the precise manner in which men should build up His Church" (*Messenger and Advocate,* vol. 1, no. 1, October 1834, 15).

13. See ibid.

14. *Times and Seasons,* vol. 3, no. 19, 1 August 1842, 865–66.

15. See Larry C. Porter, "Dating the Restoration of the Melchizedek Priesthood," *Ensign,* June 1979, 5–10; Larry C. Porter, "The Priesthood Restored," in Robert L. Millet and Kent P. Jackson, eds., *Studies in Scripture, Volume 2: The Pearl of Great Price* (Salt Lake City: Randall Book, 1985), 389–409; Larry C. Porter, "The Restoration of the Aaronic and Melchizedek Priesthoods," *Ensign,* December 1996, 30–47. Addison Everett heard the Prophet say that the Melchizedek Priesthood was restored by Peter, James, and John while he and Oliver were translating the Book of Mormon in Harmony, Pennsylvania (see Brian Q. Cannon and BYU Studies Staff, "Priesthood Restoration Documents," *BYU Studies* 35, no. 4 (1995–96): 198 n. 11).

16. Addison Everett heard the Prophet say that he and Oliver were sixteen or seventeen miles away from Harmony, Pennsylvania, when the trio of angels appeared unto them (ibid., 199 n. 11).

17. President George Q. Cannon taught that Peter, James, and John "unitedly laid their hands upon the heads of Joseph and Oliver, and ordained them to the authority that they themselves held, namely, that of the Apostleship" (George D. Watt, comp., *Journal of Discourses,* 26 vols. [London: F. D. and S. W. Richards and Sons, 1854–1886], 23:360).

18. See Brian Q. Cannon and BYU Studies Staff, "Priesthood Restoration Documents," 198–99 n. 11.

19. *Times and Seasons,* vol. 3, no. 19, 1 August 1842, 866.

20. See Jessee, "Joseph Knight's Recollection of Early Mormon History," 36.

21. *Times and Seasons,* vol. 3, no. 20, 15 August 1842, 884.

CHAPTER 6

THE MOVE TO FAYETTE

Shortly after his baptism, Samuel Smith returned to his parents' home in Palmyra, New York, and brought news of Joseph and Oliver's progress. When Martin Harris heard this encouraging information, he had a great desire to go down to Pennsylvania and pay the Book of Mormon translator and his scribe a visit. But after Martin's wife, Lucy, found out his intentions, she determined to stop him from making the trip and to hinder, or even prevent, Joseph Smith from accomplishing his work. She mounted her horse and flew through the neighborhood for several miles distant, says Joseph's mother, seeking to collect any evidence that the Prophet did not really have the gold plates he claimed to possess but was instead just out to obtain other people's money by fraudulent means.

After Mrs. Harris found a few individuals who agreed with her skeptical point of view, she went to Lyons, New York—the county seat fifteen miles east of Palmyra—and entered a complaint before a magistrate. She then sent word to Lyman Cowdery (Oliver Cowdery's older brother, who served as a marshal of the court), requesting him to come to Lyons with a good horse ready to travel quickly to Pennsylvania—in company with other officers—in order to arrest and imprison Joseph Smith if the court ruled against him. Lucy Harris then swore out an affidavit and told the officers of others they should subpoena, including her husband Martin.

On the day of Joseph's absentee trial, some of the neighbors who were friendly to the Smith family informed them that the witnesses had left for Lyons. This whole situation gave Lucy Mack Smith a great deal of anxiety, but her son Hyrum told her to look to the Lord. Lucy took this advice seriously. She retired to a secluded place and prayed at length for the safety of Joseph. In time, she says, the Spirit of the Lord rested upon her, and the feelings of foreboding that she had previously experienced were entirely removed. A voice then spoke to her, saying that not one hair of his head would be harmed. Lucy arose from her entreaties to the throne of grace with a feeling of happiness. Her heart was light and her mind completely at ease.

At the court proceedings the first witness to be called claimed that Joseph Smith told him the box that supposedly contained the golden plates was really just filled with sand and admitted that he was a deceiver. The second witness swore that Joseph Smith said the box was filled with lead, and he would use the prop in whatever way he saw fit. The third witness testified that Joseph Smith told him there was actually nothing in the box, that he had made fools out of everybody, and that all he wanted to do was get Martin Harris's money away from him—adding that he had already gotten two or three hundred dollars from the man. Lucy Harris's affidavit was then read in the courtroom. In this document she said that she believed Joseph Smith only had one overall objective, and that was to defraud her husband of his property. She also declared that she didn't believe Joseph Smith really had any gold plates. Following the recitation of this document the magistrate announced that before he would allow any other witnesses to testify he wanted to hear from Martin Harris. When Martin was sworn in he took the opposite stance that the previous witnesses had taken. He boldly and energetically testified that Joseph Smith had never taken a single dollar from him. He stated that he had, in fact, once given the Prophet fifty dollars, but that was given freely by him in order to do the work of the Lord. He further affirmed that Joseph Smith had never shown any disposition to get any other person's money. Finally, Martin told the people in the room that if they continued to resist the truth that Joseph possessed the golden plates it would someday be the means of damning their souls.

It is reported that at this point in the proceedings the judge who was overseeing the case announced that no more witnesses would be called. He instructed the clerk of the court to hand him the notes of what had just taken place. He then tore them into pieces and told the people to go home and mind their own business.[1]

A DIVINE WARNING

Joseph Smith and Oliver Cowdery were unaware of the legal actions that were occurring in the upper part of the state of New York. But one morning as Joseph was preparing to work, he was informed through his translating device that evil-designing people were endeavoring to thwart the work of God. Therefore, he was commanded to write a letter to a man named David Whitmer (who was one of Oliver Cowdery's acquaintances) and tell him to come immediately with a team of horses to move him and Oliver to the Whitmer residence in Fayette, New York. There the two men would complete the translation of the Book of Mormon plates. Joseph had never seen David Whitmer before in his life, but being acquainted with his father, Peter Whitmer Sr., he complied with the command nevertheless.

When David Whitmer first received the letter from Joseph, he was uncertain as to how he should react. He showed it to his father, mother, sisters, and brothers and asked their advice as to what it would be best for him to do. His father responded,

> Why David, [you] know you have sowed as much wheat as you can harrow in tomorrow and [the] next day and then you have a quantity of plaster to spread that is much needed on your land and you cannot go unless you get an evidence from God that it is very necessary.

This suggestion was pleasing to David, and so he asked the Lord to grant him a testimony of the fact that this was indeed His will.[2] David reports in his own words what happened next.

> I did not know what to do, I was pressed with my work. I had some 20 acres to plow, so I concluded I would finish plowing and then go. I got up one morning to go to work as usual and, on going to the field, found between five and

seven acres of my ground had been plowed during the night.

I don't know who did it; but it was done just as I would have done it myself, and the plow was left standing in the furrow.[3]

Lucy Mack Smith provides a few details concerning the events that followed. She says, "When [David] informed his father of the fact his father could not believe it till he examined [the field] for himself." His father then told him, "There must be some overruling power in this thing and I think you had better go as soon as you get your plaster paris sown." David agreed with these sentiments. "The next morning, as soon as breakfast was over, he took the half-bushel measure under his arm and went out to the place where he supposed the plaster to be." But the lime fertilizer had entirely disappeared from the location where he had left it the previous day.

David ran over to his sister's house, which was only a short distance away, and asked her if she knew where the fertilizer had gone. She was surprised at his question and informed him that it had all been sown by three men the previous day. Her children had begged her to go outside and watch them because they were doing their job faster than anybody they had ever seen do it before. The woman went outside to take a look but, supposing that David had hired the men, she went back into the house and didn't give it a second thought.

David was unable to find out who these swift workers were, and his father was equally puzzled when he was told of this deed, but the entire Whitmer family was now convinced that a higher power was connected with these events, and they all pitched in to prepare David for his journey to Pennsylvania.[4]

TO PENNSYLVANIA AND BACK

David Whitmer and the team of horses that were pulling his wagon moved rapidly along the rough dirt roadway. David reports that he traveled over forty miles on the first day of his long journey,[5] and it was necessary for him to put up at inns as he made his way south.[6] After two and a half days of travel, David reached the head of Cayuga Lake and there, unexpectedly, was met by both the Prophet and his scribe.[7] Whitmer relates, "When I arrived at Harmony, Joseph and Oliver were coming toward me, and met me some distance from the house. Oliver told me that Joseph had informed him . . . that I would be there that day before dinner, and this was why they had come out to meet me."[8] But this was not the only surprise for David. He says,

> Oliver told me they knew just when I started, where I put up at night and even the name on the sign board of the hotel where I stayed each night, for he asked Joseph to look in the seerstone, that [Joseph] did so, and told [Oliver] all these particulars of my journey, which Oliver had carefully noted in his book.

> Oliver asked me—when I first met them—when I [had] left home, where I stayed on the road, and the names of the persons keeping the hotels. I could not tell the names, but as we returned I pointed out the several houses where I had stopped, [and] he pulled out his book and found it to be correct even to the names.[9]

Joseph's demonstration of the gift of seership greatly astonished David Whitmer,[10] and he said on one occasion that it "strengthened his faith in the Prophet."[11]

Joseph was naturally concerned with the transportation of the golden plates during this journey to New York, so he "inquired of the Lord [to know] in what manner the plates should be conveyed to their point of destination. His answer was that he should give himself no trouble about [the matter] but hasten to [Fayette] and after he arrived [at] Mr. Whitmer's house if he would repair immediately to the garden he would receive the plates from the hand of an angel to whose charge they must be committed for their safety."[12] David tells a fascinating story about an encounter these men had with this particular angel during their trip. He says,

When I was returning to Fayette, with Joseph and Oliver—all of us riding in the wagon, Oliver and I on an old-fashioned, wooden spring seat and Joseph behind us—[and] while [we were] traveling along in a clear open place, a very pleasant, nice-looking old man suddenly appeared by the side of our wagon and saluted us with, "Good morning, it is very warm" (at the same time wiping his face or forehead with his hand). We returned the salutation and, by a sign from Joseph, I invited him to ride if he was going our way. But he said very pleasantly, "No, I am going to Cumorah." This name was something new to me; I did not know what Cumorah meant. We all gazed at him and at each other, and as I looked around inquiringly [at] Joseph the old man instantly disappeared so that I did not see him again. . . .

He was . . . about 5 feet 8 or 9 inches tall and heavy set. . . . [H]e was dressed in a suit of brown woolen clothes, his hair and beard were white, like Brother [Orson] Pratt's, but his beard was not so heavy. I also remember that he had on his back a sort of knapsack with something in [it], shaped like a book.[13]

David and Oliver "asked the Prophet to inquire of the Lord who this stranger was. Soon David said they turned around and Joseph looked pale, almost transparent, and said that was one of the Nephites and he had the plates of the Book of Mormon in the knapsack."[14]

David Whitmer relates that as they traveled along their way they all conversed freely about the great work that was being brought about. He also indicates that he was informed by Joseph and Oliver that they had baptized each other—seeking by that action to fulfill the command they had received in regard to that important gospel ordinance.[15]

THE TRANSLATION RECOMMENCES

The Prophet's mother says that Joseph, Oliver, and David arrived at the Whitmer home in Fayette, New York, "in health and fine spirits" after a "short and pleasant journey."[16] No time was wasted in getting back to the Lord's business, however. The day after their arrival the translation was commenced on the remainder of the golden plates.[17] According to David Whitmer this was around the first of June in 1829.[18]

The Whitmer family was "very anxious concerning the work" that Joseph and Oliver were engaged in and were "very friendly" towards them as individuals. Joseph Smith notes that John Whitmer in particular assisted them "very much in writing during the remainder of the work."[19] Indeed, John states that he acted as scribe for sixty pages' worth of material.[20]

It is apparent from several historical sources that during part of the translation process the Whitmer family was granted a great deal of access to the translator and his scribe. David Whitmer reports: "I, as well as all of my father's family, Smith's wife [Emma], Oliver Cowdery, and Martin Harris were present during the translation. I did not wish to be understood as saying that those referred to as being present were all the time in the immediate presence of the translator, but were at the place and saw how the translation was conducted."[21]

According to one late, secondhand account, there were other times when nonparticipants were not allowed to be present during the work of translation. Oliver B. Huntington recorded in his journal:

> I conversed with one old lady 88 years old [whose name was Sarah or "Sally" H. Conrad] who lived with David Whitmer when Joseph Smith and Oliver Cowdery were translating the Book of Mormon in the upper room of the house, and she, only a girl, saw them come down from [the] translating room several times when they looked so exceedingly white and strange that she inquired of Mrs. Whitmer the cause of their unusual appearance. But Mrs. Whitmer was unwilling to tell the hired girl the true cause as it was a sacred, holy event connected with a holy, sacred work which was opposed and persecuted by nearly everyone who heard of it. The girl felt so strange and unusual [about their] appearance [that] she finally told Mrs. Whitmer that she would not stay with her until she

knew the cause of the strange looks of these men. Sister
Whitmer then told her what the men were doing in the
room above and that the power of God was so great in the
room that they could hardly endure it; at times angels were
in the room in their glory which nearly consumed them.
This satisfied the girl and opened the way [for her] to
embrace the gospel.[22]

Either on or shortly before 11 June 1829, the Prophet Joseph
Smith translated the title page of the Book of Mormon and took it
with him to Palmyra in order to use it in securing the copyright for
the book.[23] In his published history Joseph made special note of this
document, saying:

> I wish also to mention here, that the title page of the Book
> of Mormon is a literal translation, taken from the very last
> leaf, on the left hand side of the collection or book of
> plates, which contained the record which has been trans-
> lated; the language of the whole running the same as all
> Hebrew writing in general [i.e., from right to left]; and
> that said title page is not by any means a modern composi-
> tion either of mine or of any other man's who has lived or
> does live in this generation. . . . [It] is a genuine and literal
> translation of the title page of the original Book of
> Mormon, as recorded on the plates.[24]

This published statement is a strong and forthright testimony by
the Prophet that he did not have anything to do with the origin of
the Book of Mormon, as many of his critics have claimed. (An examination and rebuttal of this type of claim can be found in appendix 4
of this book.)

Sometime before 14 June 1829, Joseph Smith received a revelation
for Oliver Cowdery that is now known as section 18 of the Doctrine
and Covenants.[25] This revelation is particularly interesting because it
seems to be connected in several ways to the translation of the Book of
Mormon. First of all, it is obvious from the text that Oliver had a question that he wanted answered (see D&C 18:1). The Lord, in His reply,

confirmed to the primary scribe that the words which he had written down were true, and that fact had been established "in many instances" by the manifestation of the Spirit (v. 2). Next, Oliver was admonished to rely upon the things which he had transcribed (v. 3), as they were connected with the "foundation" of the Lord's Church (v. 4). It appears from verses 7, 22, 29, and 42 that Oliver was struggling with something that he had written down concerning baptism, specifically the baptism of children who have arrived at the years of accountability. It seems possible, from this perspective, that Doctrine and Covenants section 18 was delivered shortly after the translation of Moroni 8:5–23 since that text addresses the very same issue—the baptism of children.[26] If this deduction were to prove accurate, then it would seem safe to date Doctrine and Covenants section 18 in the first half of the month of June.

During the same month, the Lord also addressed a revelation to David Whitmer, the man who had heard and seen so much in such a short period of time. In what is now known as Doctrine and Covenants section 14, the Savior rehearsed to David the same Old Testament prophecy that the angel Moroni had quoted to Joseph Smith on 22 September 1823, saying, "A great and marvelous work is about to come forth unto the children of men" (D&C 14:1). And in direct reference to the Book of Mormon, the Redeemer told David, "I must bring forth the fullness of my gospel from the Gentiles unto the house of Israel" (v. 10)—another message that Moroni had delivered to young Joseph long before. The Lord then informed David that he was called to assist in this great work (v. 11). The exact timing of this revelation is not known, but it is recorded that in the middle of June 1829 David decided to cast his lot with the Saints.[27] He went with a small group of converts to the shores of Seneca Lake and there he was baptized by the Prophet Joseph Smith.[28]

Soon David Whitmer would participate in an event that would be far more glorious, one that would cause his name to be held up before the nations of the earth and forever validate the Prophet's testimony regarding how the Book of Mormon came forth.

NOTES TO CHAPTER 6

1. See Lavina F. Anderson, ed., *Lucy's Book: A Critical Edition of Lucy Mack Smith's Family Memoir* (Salt Lake City: Signature Books, 2001), 440–45.

2. Ibid., 446–47. David Whitmer had previously received a letter from Oliver Cowdery wherein he not only provided a few lines of the words translated from the golden plates but also testified that he had a revealed knowledge that these things were true (see *Kansas City Journal,* 5 June 1881).

3. *Millennial Star,* vol. 40, no. 49, 9 December 1878, 772.

4. Anderson, ed., *Lucy's Book,* 448–49. Peter Whitmer Sr. offered Joseph and Oliver free room and board while they stayed at his house in Fayette, New York. They were also offered the assistance of David and one of the other sons in carrying out scribal duties (see *Times and Seasons,* vol. 3, no. 20, 15 August 1842, 884–85).

5. See *Deseret News,* 25 March 1884.

6. See *Juvenile Instructor,* vol. 22, no. 4, 15 February 1887, 55.

7. Whitmer: "I was a little over two and a half days going, and traveled over 40 miles the first day, and met them on the third day at the head of Cayuga Lake" (*Deseret News,* 25 March 1884). Whitmer told Edward Stevenson that it was "about 2 1/2 days drive" (Edward Stevenson Diary, 9 February 1886, Historical Department Archives, The Church of Jesus Christ of Latter-day Saints, Salt Lake City, Utah).

8. *Millennial Star,* vol. 40, no. 49, 9 December 1878, 772.

9. *Deseret News,* 25 March 1884.

10. See *Millennial Star,* vol. 40, no. 49, 9 December 1878, 772.

11. Edward Stevenson Diary, 2 January 1887, Historical Department Archives, The Church of Jesus Christ of Latter-day Saints, Salt Lake City, Utah.

12. Anderson, ed., *Lucy's Book,* 450.

13. *Millennial Star,* vol. 40, no. 49, 9 December 1878, 772.

14. Edward Stevenson Diary, 9 February 1886, Historical Department Archives, The Church of Jesus Christ of Latter-day Saints, Salt Lake City, Utah.

15. See Zenas H. Gurley, interview of David Whitmer, 14 January 1885, Gurley Collection, Historical Department Archives, The Church of Jesus Christ of Latter-day Saints, Salt Lake City, Utah.

16. Anderson, ed., *Lucy's* Book, 450.

17. See *Kansas City Journal,* 5 June 1881. David Whitmer provides a few details about the translation as it took place in his family's home. He says, "In regard

to the translation, it was a laborious work for the weather was very warm, and the days were long and they worked from morning till night. But they were both young and strong and were soon able to complete the work" (*Deseret News,* 25 March 1884). Again, David reports, "Joseph and Oliver worked hard, early and late, while translating the plates. It was slow work, and they could write only a few pages a day" (*Saints' Herald,* vol. 31, 21 June 1884).

18. See *Kansas City Journal,* 5 June 1881.

19. *Times and Seasons,* vol. 3, no. 20, 15 August 1842, 885.

20. See *Saints' Herald,* vol. 26, 15 December 1879, 370.

21. The two parts of this quotation can be found in the *Kansas City Journal,* 5 June 1881, and ibid., 19 June 1881.

22. Diary of Oliver B. Huntington, 415–16, L. Tom Perry Special Collections Library, Harold B. Lee Library, Brigham Young University, Provo, Utah.

23. Joseph Smith: "Our translation drawing to a close, we went to Palmyra, Wayne County, [New York, and] secured the copyright" (*Times and Seasons,* vol. 3, no. 24, 15 October 1842, 943). For further reading see Miriam A. Smith and John W. Welch, "Joseph Smith: 'Author and Proprietor,'" in John W. Welch, ed., *Reexploring the Book of Mormon* (Salt Lake City: Deseret Book; Provo, Utah: FARMS, 1992), 154–57.

24. *Times and Seasons,* vol. 3, no. 24, 15 October 1842, 943.

25. Dating parameters for this revelation can be found in Lyndon W. Cook, *The Revelations of the Prophet Joseph Smith* (Salt Lake City: Deseret Book, 1985), 29.

26. Notice also the word grouping of "faith, hope, [and] charity" in Moroni 8:14 and the same grouping in Doctrine and Covenants 18:19.

27. See Edward Stevenson Diary, 2 January 1887, Historical Department Archives, The Church of Jesus Christ of Latter-day Saints, Salt Lake City, Utah.

28. See *Times and Seasons,* vol. 3, no. 21, 1 September 1842, 897.

CHAPTER 7

BOOK OF MORMON WITNESSES

Joseph Smith notes in his published history of the Church that during the course of the work of translation, he and his associates learned that "three special witnesses were to be provided by the Lord, to whom He would grant that they should see the plates from which . . . the Book of Mormon . . . [was] translated, and that these witnesses should bear record of the same" (see Ether 5:2–4; 2 Ne. 27:12–13). "Almost immediately after we had made this discovery," said the Prophet, "it occurred to Oliver Cowdery, David Whitmer and . . . Martin Harris (who had come to inquire after our progress in the work) that they would have me inquire of the Lord, to know if they might not obtain of Him [the privilege] to be these three special witnesses; and finally they became so very solicitous, and teased me so much, that at length I complied."[1]

The answer that was given by the Lord in response to this inquiry is known today as Doctrine and Covenants section 17. In verses 1 through 9 of this latter-day revelation, Jesus Christ testifies to the three supplicants that the Book of Mormon translation is true. He also names the Nephite relics that they will be privileged to see in the capacity of witnesses (the golden plates, the breastplate, the sword of Laban, the Urim and Thummim, and "the miraculous directors," or Liahona) and tells them that they must obtain faith like the ancient prophets before this great privilege will be granted.[2]

It was not many days after section 17 of the Doctrine and Covenants had been received that the Lord fulfilled His promise to

exhibit the golden plates and the other ancient relics.[3] David
Whitmer said that "it was in June 1829, the very last part of the
month" when this important event took place.[4] David also revealed
that this experience happened "shortly before the completion of the
translation when there were but a few pages left."[5]

Mother Smith indicates that on the morning of the day when the
Three Witnesses saw the golden plates and other items, Joseph Smith
was attending to prayer in the Whitmer home in Fayette, New York.
When he had finished praying he said, "Martin Harris, . . . you have got
to humble yourself before your God this day and obtain, if possible, a
forgiveness of your sins for if you will do this it is His will that you and
Oliver Cowdery and David Whitmer should look upon the plates."[6]

At about eleven in the morning, David Whitmer was out working
in the field of his farm.[7] "I was plowing in my field," said David, "when
I heard a voice saying, 'Blessed is the name of the Lord and those that
keep His commandments.' After I had plowed one more round, the
Prophet and Oliver Cowdery [and Martin Harris] came along, and
said: 'Come and be one of the witnesses.'"[8] The Prophet reportedly
explained that he had received a "revelation stating that [David] was to
be one of the witnesses to the Book of Mormon."[9] Joseph also apparently told David that "the angel would show the plates . . . [and] that
the Lord had promised to make this manifest and now was the time."[10]

When he was questioned about this event later in his life, David said
that he "left his team tied up to the fence"[11] and then "got over the
fence."[12] Together David, Joseph, Oliver, and Martin all "agreed to retire
into the woods and try to obtain, by fervent and humble prayer, the
fulfillment of the promises given in [Doctrine and Covenants section
17]; that they should have view of the plates, etc."[13] They went into the
edge of the forest and reached a "pasture, cleared of underbrush, at a
point equally distant between two public highways." According to
David this spot was "about 40 rods" from Peter Whitmer Sr.'s home.[14]

THE EXPERIENCE OF
OLIVER COWDERY AND DAVID WHITMER

Once this group arrived at their destination, they knelt down and,
says the Prophet, "according to previous arrangements I commenced,

by vocal prayer to our Heavenly Father, and was followed by each of the rest in succession." The group prayed "in much faith, to Almighty God" to bestow upon them the fulfillment of the promises made to them.[15] But something was not right. The Prophet relates:

> [W]e did not . . . obtain any answer or manifestation of the divine favor in our behalf. We again observed the same order of prayer, each calling on and praying fervently to God in rotation; but with the same result as before.

> Upon this, our second failure, Martin Harris proposed that he would withdraw himself from us believing, as he expressed himself, that his presence was the cause of our not obtaining what we wished for. He accordingly withdrew from us.[16]

After Martin had gone, the remaining participants "knelt down again, and had not been many minutes engaged in prayer when presently [they] beheld a light above [them] in the air of exceeding brightness."[17] David Whitmer indicated that about this time the three men got up from their kneeling position and sat down on a nearby log.[18] In describing the light David explained that it "was not like the light of the sun, nor like that of a fire, but more glorious and beautiful." He said, "It extended away round us, I cannot tell how far."[19] Whitmer also said that once the "light from heaven" began to shine, solemnity pervaded the minds of those who were present.[20] In another recital of this event he is represented as saying that "simultaneous with the light came a strange entrancing influence which permeated [David] so powerfully that he felt chained to the spot, while he also experienced a sensation of joy absolutely indescribable."[21]

The otherworldly light "grew brighter and brighter,"[22] and then suddenly a radiant angel appeared before the three men, dressed in white and standing above the ground.[23] Between the trio of mortals and the heavenly visitor was a table that appeared to be made of wood,[24] and on top of the table were a variety of objects, including the following:

- the golden plates of the Book of Mormon
- the breastplate
- the sword of Laban
- the directors, or Liahona
- the brass plates
- the plates of the book of Ether
- plates containing records of wickedness and secret combinations
- many other plates[25]

The interpreters, or Urim and Thummim, were not on top of the table, according to Whitmer, but were "a little way off, and in a receptacle which held them."[26] David is quoted as saying that the "Interpreters" which he saw "in the holy vision . . . looked like whitish stones put in the rim of a bow . . . like spectacles, only much larger."[27]

Joseph Smith relates that the angel[28] held the golden plates of the Book of Mormon in his hands and turned over the leaves of the unsealed portion one by one so that the witnesses could have a distinct view of the engravings that covered their surfaces.[29] David Whitmer reportedly said that as the angel "turned over [the plates] leaf by leaf, [he] explain[ed] the contents, here and there."[30] But this is apparently not all that the heavenly being said. David Whitmer recalled that the angel "declared to us . . . that the Book of Mormon is true."[31] According to an account of Oliver Cowdery's words, the angel testified "that the translation from the plates in the Book of Mormon was accepted of the Lord." In addition, said Cowdery, the angel stated that the translation would "go forth to the world, and no power on earth should stop its progress."[32] Oliver is further represented as saying that the angel "commanded [them] as witnesses to bear a faithful testimony to the world of the vision that they were favored to behold,"[33] and, said Oliver, "this personage told us if we denied that testimony there [would be] no forgiveness in this life nor in the world to come."[34] Finally, the angel "addressed himself to David Whitmer and said, 'David, blessed is the Lord, and he that keeps His commandments,'"[35] thus repeating the message that he heard in the field right before Joseph, Oliver, and Martin had joined him there.[36]

The Prophet Joseph Smith states in his published notes that immediately after the angel had addressed David, the group "heard a voice from out of the bright light" above them saying, "These plates have been revealed by the power of God, and they have been translated by the power of God; the translation of them which you have seen is correct, and I command you to bear record of what you now see and hear."[37] "We know it was the voice of God," said David to one of many curious interviewers who sat down to listen to his story. "I knew it was the voice of God just as well as I knew anything."[38]

Whitmer remarked that "the vision was closed at once, and exactly as it came even so did the sight disappear."[39] He also mentions something that is rarely brought up in LDS discussions on this event and that may possibly be the core of certain stories that emerged after the Church moved to Utah. He asserts that the objects on the table "were taken away by the angel to a cave, which [the witnesses] saw by the power of God while [they] were yet in the Spirit."[40] This was not the only time that David made mention of the cave. He was asked on another occasion,

> Where are the plates now?
> He [answered,]In a cave, where the angel has hidden them up till the time arrives when the plates, which are sealed, shall be translated. God will yet raise up a mighty one, who shall do his work till it is finished and Jesus comes again.
> [He was then asked,]Where is that cave?
> He [responded,]In the state of New York.
> [The next question was,]In the Hill Cumorah?
> [The answer was,] No, but not far from that place.[41]

THE EXPERIENCE OF MARTIN HARRIS

Martin Harris had removed himself from the presence of Joseph, Oliver, and David before they received their remarkable manifestation. Martin is represented as saying in one source, "I withdrew from them, telling them that it was on my account that their prayer was not answered. After they had been visited by the angel, the Prophet then came over to me where I was praying."[42] According to Joseph Smith's published account, Martin was a considerable distance from where the other group was and had been fervently engaged in prayer. He told the Prophet that he had not yet prevailed with the Lord, and earnestly requested Joseph to join him in prayer so that he might also receive the same blessings that the others had obtained.[43]

The two men knelt down,[44] and "after praying some time, the angel appeared."[45] "I saw the angel descend from heaven," Martin reportedly said,[46] and as in the manifestation given to Oliver Cowdery and David Whitmer, the angel stood on the opposite side of a table to present the objects. This time sources indicate that the angel revealed the plates of the Book of Mormon, the breastplate, the sword of Laban, as well as the interpreters.[47]

Some of the people who spoke to Martin about his experience quoted him, long after his passing, as saying, "[T]he angel stood before me and said, 'Look' and when I glanced at the angel, I fell, but [then] I stood on my feet."[48] "I saw with these two eyes the angel stand with the gold plates in his hands," he said, "and I saw him turn leaf by leaf the plates of gold."[49] Like the other witnesses, Harris's view of the Book of Mormon plates was evidently so clear that he was able to testify that he saw the engravings on them.[50]

From other records that are available it would seem that the messenger from beyond the veil said a few other significant things to Martin Harris. These sources say, "The angel declared that the Book of Mormon was correctly translated by the power of God and not of man," and also that "it contained the fullness of the gospel of Jesus Christ to the Nephites, who were a branch of the lost sheep of the house of Israel, and had come from the land of Jerusalem to America."[51] The angel apparently also "command[ed] him to bear a testimony of these things to all people whenever opportunity was afforded him to do so."[52] "When [the angel] had finished his message," according to one rehearsal of Harris's statement, he "saw him ascend up into heaven."[53]

"[A]fter the angel ascended into heaven, [Martin] saw the heavens open," says another source, "and heard the voice of God declare that everything was correct that the angel had told them, and that the Book of Mormon was translated correctly."[54] Martin also related to an acquaintance, "I was commanded by God's voice to testify to the whole world [of] what I had seen and heard."[55]

Finally, Martin is represented as saying of his experience, "I cried out in my ecstasy—'Tis enough; tis enough; mine eyes have beheld of the glories of God. Hosanna; hosanna; hosanna, to God and the Lamb.' And I fell on my face on the ground. The next thing I knew, the Prophet was helping me up."[56] Joseph Smith reports in his history that after Martin's petition to heaven had been answered in such a glorious and overwhelming manner he rejoiced exceedingly.[57]

THE MANIFESTATION'S AFTERMATH

After Joseph and Martin had rejoined Oliver and David, "Harris described the angelic visitant to Whitmer, who recognized it as the same person that he and Cowdery had seen."[58] The four witnesses then returned to the Peter Whitmer homestead. Lucy Mack Smith remembered that when they returned it was between three and four o'clock in the afternoon. She says in regard to this episode,

> Mrs. Whitmer and Mr. Smith and myself were sitting in a bedroom. I sat on the bedside. When Joseph came in, he threw himself down beside me [and exclaimed], "Father! Mother! . . . you do not know how happy I am. The Lord has caused the plates to be shown to three more besides me who have also seen an angel and will have to testify to the truth of what I have said, for they know for themselves that I do not go about to deceive the people and I do feel as though I [have been] relieved of a dreadful burden which was almost too much for me to endure. But they will now have to bear a part, and it does rejoice my soul that I am not any longer to be entirely alone in the world."

> Martin Harris then came in. He seemed almost overcome with excess of joy. He then testified to what he had seen and heard, as did also the others—Oliver and David.[59]

The Three Witnesses then obeyed the divine commandment that they had received and subscribed their names to a document declaring that they had indeed seen the Book of Mormon plates and heard the voice of God.[60] The document that these men drafted and signed is included in every copy of the Book of Mormon. It says without equivocation that they did indeed see the angel and the plates and heard God's voice bear witness of the truth.

There is a fascinating episode connected with the published declaration of the Three Witnesses that is rarely mentioned in discussions on this matter. David Whitmer told a man named James H. Hart that

> when they were first commanded to testify of these things they demurred and told the Lord [that] the people would not believe them for the [Book of Mormon], concerning which they were to bear record, told of a people who were educated and refined, dwelling in large cities; whereas all that was then known of the early inhabitants of this country was the filthy, lazy, degraded and ignorant savages that were roaming over the land.

> [David Whitmer said,] "The Lord told us in reply that He would make it known to the people that the early inhabitants of this land had been just such a people as they were described in the [Book of Mormon] and He would lead them to uncover the ruins of the great cities, and they should have abundant evidence of the truth of that which is written in the book."[61]

THE THREE WITNESSES TESTIFY

The Three Witnesses of the Book of Mormon testified of the truth of their published statement on countless occasions, both in public and in private. The following testimonies are especially notable because they were each expressed after a challenge had been issued.

Colonel Giles of Richmond, Missouri, paid a visit to David Whitmer in July 1884 and at first discussed the latter's printed testimony "in an affable and friendly manner." But then,

> rather suggestively [Colonel Giles] asked if it might not have been possible that he, Mr. Whitmer, had been

mistaken and had simply been moved upon by some mental disturbance, or hallucination, which had deceived him into *thinking* he saw the . . . angel, the plates, the Urim and Thummim, and the sword of Laban. . . .

Elder Whitmer arose and drew himself up to his full height—a little over six feet—and said, in solemn and impressive tones:

"No, sir! I was not under any hallucination, nor was I deceived! I saw with these eyes and I heard with these ears! *I know whereof I speak!*"[62]

On 27 June 1858, President Brigham Young spoke to a group of Latter-day Saints about Oliver Cowdery and related that several years after Cowdery had become disaffected from the Church,

a gentleman walked into his law office and said to him, "Mr. Cowdery, what do you think of the Book of Mormon now? Do you believe that it is true?" He replied, "No sir, I do not." "Well," said the gentleman, "I thought as much; for I concluded that you had seen the folly of your ways and had resolved to renounce what you once declared to be true." [Oliver replied,] "Sir, you mistake me: I do not *believe* that the Book of Mormon is true; I am past *belief* on that point, for I KNOW that it is true, as well as I know that you now sit before me." "Do you still testify that you saw an angel?" [asked the interrogator]. [The reply was,] "Yes, as much as I see you now; and I know the Book of Mormon to be true."[63]

George Godfrey of Clarkston, Utah, became one of Martin Harris's neighbors when the third witness of the Book of Mormon settled in that area in 1874. George recalled that he had heard Martin "bear witness to the truthfulness and genuineness of the Book of Mormon" many times during his final years. That testimony "never varied," even though several individuals "tried to entrap him relative to the testimony which he bore by cross questioning him relative to . . . scenes and events . . . in connection with the bringing forth of the Book of Mormon." George states,

> A few hours before [Martin's] death, and when he was so weak and enfeebled that he was unable to recognize me or anyone, and knew not to whom he was speaking, I asked him if he did not feel that there was an element at least of fraudulence and deception in the things that were written and told of the coming forth of the Book of Mormon. And he replied as he had always done so many, many times in my hearing and with the same spirit he always manifested when enjoying health and vigor and said: "The Book of Mormon is no fake. I know what I know. I have seen what I have seen and I have heard what I have heard. I have seen the gold plates from which the Book of Mormon is written. An angel appeared to me and others and testified to the truthfulness of the record, and had I been willing to have perjured myself and sworn falsely to the testimony I now bear I could have been a rich man, but I could not have testified other than I have done and am now doing for these things are true."[64]

THE EIGHT WITNESSES

Lucy Mack Smith recollects in her dictated history that the day after the Three Witnesses had their experience with the angel in the forest she and her husband (and probably Martin Harris) left Fayette, New York, and returned to the Smith family home in Palmyra. Lucy says that they were a cheerful, rejoicing little company as they traveled along the roadway. Lucy also states that a few days after their departure from Fayette, the Prophet Joseph Smith, Oliver Cowdery, and the Whitmers arrived at their farm with the view of making arrangements to get the Book of Mormon printed.[65]

While translating the Book of Mormon text, Joseph and his associates learned that in addition to the "three witnesses"—who would see the golden plates "by the power of God"—there would also be "a few" other people who would be permitted to view the plates "according to the will of God" in order "to bear testimony of His word to the children of men" (2 Ne. 27:12–13). At some point it was determined that eight individuals would be allowed to view and handle the Book of Mormon plates without any supernatural display involved. The men chosen for this experience were Joseph Smith Sr., Hyrum Smith, Samuel H. Smith, John Whitmer, Peter Whitmer Jr., Jacob Whitmer, Christian Whitmer, and Hiram Page.

On a Thursday, possibly 25 June 1829, the Prophet Joseph Smith led these eight men to "a little grove where it was customary for the [Smith] family to offer up their secret prayers—as Joseph had been instructed that the plates would be carried there by one of the ancient Nephites."[66] John Whitmer said that when they arrived at the spot, Joseph Smith handed the plates uncovered into the witnesses' hands, and they were allowed to turn the leaves and otherwise examine the plates sufficient to satisfy them.[67]

The Eight Witnesses then fulfilled their duty by subscribing their names to a solemn declaration of what they had experienced. This document, which is also included in every copy of the printed Book of Mormon, states forthrightly that these gentlemen handled the curious[68] looking set of golden plates with their hands and plainly saw the hieroglyphics that were engraved upon them.

The Eight Witnesses of the Book of Mormon reaffirmed their published testimony throughout their lives. John Whitmer, for instance, wrote the following for a Church newspaper article:

> [T]o say that the Book of Mormon is a revelation from God, I have no hesitancy; but with all confidence have signed my name to it as such. . . . I desire to testify to all that will come to the knowledge of this address, that I have most assuredly seen the plates from whence the Book of Mormon is translated, and that I have handled these plates and know of a surety that Joseph Smith, Jr. has translated the Book of Mormon by the gift and power of God, and in this thing the wisdom of the wise most assuredly has perished.[69]

After Christian Whitmer and Peter Whitmer Jr. had both passed away, Oliver Cowdery stated in an editorial that they were the first to embrace the new covenant, on hearing it, and during a constant scene of persecution and perplexity, to their last moments, maintained its truth. They were both included in the list of the eight witnesses in the Book of Mormon and, though they have departed, it is with great satisfaction that we reflect that they proclaimed to their last moments the certainty of their former testimony. . . . May all who read remember the fact that the Lord has given men a witness of Himself in the last days, and that they have faithfully declared it till called away.[70]

John C. Whitmer, Jacob Whitmer's son, reported that his father "was always faithful and true to his testimony to the Book of Mormon, and confirmed it on his deathbed."[71] Those who visit Jacob's final resting place will notice that on top of the fine marble stone that marks his grave is a representation of "the Book of Mormon laid open, with a blooming rose resting on the divide, and the book resting upon the closed-up Bible."[72]

Philander Page, the son of Hiram Page, told Andrew Jenson in September 1888: "I knew my father to be true and faithful to his testimony of the divinity of the Book of Mormon until the very last. Whenever he had an opportunity to bear his testimony to this effect, he would always do so, and seemed to rejoice exceedingly in having been privileged to see the plates and thus become one of the Eight Witnesses."[73]

In the spring of 1832, Samuel Smith was spreading the message of the restored gospel in Daniel Tyler's neighborhood. Tyler said that Samuel "read the 29th chapter of Isaiah at the first meeting and delineated the circumstances of the coming forth of the Book of Mormon, of which he said he was a witness. He knew his brother Joseph had the plates, for the Prophet had shown them to him, and he had handled them and seen the engravings thereon."[74]

Hyrum Smith confirmed his 1829 signed testimony in an 1839 article published in the Church's Nauvoo newspaper. In the article he said,

Having given my testimony to the world of the truth of the Book of Mormon, the renewal of the everlasting covenant, and the establishment of the Kingdom of heaven, in these last days; and having been brought into great afflictions and distresses for the same, I thought that it might be strengthening to my beloved brethren, to give them a short account of my sufferings, for the truth's sake, and the state of my mind and feelings, while under circumstances of the most trying and afflicting nature. . . .

I had been abused and thrust into a dungeon, and confined for months on account of my faith, and the "testimony of Jesus Christ." However, I thank God that I felt a determination to die rather than deny the things which my eyes had seen, which my hands had handled, and which I had borne testimony to . . . and I can assure my beloved brethren that I was enabled to bear as strong a testimony, when nothing but death presented itself, as ever I did in my life.[75]

And finally, there is the steadfast refusal of Joseph Smith Sr. to deny what he knew to be absolutely true. The Prophet's mother relates that around October 1830 all of the Smiths' children, except for their young daughter Lucy, were out of town. An old Quaker gentleman came to the door asking for Father Smith, stating that he had bought a fourteen-dollar note against him, and had come to collect on it. When asked why he had purchased the note, the Quaker said it was his own business and that he wanted the money right then. Father Smith said he could give him six dollars but would have to provide him the rest at a later time. This was not satisfactory to the Quaker, however. He replied that if he didn't get the money immediately he would have Father Smith thrown in jail—unless he would burn the Book of Mormon, in which case the debt would be forgiven. Father Smith replied "in a cool, decided manner, 'No sir, I shall not do that.'" Lucy Mack Smith offered the Quaker her gold bead necklace as a payment, but the man refused to accept it, saying triumphantly that unless the debt was paid in full Father Smith would go to jail. Mother Smith accused the Quaker of harassing their family in an attempt to compel them to deny the work of God, and she said, "We shall not burn the Book of Mormon nor deny the inspiration of the Almighty." The Quaker then summoned a constable that was waiting nearby and Father Smith was taken as a prisoner.

After the Prophet's father had been secured inside of a carriage and carted away, his captors tried every possible argument to induce him to renounce the Book of Mormon, promising that if he did his debt would be canceled. But Father Smith did not reply to their continual urgings, and as he was thrown into the dungeon he thought to himself that he was not the first man who had been imprisoned for the truth's sake.[76]

The testimonies of the Book of Mormon witnesses form a solid foundation upon which Latter-day Saints can build their faith. These straightforward declarations ring out with the sound of certainty and conviction. And even though only a few mortals have been privileged to confirm the reality of the golden plates by their sight and touch, the Book of Mormon itself invites all men and women to become personal witnesses of its truth through the power of the Holy Ghost.

NOTES TO CHAPTER 7

1.   *Times and Seasons,* vol. 3, no. 21, 1 September 1842, 897.

2.   It is not known whether it was 2 Nephi 27:12–13 or Ether 5:2–4 that triggered Cowdery, Whitmer, and Harris's request to serve as the Three Witnesses. In connection with this question, it is perhaps relevant that both 2 Nephi 27:11, 13 and Doctrine and Covenants 17:4, 9 contain the phrase "the children of men." In other words, it may be that in the Lord's revelation on the subject He made reference to the material that had sparked the request.

3.   See *Times and Seasons,* vol. 3, no. 21, 1 September 1842, 897.

4.   Joseph F. Smith Diary, 7–8 September 1878, Historical Department Archives, The Church of Jesus Christ of Latter-day Saints, Salt Lake City, Utah.

5.   George Q. Cannon Journal, 27 February 1884, Historical Department Archives, The Church of Jesus Christ of Latter-day Saints, Salt Lake City, Utah.

6.   Lavina F. Anderson, ed., *Lucy's Book: A Critical Edition of Lucy Mack Smith's Family Memoir* (Salt Lake City: Signature Books, 2001), 452.

7. See the letter written by Edward Stevenson to Orson Pratt, 23 December 1877, Journal History, Church Office Building Library, The Church of Jesus Christ of Latter-day Saints, Salt Lake City, Utah.

8. *Salt Lake Herald*, 2 February 1878.

9. *Saints' Herald*, vol. 29, 1 March 1882.

10. George Q. Cannon Journal, 27 February 1884.

11. Edward Stevenson Diary, 9 February 1886, Historical Department Archives, The Church of Jesus Christ of Latter-day Saints, Salt Lake City, Utah.

12. *Saints' Herald*, vol. 29, 1 March 1882.

13. *Times and Seasons*, vol. 3, no. 21, 1 September 1842, 897.

14. Edward Stevenson Diary, 2 January 1887. Orson Pratt declared, "I am individually acquainted . . . with the translator and the Three Witnesses . . . [and] I have seen the place where the angel descended and showed them the plates" (George D. Watt, comp., *Journal of Discourses*, 26 vols. [London: F. D. and S. W. Richards and Sons, 1854–1886], 7:30).

15. *Times and Seasons*, vol. 3, no. 21, 1 September 1842, 897.

16. Ibid., 897–98.

17. Ibid., 898. David Whitmer confirmed that it was "a bright light" (David Whitmer to Anthony Metcalf, 2 April 1887, in Lyndon W. Cook, ed., *David Whitmer Interviews: A Restoration Witness* [Orem, Utah: Grandin Book, 1993], 247) and also confirmed that this light "came down from above" the group (*Saints' Herald*, vol. 29, 1 March 1882).

18. See *Saints' Herald*, vol. 29, 1 March 1882.

19. Joseph F. Smith Diary, 7–8 September 1878, Historical Department Archives, The Church of Jesus Christ of Latter-day Saints, Salt Lake City, Utah; in *Deseret News*, 16 November 1878.

20. *Saints' Herald*, vol. 31, 21 June 1884.

21. *The Omaha Herald*, 17 October 1886. David Whitmer connected the unearthly light and its accompanying rapturous feeling with the Spirit of God. "[W]e were in the Spirit when we had the view, for no man can behold the face of an angel, except in a spiritual view, but we were in the body also, and everything was as natural to us as it is at any time" (David Whitmer to Anthony Metcalf, 2 April 1887, in Cook, ed., *David Whitmer Interviews*, 247). Whitmer "explained that he saw the plates . . . with his natural eyes, but he had to be prepared for it—that he and the other witnesses were overshadowed by the power of God, and a halo of brightness indescribable" (Nathan Tanner Jr. Journal, 13 April 1886, Historical Department Archives, The Church of Jesus

Christ of Latter-day Saints, Salt Lake City, Utah). These descriptions of the event are in accordance with the Lord's promise that the Three Witnesses would see the plates "as they are" (D&C 5:13) yet have their experience "by the power of God" (vv. 25–26).

22. Edward Stevenson Diary, 9 February 1886.

23. Oliver Cowdery reportedly said that the angel was "dressed in white [and] standing above the ground, in a glory I have never seen anything to compare with, the sun [being] insignificant in comparison" (*Deseret News,* 21 February 1910). David Whitmer also said that the angel "was dressed in white, and spoke and called me by name and said, 'Blessed is he that keepeth His commandments'" (*Saints' Herald,* vol. 29, 1 March 1882, 68). Whitmer said the "personage [was] clothed in white" (*Omaha Herald,* 17 October 1886).

24. David Whitmer noted, "Between us and the angel there appeared a table" (*Saints' Herald,* vol. 31, 21 June 1884); there was "a table in front of [the angel]" (Edward Stevenson Diary, 9 February 1886 and 2 January 1887). This table was about five or six feet away (see *Saints' Herald,* vol. 31, 21 June 1884). David Whitmer: "In the midst of this light, but a few feet from us, appeared a table" (*Millennial Star,* vol. 43, no. 28, 11 July 1881, 437). Whitmer: "The table had the appearance of literal wood" (Zenas H. Gurley, interview of David Whitmer, 14 January 1885, Gurley Collection, Historical Department Archives, The Church of Jesus Christ of Latter-day Saints). Whitmer: The table "appeared to be [tangible], but they did not touch it" (Nathan Tanner Jr. Reminiscence, 17 February 1909, Historical Department Archives, The Church of Jesus Christ of Latter-day Saints).

25. These items are identified in the following sources: Edward Stevenson to Daniel H. Wells, 16 February 1886, cited in Andrew Jenson, *Historical Record,* May 1887, 6:212; *Millennial Star,* vol. 40, no. 49, 9 December 1878, 771–72; ibid., vol. 43, no. 28, 11 July 1881, 437; Edward Stevenson to Orson Pratt, 23 December 1877, 3–4; *Deseret News,* 16 August 1878, 2; Nathan Tanner Jr. to Nathan A. Tanner, 17 February 1909, Historical Department Archives, The Church of Jesus Christ of Latter-day Saints, Salt Lake City, Utah.

26. Ibid.

27. Zenas H. Gurley, interview of David Whitmer, 14 January 1885.

28. When David Whitmer was asked, "Did the personage or angel who showed you the plates tell you his name?" he replied, "No, he did not." Whitmer speculated that it may have been Moroni or even one of the three Nephite Apostles who were promised that they would not taste of death (*Deseret Evening News,* 4

September 1883). When asked, "Who was the angel that showed the plates to you?" Whitmer replied, "I do not know as no name was given" (Zenas H. Gurley, interview of David Whitmer, 14 January 1885).

29. "In his hands he held the plates which we had been praying for these [witnesses] to have a view of: he turned over the leaves one by one, so that we could see them, and discover the engravings thereon distinctly" (*Times and Seasons,* vol. 3, no. 21, 1 September 1842, 898). David Whitmer said that the angel showed them the plates "one by one, which were to be translated" (*Deseret Evening News,* 16 August 1878).

30. *Fall River Herald,* 28 March 1879. David Whitmer specifically states that he, Joseph Smith, and Oliver Cowdery "did not" handle the Book of Mormon plates during this manifestation (*Deseret Evening News,* 16 August 1878, 2). Whitmer: "We did not touch nor handle the plates" (Zenas H. Gurley, interview of David Whitmer, 14 January 1885). "I then asked [David Whitmer] if he ever handled the plates, and he said that he did not at any time" (Nathan Tanner Jr. Journal, 13 April 1886, Historical Department Archives, The Church of Jesus Christ of Latter-day Saints, Salt Lake City, Utah).

31. David Whitmer to Anthony Metcalf, 2 April 1887, in Cook, ed., *David Whitmer Interviews,* 247.

32. *Millennial Star,* vol. 48, no. 27, 5 July 1886, 420.

33. Ibid. David Whitmer said, "The angel told us that we must bear testimony to the world, as contained in my testimony written in the Book of Mormon" (David Whitmer to Susa Young Gates, 11 February 1887, David Whitmer Papers, Community of Christ Archives, Independence, Mo.).

34. *Deseret News,* 21 February 1910.

35. *Times and Seasons,* vol. 3, no. 21, 1 September 1842, 898. Whitmer verifies that the angel "called [him] by name and said, 'Blessed is he that keepeth His commandments'" (*Saints' Herald,* vol. 29, 1 March 1882).

36. See *Salt Lake Herald,* 2 February 1878.

37. *Times and Seasons,* vol. 3, no. 21, 1 September 1842, 898.

38. *Saints' Herald,* vol. 29, 1 March 1882.

39. *Deseret Evening News,* 16 August 1878, 2.

40. *Saints' Herald,* vol. 31, 21 June 1884.

41. *Deseret Evening News,* 16 August 1878, 2.

42. John E. Godfrey, affidavit, 2 June 1933, L. Tom Perry Special Collections Library, Harold B. Lee Library, Brigham Young University, Provo, Utah.

43. See *Times and Seasons,* vol. 3, no. 21, 1 September 1842, 898.

44. Martin Harris remarked to an acquaintance, "In my desperation I asked the prophet [and] seer to kneel down with me and to pray for me also that I [might] also see the plates, and we did kneel down and pray" (Ole A. Jensen, "Testimony of Harris," L. Tom Perry Special Collections Library, Harold B. Lee Library, Brigham Young University, Provo, Utah).

45. John E. Godfrey, affidavit, 2 June 1933. Joseph Smith specified that the angel appeared "before [they] had yet finished" praying (*Times and Seasons,* vol. 3, no. 21, 1 September 1842, 898).

46. William Pilkington, statement sworn before Joseph W. Peterson, 3 April 1934, L. Tom Perry Special Collections Library, Harold B. Lee Library, Brigham Young University, Provo, Utah.

47. "[T]he angel stood on the opposite side of the table on which were the plates, the Interpreters, etc." (*Millennial Star,* vol. 48, no. 25, 21 June 1886, 390). Martin says he "saw the Urim and Thummim, the breastplate, and the sword of Laban" (William Pilkington to Vern C. Poulter, 28 February 1930, L. Tom Perry Special Collections Library, Harold B. Lee Library, Brigham Young University, Provo, Utah). David Whitmer said of Martin Harris, "I don't think he saw all that we did" (Joseph F. Smith Diary, 7–8 September 1878, Historical Department Archives, The Church of Jesus Christ of Latter-day Saints, Salt Lake City, Utah). In connection with this last statement, it should be remembered that Whitmer said he, Joseph, and Oliver saw the angel take the objects on the table to a cave. It may be that when the angel visited Martin and Joseph he brought fewer items with him. This is evidenced by the fact that Martin never mentions the various sets of plates that David does in his narratives.

48. Ole A. Jensen, "Testimony of Harris."

49. John E. Godfrey, affidavit, 2 June 1933.

50. See William Pilkington to Vern C. Poulter, 28 February 1930.

51. *Millennial Star,* vol. 48, no. 25, 21 June 1886, 390. Harris: "With these ears (pointing to them) I heard [the angel] say it was a true and correct record of an ancient people that dwelt upon this the American continent" (Alma L. Jensen, affidavit, 1 June 1936).

52. *Millennial Star,* vol. 44, no. 5, 30 January 1882, 78.

53. William Pilkington, statement, 3 April 1934.

54. William Pilkington to Vern C. Poulter, 28 February 1930. "I also heard the voice of the Lord saying that these words [on the plates] were true" (John E. Godfrey, affidavit, 2 June 1933). "I then heard the voice of God say, 'The book is true and translated correctly'" (Ole A. Jensen, "Testimony of Harris").

55. William Pilkington, statement, 3 April 1934.

56. Ibid.

57. See *Times and Seasons,* vol. 3, no. 21, 1 September 1842, 898. Oliver Cowdery, David Whitmer, and Martin Harris were not the only persons to be shown the Book of Mormon plates by an angel of God. Consider the following three examples.

Mary Musselman Whitmer: John C. Whitmer relates, "I have heard my grandmother (Mary Musselman Whitmer) say on several occasions that she was shown the plates of the Book of Mormon by a holy angel. . . . It was at the time, she said, when the translation was going on at the house of the elder Peter Whitmer, her husband [in June 1829]. Joseph Smith with his wife and Oliver Cowdery—whom David Whitmer a short time previous had brought up from Harmony, Pennsylvania—were all boarding with the Whitmers and my grandmother, in having so many extra persons to care for, besides her own large household, was often overloaded with work to such an extent that she felt it to be quite a burden. One evening, when (after having done her usual day's work in the house) she went to the barn to milk the cows, she met a stranger carrying something on his back that looked like a knapsack. At first she was a little afraid of him, but when he spoke to her in a kind, friendly tone and began to explain to her the nature of the work which was going on in her house, she was filled with inexpressible joy and satisfaction. He then untied his knapsack and showed her a bundle of plates, which in size and appearance corresponded with the description subsequently given by the witnesses to the Book of Mormon. This strange person turned the leaves of the book of plates over, leaf after leaf, and also showed her the engravings upon them; after which he told her to be patient and faithful in bearing her burden a little longer, promising that if she would do so she should be blessed; and her reward would be sure, if she proved faithful to the end. The personage then suddenly vanished with the plates, and where he went, she could not tell. From that moment my grandmother was enabled to perform her household duties with comparative ease, and she felt no more inclination to murmur because her lot was hard" (Andrew Jensen, *LDS Biographical Encyclopedia* [Salt Lake City: Andrew Jenson History Company, 1901], 1:283).

Lyman E. Johnson: President Brigham Young made note of the fact that "one of the Quorum of Twelve—a young man full of faith and good works—prayed, and the vision of his mind was opened, and the angel of God came and laid the plates before him, and he saw and handled them, and saw the angel, and conversed with him as he would with one of his friends; but after all this, he was left to doubt, and plunged into apostasy, and has continued to contend against this work" (*Journal of Discourses*, 7:164). Compare this information with an article in the *Catholic Telegraph* that states that when Lyman Johnson and Orson Pratt were preaching on 8 April 1832, one of them said that "an angel brought the Mormonite Bible and laid it before him (the speaker); he therefore *knows* these things to be true" (*Catholic Telegraph*, vol. 1, no. 26, 14 April 1832; emphasis in original. My thanks to Matt Roper for bringing this source to my attention).

    Harrison Burgess: "On the third Sabbath in May [1833] while speaking to a congregation I declared that I knew the Book of Mormon was true and the work of God. The next day while I was laboring in the community something seemed to whisper to me 'Do you know the Book of Mormon is true?' My mind became perplexed and darkened, and I was so tormented in spirit that I left my work and retired into the woods. The misery and distress that I there experienced cannot be described. The tempter all the while seemed to say, 'Do you know the Book of Mormon is true?' I remained in this situation about two hours. At last it came into my mind the faith that the brother of Jared had in obtaining a knowledge of God for himself, and others also. I resolved to know whether I had proclaimed the truth or not and commenced praying to the God of heaven for a testimony of these things. When all at once the vision of my mind was opened and a glorious personage clothed in white stood before me and exhibited to my view the plates from which the Book of Mormon was proclaimed and taken" (Harrison Burgess, autobiography, "Sketch of a Life Well Spent," Historical Department Archives, The Church of Jesus Christ of Latter-day Saints, Salt Lake City, Utah, 65–66).

58. *Chicago Times*, 17 October 1881.

59. Anderson, ed., *Lucy's Book*, 453.

60. Joseph Smith: "Having thus, through the mercy of God, obtained these glorious manifestations it now remained for these three individuals to fulfill the commandment which they had received, viz.: to bear record of these things" (*Times and Seasons*, vol. 3, no. 21, 1 September 1842, 898).

61. *Deseret News*, 4 September 1883.

62. *Saints' Herald*, vol. 83, no. 2, 28 January 1936; emphasis in original.

63. *Journal of Discourses*, 7:55; emphasis in original.

64. George Godfrey, affidavit, 29 October 1921, in Eldin Ricks, *The Case of the Book of Mormon Witnesses* (Salt Lake City: Deseret News Press, 1971), 21.

65. See Anderson, ed., *Lucy's Book,* 455.

66. Ibid., 455–56.

67. See *Deseret News,* 6 August 1878.

68. Richard L. Anderson writes, "In 1829 the word *curious* carried the meaning of the Latin word for 'careful,' suggesting that the plates were wrought 'with care and art'" (Daniel H. Ludlow, ed., *Encyclopedia of Mormonism* [New York: Macmillan, 1992], 1:214).

69. *Messenger and Advocate,* vol. 2, no. 6, March 1836, 286–87.

70. Ibid., vol. 3, no. 3, December 1836, 426.

71. *Deseret News,* 17 September 1888, 2.

72. Ibid., 16 August 1878, 2.

73. Jenson, *LDS Biographical Encyclopedia,* 1:277. Philander Page once said, "I have heard Oliver Cowdery, David Whitmer, Jacob Whitmer, John Whitmer, and my father, Hiram Page, reaffirm their testimonies as published in the Book of Mormon" (*Improvement Era,* vol. 15, no. 3, January 1912, 257).

74. Abraham H. Cannon, ed., *Scraps of Biography* (Salt Lake City, Juvenile Instructor Office, 1883), 23–24.

75. *Times and Seasons,* vol. 1, no. 2, December 1839, 20, 23.

76. Anderson, ed., *Lucy's Book,* 488–91, 496.

CHAPTER 8

PUBLICATION AND CONFRONTATION

On the north side of Main Street in Palmyra, New York, stood a group of buildings known as "Exchange Row." At the western end of this complex was a three-storied building rented out by Philip Grandin to his twenty-two-year-old brother, Egbert B. Grandin. On the top floor of this building Egbert had constructed a print shop with two small presses (the *Wayne Sentinel* newspaper was published here); on the second floor was a book bindery run by Luther Howard (a newspaper printer who hailed from Ithaca, New York); and on the first floor was Howard and Grandin's bookstore.

Sometime in the forepart of June 1829, Joseph Smith, Hyrum Smith, Oliver Cowdery, and Martin Harris all went to see young Mr. Grandin at his printing establishment and asked him what he would charge to produce a set of five thousand books. They presented Egbert with the title page of the Book of Mormon and a few sheets of manuscript, and then Martin Harris—who was one of Grandin's friends—said that he would provide payment for the books if a bargain could be made. Mr. Grandin said at once that he was not inclined to entertain their proposal at any price because he believed that the whole affair was a scheme to defraud Martin Harris. Grandin's viewpoint was kindly but firmly resisted by Mr. Harris, and resented by members of the Smith family, Oliver Cowdery taking little or no part in the conversation. Some of the other people who were present during this uncomfortable exchange also expressed their desire for Martin to stop participating in this project, but he resolutely disregarded their pleas. Pomeroy Tucker, one of the workers in Grandin's print shop, relates that after this incident

> further interviews followed, Grandin being earnestly importuned to reconsider his opinion and determination. He was assured by Harris, that if he refused to do the work, it would be procured elsewhere. And the subject was temporarily dropped, except that Grandin complied with Harris's request for an approximate estimate of the cost of the proposed edition.[1]

Immediately after these interviews took place, Joseph Smith and Martin Harris traveled to Rochester, New York, and sought out Thurlow Weed—another newspaper publisher. Thurlow recalled that Joseph Smith came into his printing office by himself "and said he wanted a book printed, and added that he had been directed in a vision to a place in the woods near Palmyra, where he resided, and that he found a 'golden Bible,' from which he was directed to copy the book which he wanted published." Mr. Weed said in reference to this remark, "I thought the man [was] either crazed or a very shallow imposter and therefore declined to become a publisher." The Prophet left the print shop after this unsuccessful encounter, but a day or two later he returned with Martin Harris, "who offered to become security for the expense of printing."[2] Mr. Weed decided at this point to read through a few of the chapters of the Book of Mormon manuscript, but to his mind it was "a jumble of unintelligible absurdities,"[3] and he once again turned down the invitation to publish it.[4]

Joseph and Martin had much better luck when they visited a Rochester book publisher named Elihu F. Marshall. This man "gave his terms for the printing and binding of the book, with his acceptance of the proffered mode of security for the payment."[5] But even after this victory had been won another problem presented itself. The distance between Palmyra and Rochester was about twenty-five miles. It would take a lot of time, cost a considerable amount of money, and also be a great inconvenience to travel between these two towns several times during the week in order to deliver and then retrieve the Book of Mormon manuscript.

With these drawbacks in mind, Joseph and Martin opted to go once again to Egbert Grandin's office in Palmyra, where they explained their dilemma to the young printer. After consulting with his neighbors—and being assured by them that this was only a business transaction and he would not be related to the Latter-day Saint religion—Grandin finally agreed to publish the Book of Mormon.[6] With this issue settled, Mr. Grandin called upon John H. Gilbert (his primary pressman) to help him estimate the cost for printing such a large run of books.[7] Joseph Smith reports in his published account of the transaction that an agreement was made between the parties to print five thousand copies of the Book of Mormon for the amount of $3,000.[8]

Lucy Mack Smith remembered that on the day that her son was to go to Palmyra to write up the contract for the publication of the Book of Mormon, Dr. Alexander McIntyre came to the Smith home and informed them that a mob of forty men had gathered together with the intent of waylaying Joseph while on his journey. Lucy implored Joseph not to go to on his errand, but the Prophet admonished her to put her trust in God and he would not be harmed.

Joseph headed off towards town, and as he approached a field belonging to David Jacaway he found the mob seated on top of the fence that ran alongside the road. The Prophet removed his hat and in a good-natured manner bid the leader a good morning. He passed on down the fence-line and addressed each of the men in the same affable way. This behavior was so unexpected and struck the mobbers with such amazement and confusion that Joseph passed them by unmolested. Joseph ended up having a successful meeting between himself and Mr. Grandin that day. Mother Smith indicates in her history that the printing contract was drawn up by the two men, but it was not signed until sometime afterward.[9]

The signing of the contract may have been delayed until the financial side of the bargain was firmly in place. It is known from existing historical documents that on 25 August 1829 Martin Harris signed a mortgage on his farm in order to finance the printing of the Book of Mormon. The agreement was for the payment of $3,000 to Egbert Grandin within the term of eighteen months, and if the money was not paid in full then Harris's 240-acre farm was to be sold at a public auction in order to satisfy the obligation.[10]

It was most likely sometime after Martin Harris signed his name to the mortgage on his farm that the formal process of publishing the Book of Mormon got under way.[11] Book publishing in the late 1820s was both a lengthy and a labor-intensive affair. (The steps that were involved in the publication process of the Book of Mormon are detailed in appendix 3 of this book.)

As soon as complete pages of the Book of Mormon began to come off of Egbert Grandin's acorn-shaped printing press, they were put to use in spreading the restored gospel of Jesus Christ. About 1 September 1829, Thomas B. Marsh—who would later become a member of the Quorum of the Twelve—was given the first sixteen pages (or one "signature") of the Book of Mormon by Martin Harris and the printer. He tells his story as follows:

> I believed the Spirit of God dictated me to make a journey west. I started in company with one Benjamin Hall, who was also led by the Spirit. I went to Lima, Livingston County, New York, where I stayed some three months, and then left for home. I called on my return at Lyonstown, [New York,] on a family whose names I do not recollect. On leaving there [the] next morning the lady inquired if I had heard of the Golden Book found by a youth named Joseph Smith. I informed her I never heard anything about it, and became very anxious to know concerning the matter. On inquiring, she told me I could learn more about it from Martin Harris, in Palmyra.
>
> I returned back westward and found Martin Harris at the printing office, in Palmyra, where the first sixteen pages of the Book of Mormon had just been struck off, the proof sheet of which I obtained from the printer and took with me. As soon as Martin Harris found out my intentions he took me to the house of Joseph Smith, Sr. where Joseph Smith, Jr. resided, who could give me any information I might wish. Here I found Oliver Cowdery, who gave me all the information concerning the book I desired. After staying there two days I started for Charleston,

Massachusetts, highly pleased with the information I had obtained concerning the new-found book.

After arriving home and finding my family all well, I showed my wife the sixteen pages of the Book of Mormon which I had obtained, with which she was well pleased, believing it to be the work of God. From this time for about one year I corresponded with Oliver Cowdery and Joseph Smith, Jr. and prepared myself to move west.[12]

Later that same month—about 20 September 1829—the first sixty-four pages (or four signatures) of the Book of Mormon had been struck off and were given to Solomon Chamberlain by Hyrum Smith. Solomon relates that in the year 1816 the Lord had shown him in a vision that all of the churches of his day had become "corrupt" and that the Lord would "soon raise up a Church, that would be after the Apostolic Order." Furthermore, he was shown in vision that "there would [be] a book come forth, like unto the Bible and the people would [be] guided by it, as well as [by] the Bible." This prophetic vision was not fulfilled until 1829, when Solomon was on a journey to Upper Canada. When his boat stopped on the Erie Canal at the town of Palmyra, Solomon felt impressed to disembark and travel south. About sundown he put up at a farmhouse and was told by the residents about Joseph Smith and the "Gold Bible." Upon hearing this story, Solomon felt a peculiar sensation, like the power of God engulfing him from his head to his feet. He soon found himself cutting across farmland and making his way toward the Smith homestead. Here Solomon found the Prophet's father, his brother Hyrum, and some of the members of the Whitmer family. He said to those present:

"If you are a visionary house, I wish you would make known some of your discoveries, for I think I can bear them." They then made known to me that they had obtained a gold record, and just finished translating it here. Now, the Lord revealed to me by the gift and power of the Holy Ghost that this was the work I had been looking for.

Here I stayed two days and they instructed me in the manuscripts of the Book of Mormon. After I had been here two days, I went with Hyrum and some others to Palmyra printing office where they began to print the Book of Mormon, and as soon as they had printed 64 pages, I took them with their leave and pursued my journey to Canada, and I preached all that I knew concerning Mormonism. . . .

I did not see anyone in traveling for 7 or 800 miles that had ever heard of the Gold Bible (so called). I exhorted all people to prepare for the great work of God that was now about to come forth.[13]

By about 1 October 1829, the printing of the Book of Mormon was considerably advanced. At this point "the first and second books of 'Nephi,' and some other portions of the forthcoming revelation were printed in sheets and, armed with a copy of these, [Joseph] Smith commenced . . . preparations for a mission to Pennsylvania where he had some relatives residing." Martin Harris bought some of the finest black cloth in Palmyra from a man by the name of David S. Aldrich and had it made into a suit for Joseph to wear during his proselytizing activities.[14]

On 22 October 1829 the Prophet wrote a letter to Oliver Cowdery, who was busy copying the Book of Mormon manuscript so that the printer could have a document to work from. Joseph indicated in his correspondence that the portions of the printed text that he had taken with him were proving useful. "There begins to be a great call for our books in this country," he said. "The minds of the people are very much excited when they find that there is a copyright obtained and that there is really [a] book about to be printed." The Prophet also noted that Josiah Stowell (who had been present in the Smith family home when the golden plates were first brought there) had a prospect for obtaining five or six hundred dollars and, if successful in doing so, desired to contribute it toward the Book of Mormon's publication. Joseph also requested in his letter that Oliver report on their progress "in the good work."[15] In his written reply, dated 6 November 1829, Oliver Cowdery said that the printer's manuscript had thus far been copied through Alma chapter 36. He also mentioned that the printing process was going slowly because the typesetter had taken sick, but Mr. Grandin was optimistic that the project could be completed by 1 February 1830.[16]

COPYRIGHT INFRINGEMENT

On 9 December 1829 a problematic situation began to develop in the town where the Book of Mormon was coming forth. Abner Cole, who published a newspaper called the *Reflector* on the same press where the Book of Mormon was being run, placed a notice upon his paper's pages signifying his intent to print extracts from the Book of Mormon. Cole justified his plan by citing a widespread and elevated level of curiosity about the volume, the large amount of requests from his readership to take such an action, and the fact that the "Gold Bible" would not be available to the public "for some months to come."[17] This public notice alarmed the individuals involved in the publication of the sacred text, and Oliver Cowdery wrote a letter to Joseph Smith on 28 December 1829 in order to inform him of the situation.[18]

Before the problem could be properly handled, however, Abner Cole went ahead and began his printing enterprise. In the 2 January 1830 issue of the *Reflector*, Cole, under the alias of Obadiah Dogberry, published 1 Nephi 1:1–20 and 1 Nephi 2:1–3. After the reproduction of this text Cole admitted that he had "no means of determining" the religious character of the Book of Mormon since he had not yet read many of its pages.[19] On 13 January 1830 Cole picked up where he had left off, publishing 1 Nephi 2:4–15. This time his editorial remarks made note of the fact that "the appellation of 'Gold Bible' is only a *cant cognomen* that has been given it by the *unbelievers*. . . . The true title of the work, as appears from the copyright, is 'The Book of Mormon.'"[20] It is interesting to note (and disconcerting to think) that even though Mr. Cole was well aware of the Book of Mormon's copyright protection, he decided to completely ignore it, and on 22 January 1830 he printed off the text of Alma 43:22–40.[21]

Lucy Mack Smith recounts that on one Sunday afternoon her son Hyrum started to feel uneasy and told Oliver Cowdery that he thought something was wrong at Grandin's printing establishment. The two men debated about whether or not they should investigate this matter on the Sabbath day, but Hyrum finally said, "I will not suffer such uneasiness any longer without knowing the cause." On this note they both headed toward Grandin's print shop, and when they arrived they found Abner Cole busily striking off his newspaper. After questioning Mr. Cole as to why he was working on a Sunday they examined the paper that was coming from the press and discovered that this man had been publishing the Book of Mormon piecemeal. Hyrum was indignant and asked Cole if he did not know that they had secured the copyright for the book. But Cole disdainfully replied, "It is none of your business, sir. . . I have hired the press and I will print what I please, so help yourself." Hyrum and Oliver reportedly argued with Cole for a long time and tried fruitlessly to dissuade him from his path. They finally abandoned the print shop and returned home to counsel with the Prophet's father. The elder Smith decided that it would be best to retrieve Joseph from Pennsylvania and so as soon as it was possible he set out to go and get him.

Father Smith and his namesake returned the following Sunday, and that same night the Prophet paid a visit to Grandin's office. Joseph introduced himself to Abner Cole in a good-natured way and then began to examine the paper that was being published. The Prophet then declared that he held the copyright for the Book of Mormon and Cole was forbidden from meddling with it in the least degree. Upon hearing this Abner threw off his coat, rolled up his sleeves, and in a roaring rage asked the Prophet if he wanted to fight—claiming as before that he could print whatever he had a mind to. Joseph told him to put his coat back on because he simply was not going to fight him. He then once again told Cole that he must stop printing extracts from the Book of Mormon. Abner is said to have hollered out, "If you think you are the best man just take off your coat and try it!"

Joseph calmly reminded Cole that this matter was governed by law and fighting over it would do no good. Even though the details are not known, it is claimed that they both eventually agreed to take the case to arbitration, and once the affair had been satisfactorily settled the Prophet returned again to his home in Harmony.[22]

FINANCIAL DIFFICULTIES

Despite the fact that Martin Harris had agreed to sell part of his farm to pay for the production of the Book of Mormon, he decided in the winter of 1830 to seek a loan for approximately half of his financial obligation. Charles Butler, a lawyer and regional loan officer for the New York Life Insurance and Trust Company in Geneva, New York, says of the meeting he had with Martin on this issue:

> He brought a letter of introduction to me from a highly respectable citizen of that town, a Mr. [Henry] Jessup, who was a leading man and an elder in the Presbyterian Church and on whose judgment I depended in respect to the character of the borrower and the value of the property in all cases of applications for loans from that quarter. From the letter of Mr. Jessup the bearer was introduced to me as a very worthy and substantial farmer, possessing a very excellent farm, which would furnish a very ample security for the amount of money which he wished to obtain, viz. $1,300.00, and he commended Mr. Harris to me as a desirable borrower.[23]

Unfortunately for Martin Harris, Charles Butler had been the founder of the Union Theological Seminary. One LDS historian makes note of the fact that "although Butler was favorably impressed with Harris's credentials, the financier decided not to grant him a loan when he learned that the money was to be used for the publication of a 'Mormon Bible.'"[24]

Some of the Prophet's associates evidently became impatient with Martin's inability to produce the money needed for the Book of Mormon's production. David Whitmer, one of the three special Book of Mormon witnesses, recalled:

When the Book of Mormon was in the hands of the printer, more money was needed to finish the printing of it. We were waiting on Martin Harris who was doing his best to sell a part of his farm, in order to raise the necessary funds. After a time Hyrum Smith and others began to get impatient, thinking that Martin was too slow and under transgression for not selling his land at once, even if at a great sacrifice. Brother Hyrum thought they should not wait any longer on Martin Harris, and that the money should be raised in some other way. . . . Hyrum said it had been suggested to him that some of the brethren might go to Toronto, Canada and sell the copyright of the Book of Mormon for considerable money.[25]

The amount of money that could be obtained from the copyright in the Canadian provinces was said to be $8,000. Hiram Page recalled that Joseph Smith planned on taking $3,000 of this money and paying for the printing and binding of the Book of Mormon.[26] "Oliver Cowdery, Joseph Knight, Hiram Page and Josiah Stowell were chosen to do the business" of going to Canada to obtain the copyright. These men were living between thirty and one hundred miles apart from each other, but after they had made preparations, they all met in Palmyra at Father Smith's house. They were all anxious to get a revelation regarding their journey.[27] David Whitmer said in one of his publications that Joseph Smith sought for such a revelation from the Lord by using his personal seerstone,[28] and Hiram Page reports that "when the revelation came [it said that they] were to go to Kingston where [they] were to sell [the copyright] *if* they would not harden their hearts."[29]

The four men reportedly went over on the ice of Lake Ontario towards Kingston.[30] Page remembered that they were treated with the utmost respect by the people that they met in this city, but they were informed that those who had authority to purchase copyrights for the province were in Toronto, 160 miles to the east.[31] One late source makes the claim that the group decided not to pursue their goal any further since they "had not money enough to bear their expenses," so they "came back nearly starved [and] completely wearied."[32] In any case, their intended goal was not accomplished.

THE DELEGATION OF RELIGIONISTS

A small delegation from Palmyra's Presbyterian church was appointed on 3 March 1830 "to visit Hyrum Smith, Lucy Smith, and Samuel Harrison Smith and report at the next meeting" in regard to their current religious standing. The three Smiths had not attended services in the Presbyterian church for the previous eighteen months.[33]

In her dictated history, Lucy Mack Smith provides an account of a meeting where this delegation seems to have been initially contemplated. She also provides insight into the underlying reason for the delegation's visit. The Prophet's mother says that a group of men gathered for a council meeting in the room adjoining the one where Oliver Cowdery was working with Dr. Robinson's son. Oliver suspected that something was not right with this situation, so he encouraged the young man to listen to the other group's conversation through a hole that was in the wall. Robinson heard these men say that the Smiths' "Golden Bible" would be "a serious injury to all religious denominations," and therefore it had to be stopped. If not, they felt it would imperil the livelihood of many ministers. It was proposed that in order to put a stop to the printing of the Book of Mormon a committee of three people would go to the Smith house on the Tuesday or Wednesday following and request Mother Smith to read the manuscript to them. Two of the men would then distract Lucy while the third grabbed the manuscript and tossed it into the fire. The council then decided that if this plan failed and the book was printed anyway, they would boycott its sale, thus nipping the dreadful calamity while it was still in the bud.

Oliver Cowdery was greatly troubled by this development and went off to the Smith family house so that he could tell them about it. After Oliver had explained what he knew of the nefarious plan, the Book of Mormon manuscript was placed in a large chest and hidden underneath Lucy Smith's bed.[34]

The matriarch of the Smith clan records that the delegation of religionists arrived on Wednesday after dinnertime.[35] They said, "Mrs. Smith, we hear you have a Gold Bible and we came to see [if] you [would] be so kind as to show it to us." Lucy answered, "No, gentlemen . . . we have [not] got any Gold Bible . . . but we have a translation of some gold plates which was sent to the world to bring the plainness of the gospel to the children of men." She then gave them the substance of the content of the Book of Mormon, focusing particularly on its religious principles. Not surprisingly, the Universalists, the Presbyterians, and the Methodists were all opposed to the Book of Mormon and its message.

The delegates then asked Lucy if they could see the Book of Mormon manuscript. She told them no; she had already told them what was in it and that would just have to suffice. The spokesman for the group, Deacon George Beckwith, mentioned that Lucy, Hyrum, Sophronia, and Samuel had been members of his church and he would regret losing them; but he also desired that she would say nothing publicly about the Book of Mormon, even if she truly believed in it. Lucy replied that even if she were burned at the stake she would still declare the truth that her son Joseph had possession of the record. The spokesman told his companions that they would get nowhere with Lucy (which she confirmed), so they went outside to confront Hyrum instead. They asked Hyrum if he really believed that his brother had the ancient record. Hyrum assured Deacon Beckwith that if he would read the Book of Mormon after it had been printed and ask God for a witness concerning its truth he would receive it. The delegation next approached Samuel Smith, but he just quoted Isaiah chapter 56 verses 9 through 11 to them. This passage of holy writ speaks of shepherds who do not have understanding but look to their own way and seek after gain. After this last confrontation had taken place, the delegation left the Smith property[36] and upon their return "reported that they had visited [the Smiths] and received no satisfaction . . . and that [the Smiths] did not wish to unite with [that church] anymore."[37]

NOTES TO CHAPTER 8

1. Pomeroy Tucker, *Origin, Rise, and Progress of Mormonism* (New York: D. Appleton and Co., 1867), 50–52.
2. Thurlow Weed, *Autobiography of Thurlow Weed* (Boston: Houghton and Mifflin, 1884), 1:358–59.

3. Tucker, *Origin, Rise, and Progress of Mormonism,* 52.

4. See Weed, *Autobiography of Thurlow Weed,* 1:359.

5. Tucker, *Origin, Rise, and Progress of Mormonism,* 52; see also the letter of Henry M. Allen to "the Librarian of the Palmyra Library," March 1964, Egbert B. Grandin file, King's Daughters Library, Palmyra, New York. Henry M. Allen was a grandson of Grandin.

6. The young Mr. Grandin had a lot to gain financially by taking on the Book of Mormon project and in turn he would incur a very heavy workload. In the 1830s a typical large book edition would run somewhere between five hundred and two thousand copies and Grandin was expected to produce no less than five thousand for his client (see Gayle G. Ord, "The Book of Mormon Goes to Press," *Ensign,* December 1972, 66).

7. John H. Gilbert remembered: "In the forepart of June 1829, Mr. E[gbert] B. Grandin, the printer of *The Wayne Sentinel,* came to me and said he wanted I should assist him in estimating the cost of printing 5,000 copies of a book that Martin Harris wanted to get printed, which was called the 'Mormon Bible.' It was the second application of Harris to Grandin to do the job—Harris assuring Grandin that the book would be printed in Rochester if he declined the job again. Harris proposed to have Grandin do the job, if he would, as it would be quite expensive to keep a man in Rochester during the printing of the book, who would have to visit Palmyra two or three times a week for manuscript, etc. Mr. Grandin consented to do the job if his terms were accepted" (John H. Gilbert, "Memorandum," 8 September 1892, Palmyra, New York, 1, cited in Royal Skousen, "John Gilbert's 1892 Account of the 1830 Printing of the Book of Mormon," in Stephen D. Ricks, Donald W. Parry, and Andrew H. Hedges, eds., *The Disciple as Witness: Essays on Latter-day Saint History and Doctrine in Honor of Richard Lloyd Anderson* [Provo, Utah: FARMS, 2000], 383–405).

8. See Brigham H. Roberts, ed., *History of the Church,* rev. ed., 7 vols. (Salt Lake City: The Church of Jesus Christ of Latter-day Saints, 1932–1951), 1:71. The monetary figure is confirmed in Tucker, *Origin, Rise, and Progress of Mormonism,* 52–53.

9. See Lavina F. Anderson, ed., *Lucy's Book: A Critical Edition of Lucy Mack Smith's Family Memoir* (Salt Lake City: Signature Books, 2001), 458.

10. See the Wayne County, New York, Land Records, Mortgages, Book 3, 325. Harris's mortgage came due on 5 February 1831. He redeemed it on 1 April 1831 by selling 150 acres of his farmland to Thomas Lakey for the sum of

$3,000 (see Wayne C. Gunnell, "Martin Harris: Witness and Benefactor to the Book of Mormon" [master's thesis, Brigham Young University, 1955], 38–39). Pomeroy Tucker recalled: "The farm mortgaged was sold by Harris in 1831 at private sale, not by foreclosure, and a sufficiency of the avails went to pay Grandin—though it is presumed Harris might have paid the $3,000 without the sale of the farm. This was among the best properties of the kind in the town" (Tucker, *Origin, Rise, and Progress of Mormonism,* 54–55).

11. John Gilbert said, "The work [of printing] was commenced in August 1829" (Gilbert, "Memorandum," 3).

    Joseph Smith notes: "Whilst the Book of Mormon was in the hands of the printer, we still continued to bear testimony and give information, as far as we had opportunity" (*History of the Church,* 1:74–75).

    David Whitmer indicates that this proselytizing activity occurred between the time that the printing began and the formal organization of the Church. He writes: "In August, 1829, we began to preach the gospel of Christ. . . . The Book of Mormon was still in the hands of the printer, but my brother, Christian Whitmer, had copied from the manuscript the teachings and doctrine of Christ, being the things which we were commanded to preach. We preached, baptized and confirmed members into the Church of Christ, from August, 1829, until April 6th, 1830" (David Whitmer, *An Address to All Believers in Christ* [Richmond, Mo.: David Whitmer, 1887], 32).

12. *Deseret News,* 24 March 1858.

13. Solomon Chamberlain, autobiography, L. Tom Perry Special Collections Library, Harold B. Lee Library, Brigham Young University, Provo, Utah, 4, 8.

14. Tucker, *Origin, Rise, and Progress of Mormonism,* 55–56. Joseph Smith arrived in Harmony, Pennsylvania, on 4 October 1829 (see Anderson, ed., *Lucy's Book,* 175), thus fixing the printing of 1 Nephi, 2 Nephi, and "some other portions" of the Book of Mormon at about 1 October 1829.

15. Dean C. Jessee, ed., *The Personal Writings of Joseph Smith,* rev. ed. (Salt Lake City: Deseret Book, 2002), 252.

16. See the letter written by Oliver Cowdery to Joseph Smith, 6 November 1829, Joseph Smith Collection, Historical Department Archives, The Church of Jesus Christ of Latter-day Saints, Salt Lake City, Utah.

17. *Reflector,* 9 December 1829.

18. See the letter written by Oliver Cowdery to Joseph Smith, 28 December 1829, Joseph Smith Collection, Historical Department Archives, The Church of Jesus Christ of Latter-day Saints, Salt Lake City, Utah.

19. See *Reflector,* 2 January 1830. For further reading see Russell R. Rich, "The Dogberry Papers and the Book of Mormon," *BYU Studies* 10, no. 3 (spring 1970): 315–20.

20. *Reflector,* 13 January 1830.

21. Ibid., 22 January 1830.

22. Anderson, ed., *Lucy's Book,* 470–75.

23. Manuscripts of Charles Butler, Library of Congress, Washington, D.C.

24. Milton V. Backman Jr., *Eyewitness Accounts of the Restoration* (Salt Lake City: Deseret Book, 1983), 145. Backman dates this incident in 1830.

25. Whitmer, *An Address to All Believers in Christ,* 30–31.

26. See the letter written by Hiram Page to William E. McLellin, 2 February 1848, 2–3, Community of Christ Archives, Independence, Mo.

27. See ibid., 2.

28. See Whitmer, *An Address to All Believers in Christ,* 31.

29. Hiram Page to William E. McLellin, 2 February 1848, 2; emphasis added.

30. See Wilhelm R. von Wymetal, *Joseph Smith the Prophet, His Family and His Friends* (Salt Lake City: Tribune Printing and Publishing, 1886), 311.

31. See the letter written by Hiram Page to William E. McLellin, 2 February 1848, 2–3.

32. Wymetal, *Joseph Smith the Prophet, His Family and His Friends,* 311. When the four men returned from their long journey, Oliver Cowdery and Hiram Page went to Peter Whitmer Sr.'s home in Fayette, New York, to see Joseph Smith (see Whitmer, *An Address to All Believers in Christ,* 31), while Joseph Knight and Josiah Stowell probably went to their homes in southern New York by a different route. Cowdery and Page asked Joseph why they had failed to obtain the Canadian copyright. David Whitmer—speaking fifty-seven years after the event—claims that Joseph said he did not know, but he inquired of the Lord and received the following answer: "Some revelations are of God, some revelations are of men, and some revelations are of the devil" (ibid.). Since David Whitmer considered Joseph Smith to be a fallen prophet at the time that he made this very late comment, it is difficult to gauge its completeness and reliability. Hiram Page reported that the Saints would obtain the Canadian copyright *if* the people would not harden their hearts. Perhaps the group failed in their venture because after evaluating their circumstances (harsh weather, low funds, long distance to travel) it was *they* who hardened their hearts.

33. "Records of the Sessions of the Presbyterian Church in Palmyra," 2:11–12, cited in *BYU Studies* 10, no. 4 (summer 1970): 482–84.

34. Anderson, ed., *Lucy's Book,* 460–63.

35. See ibid., 463.

36. Ibid., 467–70.

37. "Records of the Sessions of the Presbyterian Church in Palmyra," 2:11–12, 10 March 1830.

CHAPTER 9

THE BOOK OF MORMON GOES FORTH

On 26 March 1830, Egbert Grandin posted a notice in his newspaper announcing that the Book of Mormon was finally available to the public.[1] This must have been a day of great satisfaction and rejoicing for Joseph Smith and all those who had assisted him in bringing this volume of scripture before the world. Just a few days later, on 6 April 1830, The Church of Jesus Christ of Latter-day Saints was formally organized in Fayette, New York,[2] and missionaries were assigned to spread the restored gospel as contained in the ancient record.

The activities of Oliver Cowdery, Parley P. Pratt, Peter Whitmer Jr., and Ziba Peterson are representative of how the early Latter-day Saints carried out this divinely-mandated task. Oliver indicates in a signed document that they were "commanded of the Lord God to go forth . . . [and] proclaim glad tidings of great joy . . . by presenting . . . the fullness of the gospel of the Only Begotten Son of God." But before embarking on their journey, these four men each entered into a most solemn covenant before the Lord that they would walk humbly before Him and carry out their work as directed by the Holy Ghost.[3] Josiah Jones, who listened to this group of missionaries when they reached Kirtland, Ohio, gave an account of their preaching. He said that they informed the inhabitants of the town that they possessed

> a book, which they said contained what was engraven on
> gold plates found in a stone box in the ground in the town
> of Manchester, Ontario Co[unty], N[ew] Y[ork], and was

found . . . by a man named Joseph Smith, Jr. who had translated it by looking into a stone or two stones, . . . which stones he said were found in the box with the plates. They affirmed while he looked through the stone specta- cles another sat by and wrote what he told them, and thus the book was all written. The doctrines which they taught are contained in the book which the world may have recourse to. . . . [T]hey read some in their new book, and exhorted the people to repent of their pride and priestcraft and all other sins, and be baptized by them *for the remission of them*, for they said that if they had been baptized it was of no avail, for there was no legal administrator, neither had been for fourteen hundred years, until God had called them to the office, and had sent them into the world to publish it to this generation.[4]

As the Book of Mormon was taken out into the world by missionaries, it played a central role in the conversion of those who studied its teachings. Some of the converts recorded in autobiogra- phies and journals how they were brought into the restored Church through the instrumentality of the sacred writing. Following are the stories of five of these individuals, chosen not necessarily for their extraordinary nature but for the prominent role each person would eventually play in spreading the Book of Mormon among the inhabi- tants of the earth.

BRIGHAM YOUNG

Brigham Young lived only forty miles away from Joseph Smith's hometown of Palmyra, New York. Shortly after the restored Church of Jesus Christ was formally organized in April 1830, Brigham began to hear rumors of the Prophet and his Gold Bible. His daughter Susa reports that he was attracted by the audacious nature of the new American religion and was one of many at the time looking for "new light on old doctrines." He therefore resolved to investigate the matter on his own.

Upon making inquiries Brigham learned that a new revelation had come to the earth, that a new set of scriptures stood alongside the

Bible. He desired to follow the biblical admonition to prove all things, so for nearly two years he studied the book and its religious precepts. According to his daughter,

> He listened to the reports and considered the testimony of already converted friends. "I weighed the matter studiously for nearly two years," he once declared, "before I made up my mind to receive that book. I looked at it on all sides. All other religions I could fathom . . . but this new one I reasoned on month after month, until I came to a certain knowledge of its truth. Had this not been the case I never would have embraced it to this day. I wished time sufficient to prove all things for myself." He told of his own conversion by answering his daughter who had expressed a longing desire to know that the gospel was true, that Jesus was the Christ and that Joseph Smith was divinely ordained to re-establish His Church in latter days; not merely to hope and try to believe it, but to know as her father *knew* its truth. He said, "Daughter, there is only one way to find it out. And that is the way I found it out and the way your mother found it. Get down on your knees and ask God to give you that testimony and knowledge which Peter had when Christ asked the Apostles: Whom do ye say I am?"

> Finally, on April 14, 1832, when he was thirty-one years of age, he was baptized into the Church at Mendon, Monroe County, New York. After his own acceptance of the new gospel, he was instrumental in bringing about the conversion of all his brothers and sisters, his aged father, and his own dying wife.[5]

WILFORD WOODRUFF

On 29 December 1833, two elders of the Church visited the home of Wilford Woodruff in Richmond, New York. Wilford was away at the time, but his sister-in-law knew that he and her husband would want to hear of a meeting where the elders were scheduled to preach.

When Wilford returned home and heard of the meeting, he immediately turned out his horses and without even waiting for supper headed off for the schoolhouse. "On my way," says Wilford, "I prayed most sincerely that the Lord would give me His Spirit, and that if these men were the servants of God I might know it, and that my heart might be prepared to receive the divine message they had to deliver."

Wilford reached the schoolhouse and found that his brother had already arrived, eager to hear what was to be said. But since the building was full, Wilford had to sit on top of a writing desk in order to see the speakers.

When one of the elders knelt down to begin the meeting with prayer, Wilford was greatly impressed because the Spirit rested down upon him and bore witness that this man was a servant of God. The Spirit then rested mightily upon this same man for an hour and a half as he taught his audience about the divine authenticity of the Book of Mormon and the mission of the Prophet Joseph Smith. "I believed all that he said," relates Wilford. "The Spirit bore witness of its truth."

After the second elder bore his testimony, the floor was opened for comments, either for or against what had been said. Wilford almost immediately found himself on his feet and confirming the truth of the message that had been delivered—the Spirit urging him to do so. He was followed by similar remarks from his brother and also from several other people who were in the room.

The Woodruff brothers took the two elders to their home and stayed up late into the night conversing upon the principles of the gospel. Wilford began at once to read from the pages of the Book of Mormon, and as he did, he says, "the Spirit bore witness that the record which it contained was true. I opened my eyes to see, my ears to hear, and my heart to understand. I also opened my doors to entertain the servants of God."[6]

PARLEY P. PRATT

Parley P. Pratt first learned of the Book of Mormon from an old Baptist deacon in Palmyra, New York. From Parley's perspective, this was a "strange book, a VERY STRANGE BOOK!" His interest piqued, he borrowed the deacon's copy. He writes of this volume:

I opened it with eagerness, and read its title page. I then read the testimony of several witnesses in relation to the manner of it being found and translated. After this I commenced its contents by course. I read all day; eating was a burden, I had no desire for food; sleep was a burden when the night came, for I preferred reading to sleep.

As I read, the Spirit of the Lord was upon me, and I knew and comprehended that the book was true, as plainly and manifestly as a man comprehends and know that he exists.

With a fullness of joy in his heart, Parley determined that he would seek out Joseph Smith—the discoverer and translator of the volume. He sought for the Prophet in Palmyra, New York, but was informed that he had moved to Pennsylvania. But as compensation for his efforts, he was able to speak with Hyrum Smith, the Prophet's brother. The two men conversed together for many hours, and during their conversation Parley was able to learn details about the discovery and translation of the book that he had recently read with such interest. In addition, he was informed of the rise of the restored Church and the priesthood authority that had been returned to the earth.

Before they parted company, Hyrum presented Parley with a copy of the first edition of the Book of Mormon. Parley was especially grateful to receive this gift because he had not yet had the opportunity to completely peruse its pages. He was so anxious to finish this task that he commenced reading the book again during his journey home.[7] Parley was soon baptized and immediately became a zealous preacher of the Book of Mormon and the restored gospel.

JOHN TAYLOR

John Taylor was a resident of Toronto, Canada. In the church he attended, there was a group of gentlemen with whom he investigated the doctrines of Christianity as found in the Bible. According to his biographer, they met several times a week to compare what they read with what they saw among the various Christian denominations. As a result of this exercise they came to the conclusion that none of the churches of the time were true as they lacked the authority to preach the gospel. With this realization before them, they could only pray that if God had a Church somewhere on the earth He would send them a messenger.

This prayer was heard by the Lord, and He sent them a messenger in the person of Parley P. Pratt. But when John learned that Parley was a "Mormon," he was inclined to turn him away because of the negative rumors he had heard of the religion. Nevertheless, Parley was allowed to preach.

The message Elder Pratt delivered was strange to the ears of the listeners. He spoke of how God had chosen a backwoods farm boy in upstate New York to restore the gospel to the earth, and He had sent an angel to this youth who revealed the whereabouts of a hidden record—a chronicle of ancient America no less. This volume had been translated into English by the gift and power of God and was called the Book of Mormon.

This curious message captured John's interest, and he began to study it thoroughly. He compared transcribed notes of Elder Pratt's sermons with the Bible and also scrutinized evidences of the divine authenticity of the Book of Mormon. "I made a regular business of it for three weeks," he said, "and followed Brother Parley from place to place." After this careful investigation, John Taylor had feelings of conviction. On 9 May 1836 he and his wife entered into the waters of baptism and joined themselves with the Latter-day Saints.[8]

GEORGE A. SMITH

In August 1830, the Prophet's father and brother Don Carlos carried some copies of the Book of Mormon to their relatives who lived 250 miles away from Palmyra. Some of them fully accepted the book, while others, such as Jesse Smith, fully rejected it. In fact, Jesse was so bitterly opposed to the Book of Mormon that he threatened to hew down the Prophet's father with a broadaxe if he brought copies of the book into his house. He even went so far as to follow Father Smith around and prevent him from speaking of the book in his presence.

George A. Smith, the Prophet's cousin, and George's mother read through the Book of Mormon for two days after it was given to them. And on the evening of the second day, the neighbors came to their house to see the "Golden Bible." These people commenced raising objections to the book, but as George relates,

> Although I did not believe the book, their objections looked to me so slim and foolish, that I commenced answering them and exposed the fallacy of their objections so palpably that they went away confounded, saying, "You was always a smart boy."

> I continued to read the Book of Mormon and framed in my mind a series of objections, which I supposed were sufficient to overthrow its authenticity, and on the return of my Uncle Joseph, I undertook to argue with him upon the subject, but he so successfully removed my objections and enlightened my mind that I have never since ceased to advocate the divine authenticity of that book.[9]

* * *

These stories of conversion through the Book of Mormon are but a small representation of literally millions that have been told since the days of the Prophet Joseph Smith. The book's divine authenticity has been confirmed to some by the voice of God Himself; to some it has been confirmed by the ministering of angels; and on a continual basis it is confirmed by the power of the Holy Ghost to those who seek such an assurance through humble and earnest prayer.

Today the Book of Mormon is still coming forth. But instead of being printed a few thousand at a time, as it was in 1830, it is printed by the millions. It has not yet flooded the earth like the waters of the sea, but that will surely come in the course of time. For as the angel told the witnesses who were privileged to see the plates of gold from whence the Book of Mormon came, no power on earth will stop its progress.

NOTES TO CHAPTER 9

1. See *Wayne Sentinel,* vol. 7, no. 29, 26 March 1830.
2. For information on the role that the Book of Mormon played in the formal orga-
    nization of the Church, see Robert J. Woodford, "The Articles and Covenants of
    the Church of Christ and the Book of Mormon," in *Doctrines for Exaltation* (Salt
    Lake City: Deseret Book, 1989), 262–73; Scott H. Faulring, "The Book of
    Mormon: A Blueprint for Organizing the Church," *Journal of Book of Mormon
    Studies* 7, no. 1 (1998): 60–69, 71; John A. Tvedtnes, "The Role of the Book of
    Mormon in the Restoration of the Church," transcript (Provo, Utah: FARMS,
    1997); Richard L. Anderson, "The Organization Revelations," in Robert L.
    Millet and Kent P. Jackson, eds., *Studies in Scripture, Volume 1: The Doctrine and
    Covenants* (Sandy, Utah: Randall Book, 1984), 109–23.
3. See *Ohio Star,* vol. 2, no. 49, 8 December 1831.
4. *Evangelist,* vol. 9, no. 6, 1 June 1841; emphasis in original.
5. Susa Young Gates, *The Life Story of Brigham Young* (New York: Macmillan,
    1930), 6, 9; emphasis in original. The following explains how Brigham Young
    came into possession of the copy of the Book of Mormon that helped convert
    him. "[O]ne day in April 1830, Joseph Smith's brother Samuel, the first
    Mormon missionary, came into the area. He happened to visit Tomlinson's Inn
    in Lima, eight miles southwest of Mendon, and proceeded to interrupt the
    lunch of the first person he saw who, providentially or otherwise, was Phineas
    Young, an itinerant preacher for the Methodist Episcopal Reformed Church and
    Brigham's brother. Samuel talked him into buying a copy of the Book of
    Mormon—perhaps the single most important copy ever sold. Phineas read the
    book and in quick succession so did his father, his sister Fanny, his brother
    Brigham, and 'many others,' most of whom accepted it. According to tradition,
    Heber [C. Kimball] read the same copy" (Stanley B. Kimball, "Brigham and
    Heber," *BYU Studies* 18, no. 3 [spring 1978]: 397).
6. Matthias F. Cowley, *Wilford Woodruff: His Life and Labors* (Salt Lake City:
    Deseret News Press, 1916), 32–34.
7. Parley P. Pratt, *Autobiography of Parley P. Pratt* (Salt Lake City: Deseret Book,
    1985), 36–40; emphasis in original.
8. Brigham H. Roberts, *Life of John Taylor* (Salt Lake City: George Q. Cannon
    and Sons, 1892), 30–31; emphasis in original.
9. George A. Smith Journal, L. Tom Perry Special Collections Library, Harold B.
    Lee Library, Brigham Young University, Provo, Utah, 10.

APPENDIX 1

THE STONE BOX AND ITS CONTENTS

There are a variety of firsthand and secondhand historical sources that assist in sharpening the image of Moroni's sealed box and its ancient contents (the golden plates; the interpreters, or Urim and Thummim; and the breastplate). The information that follows has been gleaned both from well-known LDS sources and lesser-known documents.

THE STONE BOX

Location

Joseph Smith states that the stone receptacle that held the Nephite relics was "on the west side of this hill not far from the top."[1] David Whitmer, who visited this location several times, likewise said that the box was situated "on the side of the hill, and a little down from the top."[2]

Appearance

The Three Witnesses of the Book of Mormon plates (Oliver Cowdery, David Whitmer, and Martin Harris) reportedly said that the box was oblong in shape.[3] Oliver Cowdery describes the receptacle as being "small" in overall size but "sufficiently large to admit a breastplate" into it.[4]

Construction

Oliver Cowdery said in the Church's official newspaper that "a hole of sufficient depth, (how deep I know not) was dug. At the bottom of this was laid a stone of suitable size, the upper surface being smooth. At each edge was placed a large quantity of cement and into this cement, at the four edges of this stone, were placed, erect, four others, their bottom edges resting in the cement at the outer edges of the first stone. The four last named, when placed erect, formed a box. The corners, or where the edges of the four came in contact, were also cemented so firmly that the moisture from without was prevented from entering. It is to be observed also that the inner surface of the four erect or side stones was smooth."[5]

"From the bottom of the box . . . arose three small pillars composed of the same description of cement used on the edges; and upon these three pillars was placed the record of the children of Joseph," or Book of Mormon plates. "Those three pillars were not so lengthy as to cause the plates and the crowning stone to come in contact."[6]

The top stone that sealed the box shut was flat on its bottom side[7] and "thick and rounding in the middle on the upper side, and thinner towards the edges." When Joseph Smith first caught a glimpse of this stone "the middle part of it was visible above the ground, but the edge all [a]round was covered with earth."[8]

THE GOLDEN PLATES

Appearance of the Volume

According to the Prophet Joseph Smith the entire set of Book of Mormon plates looked ancient. He said that the "whole book exhibited many marks of antiquity in its construction."[9]

Appearance of Plates

Joseph Smith did not say that the plates of the Book of Mormon were made of pure gold, but rather that they "had the appearance of gold."[10] Oliver Cowdery is likewise reported as saying in 1830 that the Book of Mormon was "written on golden plates, or something resembling golden plates."[11] A secondhand statement by David Whitmer in 1831 says that "the leaves were plates of metal of a whitish yellow color."[12] This coloration may be explained by William Smith who claimed that the plates consisted of "a mixture of gold and copper."[13]

Length and Width of Plates

In the fall of 1829 some of the "proselytes" of the Book of Mormon were evidently saying that "the leaves of the [book] were . . . about 8 inches long, 6 wide."[14] A report published in 1830 portrays Joseph Smith as giving these very same measurements.[15] In fact, the Prophet published his own article in 1842, which states that "each plate was six inches wide and eight inches long."[16]

Thickness of Plates

In September 1829 one newspaper article related that some Latter-day Saints were describing the plates as being "one-eighth of an inch thick."[17] Joseph Smith himself seems to have said one year later that they were "1/8 of an inch thick."[18] In 1842 the Prophet wrote that the Book of Mormon plates were "not quite so thick as common tin."[19] Oliver Cowdery had also reportedly said that they were "of the thickness of tin" in 1830,[20] while in 1831 David Whitmer was represented as saying that "the leaves were . . . of the thickness of tin plate."[21]

One record of Emma Smith's reminiscences is of great interest because it reflects the observations of someone who actually handled the plates. She says in this source that they "seemed to be pliable like thick paper, and would rustle with a metallic sound when the edges were moved by the thumb."[22]

Engravings on the Plates

According to Joseph Smith's own published account, the plates were "filled with engravings, in Egyptian characters. . . . The characters on the unsealed part were small, and beautifully engraved."[23] David Whitmer described the engravings as being "very plain and of very curious appearance."[24]

Parley P. Pratt, John Whitmer (who was an eyewitness), and an unidentified member of the Smith family each stated that the engravings could be seen on both sides of the plates.[25]

Orson Pratt provides us with a unique and very interesting detail about the golden plates. He reports that the Eight Witnesses informed him that, "Upon each side of the leaves of these plates there were fine engravings, which were stained with a black, hard stain, so as to make the letters more legible and easier to be read."[26]

It will be recalled that the Prophet copied some of the characters for Martin Harris, who showed them to Charles Anthon. David Whitmer insisted that a slip of paper in his possession was that very document. The document is now commonly referred to as the Anthon Transcript and still exists.[27]

Thickness of Entire Set

From an 1830 statement attributed to Oliver Cowdery we learn that the entire set of plates consisted of "a pile about 6 inches deep."[28] In August 1832 William McLellin was given this same measurement by some of the Saints: "altogether about 6 inches thick."[29] Joseph Smith gave the very same dimension in an 1842 article. "The volume was something near six inches in thickness," he said.[30]

In speaking of the number of the plates which made up the Book of Mormon's mass, David Whitmer simply said that they were "a great many in number."[31]

Weight of Entire Set

John Whitmer and Katherine Smith (both of whom handled the golden plates) reported that they were very heavy.[32] William Smith (another tactile witness) said that "they were much heavier than stone, and very much heavier than wood."[33] Joseph Smith allegedly said that he thought the set of plates "would weigh sixty pounds, and was sure it would weigh forty."[34] Martin Harris made the same general estimation, stating that the plates weighed "altogether, from forty to sixty pounds."[35] William Smith said in a book that he wrote, "They weighed about sixty pounds according to the best of my judgment."[36]

Rings Attaching Entire Set

According to a published statement by Joseph Smith, there were "three rings running through the whole" volume.[37]

David Whitmer specified their location. In two of his many interviews, he said that there was one "at each corner of the bundle and one in the center,"[38] and all three passed "through the back edges" of the plates.[39] Whitmer also noted that the rings were made of the same metal as the golden plates.[40] He further states that the rings were "massive" in size.[41]

Several of the early Saints, including eyewitnesses to the plates, revealed that the rings were formed like a capital letter D.[42] The shape of the rings seems to be significant. Orson Pratt asserted that "a rod might easily be passed" through these three rings, "serving as a greater convenience for carrying them."[43]

Sealed Portion

Joseph Smith indicated that "a part" of the Book of Mormon plates was sealed shut.[44] Orson Pratt expanded upon this fact when he claimed in a public discourse that two-thirds of the record had been sealed,[45] and putting this idea in opposite terms, David Whitmer (an eyewitness) said that "about one-third of [the plates] appeared to be loose."[46]

David Whitmer reports that when he saw the golden plates along with the other witnesses the sealed portion appeared to be as solid as a block of wood,[47] but he also said that there were "perceptible marks where the plates seemed to be sealed" together.[48]

THE INTERPRETERS

"With the records was found a curious instrument which the ancients called 'Urim and Thummim,'" said Joseph Smith.[49] These were the very same interpreters that the Lord gave to the brother of Jared on Mount Shelem (see Ether 3:22–24; D&C 17:1) and which were possessed by the Nephites in a later age. King Mosiah was able to translate a set of plates written in an unknown language "by the means of those two stones which were fastened into the two rims of a bow. Now these things were prepared from the beginning, and were handed down from generation to generation, for the purpose of interpreting languages" (Mosiah 28:13–14).

Description

Joseph Smith said that this ancient instrument "consisted of two transparent stones set in the rim of a bow."[50] Lucy Mack Smith claimed that the stones were "set in silver bows. [The] stones [were] connected with each other in the same way that old-fashioned spectacles are made."[51] William Smith explained that the "silver bow . . .

[was] in the shape of a horizontal figure 8, much like a pair of spectacles."[52] David Whitmer related that "the bow between the stones was more heavy, and longer apart between the stones, than we usually find it in spectacles."[53] Martin Harris provided the most detailed description of this ancient object. He said, "The two stones, set in a bow of silver, were about two inches in diameter, perfectly round, and about five-eighths of an inch thick at the center; but not so thick at the edges where they came into the bow. They were joined by a round bar of silver, about three-eighths of an inch in diameter, and about four inches long which, with the two stones, would make eight inches."[54]

Function

Joseph Smith evidently referred to this instrument as "the key,"[55] and the angel Moroni told him that its possession and use "was what constituted *seers* in ancient or former times." God had prepared these two particular stones "for the purpose of translating."[56]

But this was not their only function. Joseph Knight recalled that when Joseph Smith first received the Nephite relics from the angel Moroni, he "seemed to think more of the glasses or the Urim and Thummim than he did of the plates for, [said] he, '*I can see anything; they are marvelous.*'"[57] David Whitmer remarked, "The way that [Joseph] Smith got into the belief of his supernatural power was first by putting on the glasses; he saw his entire past history revealed to him."[58] Martin Harris said of these unusual stones, "I never dared to look into them . . . because Moses said that 'no man could see God and live' [see Ex. 33:20], and *we could see anything we wished by looking into them;* and I could not keep the desire to see God out of my mind. And beside, we had a command to let no man look into them, except by the command of God, lest he should 'look aught and perish' [see Mosiah 8:13]."[59]

THE BREASTPLATE

In the 1853 edition of Lucy Mack Smith's history, she is represented as saying that she was allowed to handle the breastplate while it was "wrapped in a thin muslin handkerchief." She says in that source that it was made of "glistening metal," was "concave on one side and convex on the other, and extended from the neck downwards, as far as the center of the stomach of a man of extraordinary size. It had four straps of the same material, for the purpose of fastening it to the breast, two of which ran back to go over the shoulders, and the other two were designed to fasten to the hips. They were just the width of two of my fingers (for I measured them), and they had holes in the end of them, to be convenient in fastening."[60]

Oliver Cowdery noted in one Church periodical that the "breastplate [was] such as was used by the ancients to defend the chest" against weaponry,[61] and Parley P. Pratt, in describing its composition, stated that it was apparently made out of copper.[62]

Joseph Smith said that the interpreters, or Urim and Thummim, could be fastened to the breastplate that was found in the stone box.[63] William Smith describes how this was done. He says that "the Urim and Thummim was attached to the breastplate by a rod which was fastened at the outer . . . edge of the [right shoulder of the] breastplate and [also fastened] to the end of the silver bow."[64] "A pocket was prepared in the breastplate on the left side, immediately over the heart," said William. "When not in use the Urim and Thummim was placed in this pocket, the rod being of just the right length to allow it to be so deposited."[65]

NOTES TO APPENDIX 1

1. *Times and Seasons,* vol. 3, no. 13, 2 May 1842, 771.
2. *Deseret Evening News,* 16 August 1878.
3. See *Le Roy Gazette,* vol. 6, no. 11, 17 March 1831.
4. *Messenger and Advocate,* vol. 2, no. 1, October 1835, 196–97.
5. Ibid., 196.
6. Ibid., 196–97.
7. See ibid., 197.
8. *Times and Seasons,* vol. 3, no. 13, 2 May 1842, 771.
9. Ibid., vol. 3, no. 9, 1 March 1842, 707. An unidentified member of the Smith family reportedly said that the plates "were in a good state of preservation" (*Peoria Register and North-Western Gazetteer,* vol. 5, no. 23, 3 September 1841).

10. *Times and Seasons,* vol. 3, no. 9, 1 March 1842, 707. An unidentified member of the Smith family likewise said that the plates "had the appearance of gold" (*Peoria Register and North-Western Gazetteer,* vol. 5, no. 23, 3 September 1841).

11. *Observer and Telegraph,* vol. 1, no. 38, 18 November 1830.

12. *Reflector,* vol. 2, no. 16, 19 March 1831.

13. *Saints' Herald,* vol. 31, no. 40, 4 October 1884, 644.

14. *Painesville Telegraph,* vol. 1, no. 15, 22 September 1829.

15. See *Republican Advocate,* 4 December 1830.

16. *Times and Seasons,* vol. 3, no. 9, 1 March 1842, 707. John Whitmer, who handled the plates for himself, said that "the leaves . . . [were] 8 by 6 or seven inches" (*Deseret News,* 6 August 1878). Oliver Cowdery apparently said that the "plates . . . [were] 7 inches in length, 6 inches in breadth" (*Observer and Telegraph,* vol. 1, no. 38, 18 November 1830). William E. McLellin heard some of the Saints say in 1832 that the "plates . . . [were] about 8 inches long, 5 or 6 wide, and altogether about 6 inches thick; each one about as thick as thin pasteboard" (William E. McLellin to Samuel McLellin, 4 August 1832, Community of Christ Archives, Independence, Mo., in Jan Shipps and John W. Welch, eds., *The Journals of William E. McLellin: 1831–1836* [Provo, Utah: BYU Studies; Urbana: University of Illinois Press, 1994], 79).

17. *Painesville Telegraph,* vol. 1, no. 15, 22 September 1829.

18. *Republican Advocate,* 4 December 1830.

19. *Times and Seasons,* vol. 3, no. 9, 1 March 1842, 707.

20. *Observer and Telegraph,* vol. 1, no. 38, 18 November 1830.

21. *Reflector,* vol. 2, no. 16, 19 March 1831. Whitmer said on another occasion, "The thickness [of each plate] was about of a common sheet of tin used by tinsmiths" (*Deseret Evening News,* 16 August 1878).

22. *Saints' Herald,* vol. 26, no. 19, 1 October 1879, 290.

23. *Times and Seasons,* vol. 3, no. 9, 1 March 1842, 707.

24. *Kansas City Journal,* 5 June 1881.

25. Parley P. Pratt: The plates "were filled with engravings on both sides" (*Millennial Star,* vol. 1, no. 2, June 1840, 30–31). John Whitmer: "Characters . . . [were] engraven on both sides" (*Deseret News,* 6 August 1878). An unidentified member of the Smith family stated that the plates "bore inscriptions in strange characters on both sides" (*Peoria Register and North-Western Gazetteer,* vol. 5, no. 23, 3 September 1841).

26. George D. Watt, comp., *Journal of Discourses,* 26 vols. (London: F. D. and S. W. Richards and Sons, 1854–1886), 7:31.

27. David Whitmer stated that this "specimen of the characters copied from the plates . . . is the identical specimen which was sent to Prof[essor] Anthon, of New York" (*St. Louis Republican,* 16 July 1884). On at least one occasion the claim was made by David Whitmer that the Anthon Transcript characters represented "a copy of the hieroglyphics made from the first of the gold plates by Joseph Smith. . . . [Joseph took] a whole week to copy [them] so particular was he that the characters should be perfectly reproduced. . . . [The characters were a] copy of the gold plate, which [Martin Harris] presented to Prof[essor] Anthon with a request for the learned linguist to read it, in fulfillment of a prophecy of Isaiah" (*Omaha Herald,* 17 October 1886). George Q. Cannon wrote in his journal, after seeing the Anthon Transcript, which was in the possession of David Whitmer, that it displayed "the characters drawn by Joseph Smith himself for Martin Harris to show to Professors Mitch[i]ll and Anthon. . . . [This] was the very paper which Isaiah saw in vision years before, and which he called the 'words of a book'" (George Q. Cannon Journal, 27 February 1884, Historical Department Archives, The Church of Jesus Christ of Latter-day Saints, Salt Lake City, Utah). For a photographic reproduction of the Anthon Transcript, see Daniel H. Ludlow, ed., *Encyclopedia of Mormonism* (New York: Macmillan, 1992), 1:43–44.

28. *Observer and Telegraph,* vol. 1, no. 38, 18 November 1830.

29. William E. McLellin to Samuel McLellin, 4 August 1832, in Shipps and Welch, eds., *The Journals of William E. McLellin: 1831–1836,* 79.

30. *Times and Seasons,* vol. 3, no. 9, 1 March 1842, 707.

31. *Kansas City Journal,* 5 June 1881.

32. See *Deseret News,* 6 August 1878; Herbert S. Salisbury, "Things the Prophet's Sister Told Me," signed transcript, 30 June 1945, cited in Richard L. Anderson, *Investigating the Book of Mormon Witnesses* (Salt Lake City: Deseret Book, 1981), 26. Herbert was the grandson of Katherine Smith (Salisbury).

33. *Saints' Herald,* vol. 31, no. 40, 4 October 1884, 644.

34. Willard Chase's reminiscence of what the Prophet said is published in Eber D. Howe, *Mormonism Unvailed* (Painesville, Ohio: Telegraph Press, 1834), 246.

35. *Daily Iowa State Register,* 28 August 1870. Martin said on another occasion, "I hefted the plates many times, and should think they weighed forty or fifty pounds" (*Tiffany's Monthly,* vol. 5, no. 4, August 1859, 166).

36. William B. Smith, *William Smith on Mormonism* (Lamoni, Iowa: Herald Steam Book and Job Office, 1883), 12. If the Book of Mormon plates were made of the ancient American eight-karat-gold and copper alloy called Tumbaga, they would have weighed approximately 53.4 pounds (see Reed H. Putnam, "Were

the Plates of Mormon of Tumbaga?" *Improvement Era,* September 1966, 788–89, 828–31; Robert F. Smith, "The 'Golden' Plates," in John W. Welch, ed., *Reexploring the Book of Mormon* [Salt Lake City: Deseret Book; Provo, Utah: FARMS, 1992], 275–77).

37. *Times and Seasons,* vol. 3, no. 9, 1 March 1842, 707.

38. *St. Louis Republican,* 16 July 1884.

39. *Kansas City Journal,* 5 June 1881.

40. See *Reflector,* vol. 2, no. 16, 19 March 1831.

41. *Kansas City Journal,* 5 June 1881.

42. Mary Whitmer, an eyewitness to the plates, "said that they were fastened with rings thus D" (Edward Stevenson Diary, 22–23 December 1877, Historical Department Archives, The Church of Jesus Christ of Latter-day Saints, Salt Lake City, Utah). An unidentified Latter-day Saint "preacher" claimed in 1831 that the "set of thin plates . . . [were] connected with rings in the shape of the letter D" (*Illinois Patriot,* vol. 1, no. 8, 16 September 1831). John Whitmer, an eyewitness to the plates, said that there were "three rings, each one in the shape of a D" (*Deseret News,* 6 August 1878).

43. George D. Watt, comp., *Journal of Discourses,* 26 vols. (London: F. D. and S. W. Richards and Sons, 1854–1886), 7:31.

44. *Times and Seasons,* vol. 3, no. 9, 1 March 1842, 707.

45. See *Journal of Discourses,* 3:347.

46. *Chicago Times,* 17 October 1881.

47. See *Deseret Evening News,* 16 August 1878.

48. *Chicago Times,* 17 October 1881.

49. *Times and Seasons,* vol. 3, no. 9, 1 March 1842, 707. Martin Harris reportedly said that "the two stones . . . were found underneath the plates" (*Tiffany's Monthly,* vol. 5, no. 4, August 1859, 165).

50. *Times and Seasons,* vol. 3, no. 9, 1 March 1842, 707. Oliver Cowdery "testified under oath" that the interpreters consisted of "two transparent stones, resembling glass, set in silver bows. That by looking through these, [Joseph Smith] was able to read in English, the reformed Egyptian characters, which were engraved on the plates" (*Evangelical Magazine and Gospel Advocate,* vol. 2, no. 15, 9 April 1831).

51. Lavina F. Anderson, ed., *Lucy's Book: A Critical Edition of Lucy Mack Smith's Family Memoir* (Salt Lake City: Signature Books, 2001), 379.

52. William Smith, interview by J. W. Peterson and W. S. Pender, 1890, from "Statement of J. W. Peterson Concerning William Smith," 1 May 1921,

Miscellaneous Letters and Papers, Community of Christ Archives, Independence, Mo.

53. *Deseret Evening News,* 16 August 1878, 2. David Whitmer: "the 'Interpreters' . . . looked like whitish stones put in the rim of a bow, looked like spectacles only much larger" (Zenas H. Gurley, interview of David Whitmer, 14 January 1885, Gurley Collection, Historical Department Archives, The Church of Jesus Christ of Latter-day Saints, Salt Lake City, Utah).

54. *Tiffany's Monthly,* vol. 5, no. 4, August 1859, 165–66.

55. Anderson, ed., *Lucy's Book,* 378; see also 389.

56. *Times and Seasons,* vol. 3, no. 12, 15 April 1842, 753; emphasis added.

57. Dean C. Jessee, "Joseph Knight's Recollection of Early Mormon History," *BYU Studies* 17, no. 1 (fall 1976): 33; emphasis added. Parley P. Pratt wrote that the interpreters, or Urim and Thummim, that Joseph Smith received were "an instrument by the use of which [seers] received revelation of things distant, or of things past or future" (*Millennial Star,* vol. 1, no. 2, June 1840, 30–31).

58. *St. Louis Republican,* 16 July 1884.

59. *Tiffany's Monthly,* vol. 5, no. 4, August 1859, 166; emphasis added.

60. Anderson, ed., *Lucy's Book,* 390.

61. *Messenger and Advocate,* vol. 2, no. 1, October 1835, 196. Oliver Cowdery says in this same source that the breastplate was placed in "the bottom of the box," while the golden plates were positioned on top of a set of pillars.

62. See *Millennial Star,* vol. 1, no. 2, June 1840, 30–31.

63. See *Times and Seasons,* vol. 3, no. 9, 1 March 1842, 707.

64. William Smith, interview by J. W. Peterson and W. S. Pender, 1890, from "Statement of J. W. Peterson Concerning William Smith," 1 May 1921, Miscellaneous Letters and Papers, Community of Christ Archives, Independence, Mo.

65. *The Rod of Iron,* vol. 1, no. 3, February 1924, 6–7.

APPENDIX 2

THE TRANSLATION PROCESS

In Mormon chapter 9 verses 32 through 34 it is stated that the Book of Mormon text was written in "reformed Egyptian" characters.[1] This particular system of language was unique among the Nephites; no other people knew this modified form of writing. Oliver Cowdery said that on one of the numerous occasions when the angel Moroni visited Joseph Smith, he told the young Prophet that the reformed Egyptian characters "cannot be interpreted by the learning of this generation; . . . Therefore . . . they are to be translated by the gift and power of God."[2] Joseph identified the means whereby the task of translation was accomplished. He said, "Through the medium of the Urim and Thummim I translated the record by the gift and power of God."[3]

There is a substantial amount of firsthand and secondhand source material that purports to describe how Joseph Smith translated the ancient Nephites' reformed Egyptian characters into the English language. This appendix presents this material in an orderly fashion for the consideration of the reader.

SPIRITUAL PREPARATION

Several requirements had to be met before the work of translation was able to go forward. According to David Whitmer, "Each time before resuming the work all present would kneel in prayer and invoke the Divine blessing on the proceeding."[4] In addition, said

David, the Prophet was required to be "just right before the Lord. . . . [otherwise] the Urim and Thummim would look dark; he could not see a thing in them."[5] David said on another occasion that Joseph

> could not translate unless he was humble and possessed the right feelings towards everyone. To illustrate so you can see: One morning when he was getting ready to continue the translation, something went wrong about the house and he was put out about it. Something that Emma, his wife, had done. Oliver and I went upstairs and Joseph came up soon after to continue the translation but he could not do anything. He could not translate a single syllable. He went downstairs, out into the orchard, and made supplication to the Lord; was gone about an hour. [He] came back to the house and asked Emma's forgiveness and then came upstairs where we were and then the translation went on all right. He could do nothing save he was humble and faithful.[6]

CONCEALMENT OF RELICS AND PARTICIPANTS

Several methods of concealing the plates, other relics, and the participants in the translation were evidently utilized during the translation of the Book of Mormon. Because the Lord had formally forbidden anyone but the Prophet from seeing the ancient relics during the translation process, it was necessary to shield them from public view. During the period when Martin Harris acted as the scribe for the book of Lehi, a curtain was hung between the translator and his assistant. An 1831 newspaper report says, "Harris declares that when he acted as [scribe], and wrote the translation, as Smith dictated, such was [the Prophet's] fear of the Divine displeasure that a screen (sheet) was suspended between the [P]rophet and himself."[7] Martin made this same detail known to another of his acquaintances, who reports, "Although in the same room, a thick curtain or blanket was suspended between them, and Smith concealed behind the blanket."[8]

When the Prophet employed his wife as a scribe, following Harris's loss of the 116 pages of the book of Lehi, no curtain was used for the purpose of concealment. Emma's comments explain why this type of barrier was not necessary. She says, "I frequently wrote day after day, often sitting at the table close by him, he sitting with his face buried in his hat, with the [seer]stone in it, and dictating hour after hour with nothing between us. . . . The plates often lay on the table without any attempt at concealment, wrapped in a small linen tablecloth, which I had given him to fold them in."[9] (Note that the interpreters were not being used.)

During the month when the translation took place at the Peter Whitmer Sr. residence in Fayette, New York, Joseph did not need to conceal the golden plates because by this time they had been given over to the safekeeping of an angel.[10] He also did not need to conceal the interpreters because he was using his personal seerstone to accomplish the translation task. A barrier was erected nevertheless. David Whitmer is represented as explaining why in these words:

> In order to give privacy to the proceeding [at the Whitmer home] a blanket, which served as a portiere, was stretched across the family living room to shelter the translators . . . from the eye of any who might call at the house while the work was in progress. This, [David] Whitmer says, was the only use made of the blanket, and it was not for the purpose of concealing . . . the translator from the eyes of the [scribe]. In fact, [Joseph] Smith was at no time hidden from his collaborators [while at the Whitmer home], and the translation was performed in the presence of not only the persons mentioned, but of the entire Whitmer household and several of Smiths' relatives besides.[11]

METHOD OF TRANSLATION

The following is a tentative model of the possible method whereby the Book of Mormon was translated into the English language. It does not in any way claim to be complete, authoritative, or final.

Manifestation of the Spirit

David Whitmer made note of the fact that when the Prophet was translating the Book of Mormon with his personal seerstone, a "spiri-

tual light would shine."[12] Orson Pratt provides a possible explanation
for this. He said that the Urim and Thummim stones glowed because
they were "illuminated by the Spirit of the living God."[13] Indeed,
Joseph Smith told Pratt that the Urim and Thummim he used in the
Book of Mormon's translation assisted him in tapping into "the Spirit
of revelation and prophecy."[14]

One person who was acquainted with the early Latter-day Saints
(a minister in another church) wrote in an 1830 letter that it was the
Holy Ghost who revealed the English translation of the Book of
Mormon to Joseph Smith through the instrumentality of the Urim
and Thummim or "spectacles."[15] This idea is supported in several
LDS sources. Orson Pratt said on several occasions that the transla-
tion was accomplished by the "power of the Holy Ghost."[16] George
Q. Cannon likewise wrote, "In translating the Book of Mormon
Joseph [Smith] was in the best school a man could attend. The Holy
Ghost, which is the spirit of intelligence, inspired his mind as he read
and understood a strange language entirely different from his own."[17]
In the early 1860s William C. Staines, who was serving as a
missionary in England, claimed to have received a revelation wherein
the Lord told him, "The Book of Mormon was translated from plates
by the power of my Spirit through Joseph Smith."[18]

The Prophet was careful to clarify that he was not the source of the
translation. Rather, he is reported to have said that it "was communicated to him, *direct from heaven*. If there was such a thing on earth as
the author of it then he (Smith) was the author; but the idea that he
wished to impress was that he had penned it as dictated by God."[19]

Reading the Hieroglyphic Characters

One resident of Kirtland, Ohio, who was not a member of the
Church asserted that "by putting his finger on one of the characters
and imploring divine aid" Joseph Smith was enabled to see its translation in the Urim and Thummim; he would then move on to the next
character.[20] David Whitmer confirms part of this statement in one of
his publications. He says that the Prophet was working with only one
character at a time.[21]

There was evidently some type of divine book-marking system in
operation during the time when the translation was taking place.

Emma Smith said of her husband that he "would dictate . . . hour after hour; and when returning after meals, or after interruptions, he could at once begin where he had left off, without either seeing the manuscript or having any portion of it read to him. This was a usual thing for him to do."[22]

Appearance of English Words

A resident of Kirtland, Ohio, who was not a member of the Church wrote in 1836 that while Joseph Smith was "looking through the Urim and Thummim" he would see words "written in plain English on a screen placed before him."[23] David Whitmer makes a similar, but much later, remark in relation to the other translation instrument that Joseph Smith used. He states that when the Prophet was using his personal seerstone he would put it "in a deep hat, and placing his face close to it, would see, not the stone, but what appeared like an oblong piece of parchment, on which the hieroglyphics would appear."[24] Joseph Smith was even more specific in his description of the translation process. He reportedly told David Whitmer and others that "the original character [from the golden plates] appeared upon parchment and under it the translation in English, which enabled him to read it readily."[25]

It was David Whitmer's understanding that there was a substantial variation in the number of English words that could be derived from each of the reformed-Egyptian hieroglyphics. Said he, "Some [hieroglyphics] represented but one word, or name, some represented several, and some from one to two lines" of written text.[26]

Orson Hyde, Joseph Knight Sr., and David Whitmer each made statements to the effect that the English translation Joseph saw had a peculiar property; it was written in letters of light or bright Roman letters. According to David Whitmer's testimony the hieroglyphics themselves were also luminous to the sight of the Prophet.[27]

Transmittal and Transcription

The words seen by Joseph Smith through either the Jaredite/Nephite interpreters or the seerstone were spoken out loud by him, and then whoever was serving as his scribe at the time would write them down on a piece of paper.

Because Joseph Smith had only a limited amount of formal education, said David Whitmer, he would sometimes "spell the words out, not knowing the correct pronunciation."[28] Oliver Cowdery, "being a schoolteacher, rendered invaluable aid in pronouncing hard words and giving their proper definition."[29]

When Martin Harris was serving as scribe during the translation of the book of Lehi in Harmony, Pennsylvania, he would write down the dictated words and say "written" when he had finished his task.[30] When the translation was taking place in the Whitmer household in Fayette, New York, however, the acting scribe would read the sentence back to the Prophet after it had been written.[31]

Verification of Transcription

Martin Harris, Oliver Cowdery, Joseph Knight Sr., and David Whitmer all stated that, "if correctly written, that sentence would disappear and another appear in its place, but if not written correctly it remained until corrected." This rule apparently also applied to the accidental omission of words in the revealed translation.[32]

Result of Translation

Martin Harris is reported to have said that the characters on the plates "assumed, through the Urim and Thummim, the forms of equivalent modern words which were familiar to the understanding of the Prophet and seer."[33] Nevertheless, said Harris, "the translation was just as it was engraven on the plates, precisely in the language then used" by the Nephites.[34] This would help to explain why there are so many ancient Hebrew literary patterns underlying the English text of the Book of Mormon.[35]

VARIATIONS IN PROCEDURE

Interpreters and Seerstone

In the beginning of the translation process it appears that Joseph Smith utilized both the breastplate and the interpreters. Joseph's brother, William Smith, reported that the Prophet "usually" used the breastplate and interpreters "when translating as it permitted him to have both hands free to hold the plates."[36]

Emma Smith recalled that the first 116 pages of the Book of Mormon were "translated by the use of the Urim and Thummim, and that was the part that Martin Harris lost." But sometime "after that [the Prophet] used a small stone," meaning his personal seerstone.[37] According to one late reminiscence of a David Whitmer statement, "Joseph . . . had the Urim and Thummim, and a chocolate-colored stone, which he used alternately, as suited his convenience."[38]

There is some evidence which suggests that Joseph Smith was still using the interpreters when Oliver Cowdery was serving as his scribe in Harmony, Pennsylvania. Oliver penned the following words for an article that was published in the Church's official newspaper:

> These were days never to be forgotten. To sit under the sound of a voice dictated by the inspiration of heaven awakened the utmost gratitude of this bosom! Day after day I continued, uninterrupted, to write from his mouth as he translated with the Urim and Thummim or, as the Nephites would have said, "Interpreters," the history or record called "The Book of Mormon."[39]

Other historical evidence suggests that there was a period of time when Joseph did not use the interpreters with the ancient breastplate but instead used them in connection with a hat, in two different ways. A newspaper article written in September 1829 reports that Joseph translated "by placing the spectacles in a hat, and looking into it,"[40] and David Whitmer is represented as saying much later that Joseph "would hold the interpreters to his eyes and cover his face with a hat, excluding all light."[41]

During the one-month time frame when the translation was taking place in Fayette, New York, it does not appear that the interpreters were being used at all. David Whitmer states that the Prophet never "translated in his presence by aid of [the] Urim and Thummim," but instead he used his "dark-colored, opaque stone called a 'Seer Stone,' which was placed in the crown of a hat."[42]

The reason for the shift between the use of the interpreters and the use of the seerstone seems to be twofold. First, Joseph began the translation process in relative isolation; he did not need to worry too much about somebody seeing the ancient Nephite relics. But when he moved to the Whitmer residence he may have switched exclusively to using the seerstone because there were so many individuals passing in and out of the house. Second, Joseph experienced too much eyestrain when he used the Urim and Thummim. William Smith reportedly said that the interpreters "were much too large for Joseph and he could only see through one [of the stones] at a time—using sometimes one and sometimes the other. By putting his head in a hat or some dark object it was not necessary to close one eye while looking through the stone with the other. In that way sometimes when his eyes grew tired he relieved them of the strain."[43]

Use and Absence of Golden Plates

As mentioned in the sections above, when Joseph Smith first began to translate the Book of Mormon plates it seems that he would hold them in his hands and point to individual hieroglyphics as he worked. But after some unspecified amount of time this method of operation changed because it was no longer necessary for him to physically look at the plates.

This change seems to have taken place either during or after the translation of the first 116 pages of the Nephite record. Emma Smith recalled that when she served as her husband's scribe "the plates often lay on the table without any attempt at concealment, wrapped in a small linen tablecloth which [she] had given him to fold them in."[44] William Smith makes a similar comment. He says that the translation with the seerstone took place with "the plates lying nearby covered up."[45] Martin Harris concurs, stating that "sometimes the plates would be on a table in the room in which Smith did the translating, covered over with a cloth."[46] Emma Smith's father, Isaac Hale, claims that Joseph said he was interpreting the Book of Mormon text "while the book of plates were at the same time hid in the woods."[47] David Whitmer also confirms this type of activity. He relates that Joseph Smith "did not use the plates in the translation" while he was staying at the Whitmer house in Fayette, New York.[48]

One late historical source may provide a clue as to how such a feat could be accomplished. In this document Joseph Smith reportedly said in 1826, while under examination in a court of law, that when he first obtained his personal seerstone he "placed it in his hat, and discovered that time, place, and distance were annihilated; that all intervening obstacles were removed, and that he possessed one of the attributes of Deity, an All-Seeing Eye."[49] Brigham Young provides us with a very similar piece of information. He says, "When Joseph had a revelation he had, as it were, the eyes of the Lord. He saw as the Lord sees."[50] Emma Smith noted evidence of this ability during the translation of the Nephite record. She said, "When my husband was translating the Book of Mormon, I wrote a part of it, as he dictated each sentence, word for word, and when he came to proper names he could not pronounce, or long words, he spelled them out, and while I was writing them, if I made any mistake in spelling, he would stop me and correct my spelling, although it was *impossible* for him to see how I was writing them down at the time."[51] The divine abilities inherent in the gift of seership may thus explain how Joseph could translate the golden plates of the Book of Mormon even while they were sitting covered by a cloth on the table next to him, in the temporary custody of an angel, or even hidden out in the woods near his home.[52]

NOTES TO APPENDIX 2

1. The Anthon Transcript preserves a sample of the reformed Egyptian characters that were engraved on the golden plates of the Book of Mormon (see Daniel H. Ludlow, ed., *Encyclopedia of Mormonism* [New York: Macmillan, 1992], 1:43–44).

2. *Messenger and Advocate,* vol. 2, no. 1, October 1835, 198. The "power to translate" the Book of Mormon was "the power of God" (D&C 1:29). Joseph Smith was given "sight and power to translate" (D&C 3:12), which would be equivalent to saying that he had the "gift and power of God" (D&C 135:3) or the gift of seership (see D&C 21:1; 107:92; 127:12). The Lord gave the Prophet "the keys of this gift" (D&C 6:28).

3. *Times and Seasons,* vol. 3, no. 9, 1 March 1842, 707.

4. *Chicago Tribune,* 17 December 1885. David Whitmer "declared that Joseph first offered prayer. . . . This was the daily method of procedure" (*Saints' Herald,* vol. 26, 15 November 1879). Orson Hyde: "The persons using [the Urim and Thummim] offered their prayers to the Lord, and [then] the answer

became visible" (Orson Hyde, *A Cry Out of the Wilderness* [Frankfurt, Germany: n.p., 1842]; English translation cited in Paul R. Cheesman, "An Analysis of the Accounts Relating Joseph Smith's Early Visions," [master's thesis, Brigham Young University, 1965], 167).

5. *Saints' Herald*, vol. 31, 21 June 1884. David Whitmer: "At times when Brother Joseph would attempt to translate, he would look into the hat in which the stone was placed, he found he was spiritually blind and could not translate. He told us that his mind dwelt too much on earthly things, and various causes would make him incapable of proceeding with the translation. When in this condition he would go out and pray, and when he became sufficiently humble before God, he could then proceed with the translation. Now we see how very strict the Lord is, and how He requires the heart of man to be just right in His sight, before he can receive revelation from Him" (David Whitmer, *An Address to All Believers in Christ* [Richmond, Mo.: David Whitmer, 1887], 30).

6. *Saints' Herald*, vol. 29, 1 March 1882.

7. *Reflector*, vol. 2, no. 16, 19 March 1831.

8. John A. Clark, *Gleanings by the Way* (Philadelphia: W. J. and J. K. Simon, 1842), 230.

9. *Saints' Herald*, vol. 26, no. 19, 1 October 1879, 289–90.

10. David Whitmer: "When Joseph was again allowed to resume the translation, the plates were taken care of by a messenger of God, and when Joseph wanted to see the plates, this messenger was always at hand" (*Kansas City Journal*, 5 June 1881).

11. *Chicago Tribune*, 17 December 1885. Elizabeth A. Whitmer (Oliver Cowdery's wife) said of the translation taking place in her family's home: "I often sat by and saw and heard them translate and write for hours together. Joseph never had a curtain drawn between him and his scribe while he was translating" (Statement on obverse of William E. McLellin letter, February 1870, Community of Christ Archives, Independence, Mo.). David Whitmer: "I, as well as all of my father's family, Smith's wife [Emma], Oliver Cowdery, and Martin Harris, were present during the translation" (*Kansas City Journal*, 5 June 1881). "I did not wish to be understood as saying that those referred to as being present were all of the time in the immediate presence of the translator, but were at the place and saw how the translation was conducted" (ibid., 19 June 1881).

12. Whitmer, *An Address to All Believers in Christ*, 12. Whitmer said on other occasions: "a spiritual light would appear before Joseph" (*Saints' Herald*, 15 November 1962, 16); "the light . . . appeared in the hat" (*Kansas City Journal*, 19 June 1881).

13. Orson Pratt, *A Series of Pamphlets* (Liverpool, England: Franklin D. Richards, 1852), 72.

14. Orson Pratt "mentioned that as Joseph used the Urim and Thummim in the translation of the Book of Mormon, he wondered why [the Prophet] did not use it in the translation of the New Testament. Joseph explained to him that the experience he had acquired while translating the Book of Mormon by the use of the Urim and Thummim had rendered him so well acquainted with the spirit of revelation and prophecy, that in the translating of the New Testament he did not need the aid that was necessary in the first instance" (Minutes of the Salt Lake City School of the Prophets, 14 January 1871, Historical Department Archives, The Church of Jesus Christ of Latter-day Saints, Salt Lake City, Utah; cf. *Millennial Star,* vol. 36, no. 32, 11 August 1874, 498–99).

15. Letter by Rev. Diedrich Villers, 1830, published in *New York History* 54 (July 1973): 326. Some commentators have argued that Joseph Smith was somehow responsible for producing the English text of the Book of Mormon in the traditional role of a "translator"—albeit a divinely inspired one. But in 2 Nephi 27:20 it is plainly stated that the Lord would "give" the words of the translation to the Prophet, and in Doctrine and Covenants 10:42 the Lord refers to the material in the 116 pages of the book of Lehi as "my words." Furthermore, the Prophet himself publicly explained that the translation "was communicated to him, *direct from heaven.* . . . [H]e had penned it as dictated by God" (Brigham H. Roberts, ed., *History of the Church,* rev. ed., 7 vols. [Salt Lake City: The Church of Jesus Christ of Latter-day Saints, 1932–1951], 4:79; emphasis in original).

16. George D. Watt, comp., *Journal of Discourses,* 26 vols. (London: F. D. and S. W. Richards and Sons, 1854–1886), 13:66; 14:299.

17. George Q. Cannon, *Young People's History of Joseph Smith* (Salt Lake City: George Q. Cannon and Sons, 1912), 104.

18. *Contributor,* vol. 12, no. 4, February 1891, 123.

19. *History of the Church,* 4:79; emphasis in original.

20. *Ohio Observer,* 11 August 1836.

21. See Whitmer, *An Address to All Believers in Christ,* 12.

22. *Saints' Herald,* vol. 26, no. 19, 1 October 1879, 290.

23. *Ohio Observer,* 11 August 1836. People who assisted in the translation, who were present during the translation, and who were members of the Prophet's family report that words were visible on the translation device. Oliver Cowdery reportedly said that "the translation appear[ed] distinctly on the instrument. . . . Every

word was distinctly visible even to every letter" (Samuel W. Richards, statement, 25 May 1907, Samuel Whitney Richards Collection, Historical Department Archives, The Church of Jesus Christ of Latter-day Saints, Salt Lake City, Utah). Elizabeth A. Whitmer (Oliver Cowdery's wife) reports, "I often sat by and saw and heard them translate and write for hours together. . . . [Joseph] would place the [stone] in his hat, and then place his face in his hat, so as to exclude the light, and then [dictate] to his scribe the words as they appeared before [him]" (Statement on obverse of William E. McLellin letter, February 1870, Community of Christ Archives, Independence, Mo.). "Martin [Harris] explained the translation as follows: By aid of the seerstone, sentences would appear and were read by the Prophet and written by Martin" (*Millennial Star,* vol. 44, no. 6, 6 February 1882, 86–87). William Smith wrote, "The manner in which [the translation] was done was by looking into the Urim and Thummim, which was placed in a hat to exclude the light . . . and reading off the translation, which appeared in the stone by the power of God" (William B. Smith, *William Smith on Mormonism* [Lamoni, Iowa: Herald Steam Book and Job Office, 1883], 11).

24. *Deseret News,* 25 March 1884.

25. Zenas H. Gurley, interview of David Whitmer, 14 January 1885, Gurley Collection, Historical Department Archives, The Church of Jesus Christ of Latter-day Saints, Salt Lake City, Utah. David Whitmer said that a piece of parchment "would appear before Joseph, upon which was a line of characters from the plates, and under it, the translation in English; at least, *so Joseph said"* (*Saints' Herald,* 15 November 1962, 16; emphasis added).

26. *Deseret News,* 25 March 1884. David Whitmer stated on another occasion that "frequently, one character would make two lines of manuscript, while others made but a word or two words" (*Chicago Times,* 17 October 1881). David Whitmer: "Sometimes the character would [represent] a single word, and frequently an entire sentence" (*Chicago Tribune,* 17 December 1885).

27. Orson Hyde: The words were "written in letters of light" (Orson Hyde, *A Cry Out of the Wilderness* [Frankfurt, Germany: n.p., 1842]; English translation cited in Cheesman, "An Analysis of the Accounts Relating Joseph Smith's Early Visions," 167). Joseph Knight: "A sentence . . . would appear in bright Roman letters" (Dean C. Jessee, "Joseph Knight's Recollection of Early Mormon History," *BYU Studies* 17, no. 1 [fall 1976]: 35). David Whitmer: "The hieroglyphics would appear, and also the translation in the English language, all appearing in bright luminous letters," which he also refers to as "the luminous writing" (*Deseret News,* 25 March 1884). David Whitmer:

"The letters appeared on [the Urim and Thummim or on the seerstone] in light, and would not go off until they were written correctly" (*Saints' Herald,* vol. 31, 21 June 1884).

28. *Chicago Tribune,* 17 December 1885. David Whitmer: "When Joseph could not pronounce the words he spelled them out letter by letter" (*Saints' Herald,* vol. 31, 21 June 1884). David Whitmer: "Sometimes Joseph could not pronounce the words correctly, having had but little education" (*Deseret News,* 25 March 1884). Emma Smith: "When he came to proper names he could not pronounce, or long words, he spelled them out" (*Journal of History,* vol. 9, no. 4, October 1916, 454).

29. *Chicago Tribune,* 17 December 1885.

30. *Millennial Star,* vol. 44, no. 6, 6 February 1882, 87.

31. See *Kansas City Journal,* 5 June 1881.

32. *Millennial Star,* vol. 44, no. 6, 6 February 1882, 87. Related by Oliver Cowdery: "If Oliver omitted a word or failed to spell a word correctly, the translation remained on the 'interpreter' until it was copied correctly" (Samuel W. Richards, statement, 25 May 1907). David Whitmer: "Brother Joseph would read off the English to Oliver Cowdery, who was his principal scribe, and when it was written down and repeated to Brother Joseph to see if it was correct, then it would disappear, and another character with the interpretation would appear" (Whitmer, *An Address to All Believers in Christ,* 12). David Whitmer: "It sometimes took Oliver several trials to get the right letters to spell correctly some of *the more difficult words,* but when he had written them correctly, the characters and the interpretation would disappear" (*Deseret News,* 25 March 1884; emphasis added). David Whitmer: "The words would appear, and if he failed to spell the word right, it would stay till it was spelled right, then pass away; another come, and so on" (*Saints' Herald,* vol. 27, no. 5, 1 March 1880). Joseph Knight: "If it was not spelled right it would not go away till it was right" (Jessee, "Joseph Knight's Recollection of Early Mormon History," 35). Since the original manuscript of the Book of Mormon contains various spelling anomalies it may be that only the words with non-English equivalents (or "more difficult words," as per Whitmer's statement) remained in view until they were transcribed correctly. And perhaps the "visible till transcribed correctly" rule only applied to the first display of such words.

33. William Pilkington to Vern C. Poulter, 28 February 1930, L. Tom Perry Special Collections Library, Harold B. Lee Library, Brigham Young University, Provo, Utah.

34. *Millennial Star,* vol. 44, no. 6, 6 February 1882, 87.
35. See John W. Welch, "Chiasmus in the Book of Mormon," *BYU Studies* 10, no. 1 (fall 1969): 69–84; John A. Tvedtnes, "Hebraisms in the Book of Mormon: A Preliminary Survey," *BYU Studies* 11, no. 1 (fall 1970): 50–60; Donald W. Parry, "Hebrew Literary Patterns in the Book of Mormon," *Ensign,* October 1989, 58–61; Royal Skousen, "Towards a Critical Edition of the Book of Mormon," *BYU Studies* 30, no. 1 (winter 1990): 41–67; John A. Tvedtnes, "The Hebrew Background of the Book of Mormon," in John L. Sorenson and Melvin J. Thorne, eds., *Rediscovering the Book of Mormon* (Salt Lake City: Deseret Book; Provo, Utah: FARMS, 1991), 77–91; Richard D. Rust, "Poetry in the Book of Mormon," in John L. Sorenson and Melvin J. Thorne, eds., *Rediscovering the Book of Mormon* (Salt Lake City: Deseret Book; Provo, Utah: FARMS, 1991), 100–13; Donald W. Parry, *The Book of Mormon Text Reformatted According to Parallelistic Patterns* (Provo, Utah: FARMS, 1992); John W. Welch, ed., *Reexploring the Book of Mormon* (Salt Lake City: Deseret Book; Provo, Utah: FARMS, 1992), 80–82, 96, 165, 167–69; Royal Skousen, "The Original Language of the Book of Mormon: Upstate New York Dialect, King James English, or Hebrew?" *Journal of Book of Mormon Studies* 3, no. 1 (spring 1994): 28–38; Kevin L. Barney, "Enallage in the Book of Mormon," *Journal of Book of Mormon Studies* 3, no. 1 (spring 1994): 113–45; Kevin L. Barney, "Poetic Diction and Parallel Word Pairs in the Book of Mormon," *Journal of Book of Mormon Studies* 4, no. 2 (fall 1995): 15–80; Brian D. Stubbs, "A Lengthier Treatment of Length," *Journal of Book of Mormon Studies* 5, no. 2 (fall 1996): 82–97; Donald W. Parry, "Power through Repetition: The Dynamics of Book of Mormon Parallelism," in Noel B. Reynolds, ed., *Book of Mormon Authorship Revisited: The Evidence for Ancient Origins* (Provo, Utah: FARMS, 1997), 295–309; Hugh W. Pinnock, *Finding Biblical Hebrew and Other Ancient Literary Forms in the Book of Mormon* (Provo, Utah: Research Press, 1999); David Bokovoy, "From Distance to Proximity: A Poetic Function of Enallage in the Hebrew Bible and the Book of Mormon," *Journal of Book of Mormon Studies* 9, no. 1 (2000): 60–63; Donald W. Parry, "Hebraisms and Other Ancient Peculiarities in the Book of Mormon," in Donald W. Parry, Daniel C. Peterson, and John W. Welch, eds., *Echoes and Evidences of the Book of Mormon* (Provo, Utah: FARMS, 2002), 155–89.
36. *The Rod of Iron,* vol. 1, no. 3, February 1924, 6–7.
37. *Saints' Herald,* 15 November 1962, 15. David Whitmer is in agreement on this point. He states that "the Prophet translated first by the Urim and Thummim

and afterwards by a seerstone" (Edward Stevenson Diary, 22–23 December 1877, Historical Department Archives, The Church of Jesus Christ of Latter-day Saints, Salt Lake City, Utah). Notice, however, that on this subject Whitmer is not stating a fact from firsthand knowledge. He says rather, "The 'interpreters' were *as I understood* taken from [Joseph] Smith and were not used by him after losing the first 116 pages [of the Book of Mormon]. It is *my understanding* that the [seer]stone . . . was furnished [to] him when he commenced translating again after losing the 116 pages" (*Kansas City Journal,* 19 June 1881; emphasis added). This last statement is an obvious error since the Prophet possessed his personal seerstone for several years before he used it in the translation process. It appears that after the loss of the 116 pages of the book of Lehi, the Lord imbued the Prophet's seerstone with the same abilities inherent in the interpreters. By this means the Prophet could translate while in the presence of persons who were formally forbidden to view the Urim and Thummim.

38. Nathan Tanner Jr., Reminiscence, 17 February 1909, Historical Department Archives, The Church of Jesus Christ of Latter-day Saints, Salt Lake City, Utah. Martin Harris likewise remarked that the Prophet started using his personal seerstone "for convenience" (*Deseret News,* 30 November 1881).

39. *Messenger and Advocate,* vol. 1, no. 1, October 1834, 14.

40. *Painesville Telegraph,* vol. 1, no. 15, 22 September 1829.

41. *Kansas City Journal,* 5 June 1881.

42. *Saints' Herald,* 15 November 1962, 16.

43. William Smith, interview by J. W. Peterson and W. S. Pender, 1890, from "Statement of J. W. Peterson Concerning William Smith," 1 May 1921, Miscellaneous Letters and Papers, Community of Christ Archives, Independence, Mo. This information helps to clarify the meaning of several curious LDS and non-LDS reports of the translation process. For instance: Oliver Cowdery, Parley P. Pratt, Peter Whitmer Jr., and Ziba Peterson reportedly said that "Joseph Smith . . . translated . . . by looking into a stone or two stones, when put *into a dark place*" (*Evangelist,* vol. 9, no. 6, 1 June 1841; emphasis added). An unidentified LDS "preacher" reported that the Prophet found "two stones with which he was enabled, by placing them over his eyes and putting his head *in a dark corner,* to decipher the hieroglyphics on the plates" (*New Hampshire Gazette,* vol. 76, no. 60, 25 October 1831; emphasis added). The translation was done with "the mammoth spectacles or Urim and Thummim . . . [*in*] *a dark corner* of a room at his residence . . . [T]he view

with the instrument used was even too brilliant for his own spiritualized eyes in the light! This was the story of the first series of translations" (Pomeroy Tucker, *Origin, Rise, and Progress of Mormonism* [New York City: D. Appleton and Co., 1867], 36; emphasis added). Alexander Campbell said, "It is a translation made through stone spectacles, *in a dark room,* and *in the hat* of the prophet Smith from the reformed Egyptian" (*Millennial Harbinger,* vol. 2, no. 2, 7 February 1831, 95; emphasis added).

44. *Saints' Herald,* vol. 26, no. 19, 1 October 1879, 290. Notice that directly after this quote Emma Smith talks twice of doing her housework, implying that the preceding information refers to her acting as scribe in Harmony, Pennsylvania.

45. William B. Smith, *William Smith on Mormonism,* 11.

46. Anthony Metcalf, *Ten Years before the Mast* (Malad, Idaho: n.p., 1888), 70–71.

47. *Susquehanna Register,* vol. 9, 1 May 1834.

48. *Kansas City Journal,* 5 June 1881. David Whitmer declared that he "did [not] see [the plates] . . . at all during the translation. He said that they were in the possession of the angel during this time" (Nathan Tanner Jr. Journal, 13 April 1886, Historical Department Archives, The Church of Jesus Christ of Latter-day Saints, Salt Lake City, Utah). David Whitmer: "When Joseph was again allowed to resume the translation, the plates were taken care of by a messenger of God, and when Joseph wanted to see the plates, this messenger was always at hand" (*Kansas City Journal,* 5 June 1881).

49. *Chenango Union,* vol. 30, no. 33, 3 May 1877. In this same source it is claimed that Joseph Smith Sr., the Prophet's father, verified this information under oath.

50. Matthias F. Cowley, *Wilford Woodruff: His Life and Labors* (Salt Lake City: Deseret News Press, 1916), 415–16.

51. *Journal of History,* vol. 9, no. 4, October 1916, 454; emphasis added.

52. Notice that the Prophet's ability to "see" without the use of the interpreters or his personal seerstone had developed to a great degree after he had translated the first 116 pages of the Book of Mormon but before he had translated the remainder of the volume. In reference to this time frame, Lucy Mack Smith says, "When we came within 3/4 of a mile of the house Joseph started off to meet us, telling his wife that father and mother were coming, although he could not see us" (Lavina F. Anderson, ed., *Lucy's Book: A Critical Edition of Lucy Mack Smith's Family Memoir* [Salt Lake City: Signature Books, 2001], 424).

APPENDIX 3

THE PUBLICATION PROCESS

There were essentially twenty different steps involved in the printing and binding of the first edition of the Book of Mormon. Thanks are due to Louis Crandall and Wallace Saling of the Crandall Historical Printing Museum in Provo, Utah, for sharing their invaluable knowledge about these processes with the author.

Step 1: Copying the Manuscript
Lucy Mack Smith preserved knowledge of the fact that the Lord dictated how the work of publication should proceed. She said,

> A revelation came to Joseph commanding him to see that Oliver [Cowdery] transcribed the whole work a second time and [he was told] never [to] take both transcripts to the [printing] office, but leave one and carry the other so that in case one was destroyed the other would be left. Furthermore, Peter Whitmer was commanded to remain at our house to assist in guarding the writings and also . . . to accompany Oliver to the office and back when no other person could be spared from the place to go and come with him—as it was necessary that Oliver should be accompanied by someone for the purpose of protecting him in case of danger. [Joseph was informed] that if this precaution was not taken his enemies would be likely to waylay him in order to get the manuscript away from him and also the

house would be infested by intrusive persons who [were] willing to sacrifice their character for the sake of putting a stop [to] the printing of the [book]. . . . This astonished us very much but we did [not] gainsay the counsel of the Most High. Wherefore we did all things according to the pattern that was given and accordingly they guarded Oliver to his work in the morning and went after him at night and kept a guard over the house all night long.[1]

Step 2: Delivering the Manuscript

John H. Gilbert was the chief compositor and pressman for the Book of Mormon's first printing. He recalled that, "When the printer was ready to commence work, [Martin] Harris was notified, and Hyrum Smith brought the first installment of manuscript, of 24 pages. . . . [H]e had it under his vest, and [his] vest and coat closely buttoned over it."[2] Pomeroy Tucker, who was working in Grandin's print shop during the publication of the book, states that "the Mormons professed to hold their manuscripts as 'sacred,' and insisted upon maintaining constant vigilance for their safety during the progress of the work, each morning carrying to the printing office the installment required for the day, and withdrawing the same at evening."[3]

Step 3: Editing the Manuscript

John Gilbert made mention of the fact that the Printer's Manuscript—which had been created by Oliver Cowdery and several other scribes—"was one solid paragraph, without a punctuation mark, from beginning to end."[4] The guardians of the manuscript told the printers that "no alteration from copy in any manner was to be made. These things were 'strictly commanded,' as they said." Mr. Gilbert, however, after "much friendly expostulation" was given a "limited" amount of discretion in providing the manuscript with punctuation, capitalization, and paragraphing.[5] Gilbert said, "I punctuated it to make it read as I supposed the Author intended, and but very little punctuation was altered in proof-reading."[6] On one occasion Gilbert asked if he should change something that he thought was a grammatical error, but he was instructed by Hyrum Smith and

Martin Harris to leave the grammar of the manuscript untouched.[7] A little known fact about the editing of the first edition of the Book of Mormon is that John Gilbert kept a copy of the Bible on his typecase so that when he ran across portions of the Book of Mormon manuscript that seemed to correspond with biblical texts he could punctuate them accordingly.[8]

Gilbert himself describes how the editing of the Printer's Manuscript was completed. He says,

> After working a few days, I said to [Hyrum] Smith on his handing me the manuscript in the morning, "Mr. Smith, if you would leave this manuscript with me, I would take it home with me at night and read and punctuate it, and I could get along faster in the daytime, for now I have frequently to stop and read half a page to find how to punctuate it." His reply was, "We are commanded not to leave it." A few mornings after this, when Smith handed me the manuscript, he said to me, "If you will give your word that this manuscript shall be returned to us when you get through with it, I will leave it with you." I assured Smith that it should be returned all right when I got through with it. For two or three nights I took it home with me and read it, and punctuated it with a lead pencil.[9]

Step 4: Setting the Type

Once Mr. Grandin decided that he would go ahead and print the Book of Mormon for Joseph Smith, he purchased a new set of type with which to accomplish the job. He "got a new font of small Pica, on which the body of the work was printed."[10]

When it came time to set the type for the text, the person assigned to this task would hold a "composition stick" in one hand and, standing at the typecases with the handwritten manuscript before him he would pick out letters, punctuation marks, and blank space dividers with his other hand. These small metallic pieces were placed one at a time, in a backward order, into the hand-held "stick" (the type had to make a mirror image of the printed words). A typical page of Book of Mormon text in the first edition contained forty-two lines of words, and it might have taken the average compositor about one minute to set each line. John Gilbert mentions that Oliver Cowdery—who had previously worked as a printer—"did several times take up a 'stick' and set a part of a page—he may have set 10 or 12 pages, all told."[11]

Once an entire line of words had been typecast, they would then be secured in a metallic "chase," or frame, and the process would be repeated until an entire page of type had been set. The person engaged in this business would then get a printer's tool called a "planer" (a wooden block with flat top and bottom surfaces), place it on top of the chase, and tap down with a mallet to ensure that all of the type was positioned at the same height.

When sixteen page forms had been completely assembled they were then placed on the "bed" of the press in a very precise arrangement and locked into place by pieces of wood that were known as "furniture." John Gilbert said that the Book of Mormon was "printed 16 pages at a time, so that one sheet of paper made two copies of 16 pages each."[12]

Step 5: Printing the Pages

In 1830, ink was not rolled across the typeset page forms but was instead applied with objects called "inkballs." These simple devices consisted of a short wooden handle attached to the top of a wooden cone. A piece of leather was then nailed around the bottom edge of the cone and stuffed with horsehair or some similar substance. Black ink was applied to the surfaces of two inkballs, and they were rolled together for several minutes in order to distribute the ink evenly. Then a person known as the "beater" would vigorously pat the inkballs across the top of the type forms until all of the letters had been sufficiently covered.

A single sheet of paper was then positioned on the "tympan," which was a rectangular platform attached with a hinge to the outside edge of the press bed. The paper was squared or registered and secured in its place by clips or "duck bills" (located at the bottom edge of the tympan) and two small gauge pins, or "points" (located near the center, outside edges of the tympan). At the top of the tympan was another hinged platform called a frisket. This device—

which was the same size and shape as the tympan—had page-sized rectangular holes cut into it and was designed to keep the ink on the paper from being smeared when an impression was made.

After the paper was positioned on the tympan, the frisket was pulled down over the paper, and the two were both pulled down on top of the press's type bed. Then the press operator would roll the press bed underneath the "platen" (or pressing mechanism), grab hold of the press lever, and pull it toward him until it stopped moving.

John Gilbert reports that it took nearly three days for each of the page forms to be printed, a form being one side of each sheet (or 16 pages worth of text). Gilbert and a man named J. H. Bortles acted as pressmen for the Book of Mormon from August 1829 until December 1829, and then a journeyman press operator named Thomas McAuley (or "Whistling Tom") was hired to finish up the presswork with Mr. Bortles.[13]

Step 6: Proofreading the First Impressions

Once the first impression of a page was made, the printed words had to be checked for accuracy. John Gilbert reports that "the title page was first set up, and after proof was read and corrected, several copies were printed for [Martin] Harris and his friends."[14] Gilbert states that Oliver Cowdery "held and looked over the manuscript when most of the proofs were read. Martin Harris [did so] once or twice, and Hyrum Smith once, Grandin supposing these men could read their own writing as well, if not better, than anyone else."[15]

Step 7: Drying the Pages and Printing Subsequent Impressions

Freshly printed pages could be hung to dry over segments of stretched-out string, or they could be straddled across suspended wooden rods. It took about one full day for the ink on each piece of paper to dry out completely.

When it was time for the pressman to make the second impression on a sheet of paper, he simply flipped the page "head to toe" and pushed the "points," or gauge pins, through the holes that had been made during the first impression. This action ensured that the blocks of words on both sides of the paper were registered (or matched each other's outside edges).

The first edition of the Book of Mormon consisted of 590 printed pages. The title page, copyright notice, and preface were located on pages 1 through 4, the Book of Mormon text was on pages 5 through 588, and the testimonies of the Three and Eight Witnesses were imprinted on pages 589 and 590. In order to print all five thousand copies of the Book of Mormon it took 185,000 individual pulls on the press arm to imprint 2,960,000 total page images on 92,500 sheets of paper.[16]

Step 8: Folding and Cutting the Pages

Once each sheet had been imprinted on both sides and sufficiently dried, it was folded down the middle and cut in half with a thin, rectangular bone knife. This action created two identical double-sided sheets of text.

Step 9: Creating the Signatures

Each of the double-sided sheets had to be folded three times (vertically, horizontally, and then vertically again) in order to create a small pamphlet, or "signature." Thirty-seven of these page sets, or "signatures," were needed in order to make just one Book of Mormon.

Step 10: Collating the Signatures

The thirty-seven signatures that made up the Book of Mormon's full text had to be collated and placed in their proper numerical order. Once this was done the gathered material formed a text-block.

Step 11: Pressing the Text-Blocks

The text-blocks had to be flattened out, and so they were taken over to a standing press. Here they were stacked (with boards or possibly some other material in between them) and subjected for several days to a substantial amount of compression.

Step 12: Channeling

Next, the text-blocks were transferred to a side press. With their spines toward the ceiling, and about an eighth of an inch of paper protruding above the level of the vise, a worker would take a small handsaw and cut four shallow channels across the text-block's horizontal axis.

Step 13: Sewing

In the sewing phase of this operation the text-blocks were taken to a small platform that had an attached framework, and they were laid flat on the platform. Two backing cords were tied along the vertical axis of the frame, and they corresponded in position to the two inside channels that were cut into the backs of the text-blocks. A very skilled artisan would weave pieces of string around the backing cords and through the four sets of small holes that were created by the cutting of the signature spines. By this step the thirty-seven individual signatures of the book were united as one large whole.

Step 14: Attaching the Endsheets

An endsheet was a thick piece of paper that had been folded once down the center; it was exactly twice the width of the text-block. Two of these sheets were attached with wheat-starch or possibly rice-starch glue to each side of a text-block. They were only attached, however, by a one-eighth-inch swath of glue located at the spine of the block.

Step 15: Rounding and Backing

In the "rounding and backing" phase of the binding process, a person would place the text-block in a floor vise and beat the spine with a large-headed hammer. This action evened out the signatures in relation to each other and also flared the edges of those that were positioned on the outside. This flaring played a role in the way that the block was secured within the book cover. At this point some book manufacturers would smear glue across the entire spine area of the block in order to ensure that all of the signatures would stay in their proper place.

Step 16: Trimming

A tool called a "plane and plow" was the next to be employed. This viselike piece of equipment held the text-block in place while a worker pushed and pulled a razor-sharp blade across its edges. The blade was not very long and so only a few of the signature sections could be cut with each pass. As a consequence, continual adjustments had to be made to the blade's position until each side of the text-block was completely trimmed. The trimming of the front and top portions of the signatures had the effect of splitting their pages apart. The bottom edges were also trimmed so that all of the sheets were uniform in size.

Step 17: Attaching the Super

The next step in the binding process was the attachment of an object called a "super." This was a piece of cloth that was used to reinforce the book hinge. It was glued about one-half of an inch on the outside of the endsheets.

Step 18: Attaching the Book Cover

The book covers for the first edition of the Book of Mormon were made out of sheepskin, and they matched the general appearance of some early-nineteenth-century Bibles. To make these covers (or "cases," as they were sometimes called) a rectangular piece of leather was laid down with its outer side toward the table. Two binder boards (which were the same dimensions as the text-block and of substantial thickness) were then glued in predesignated areas, and the excess leather was folded over and glued onto the boards.

Step 19: Connecting the Block and Cover

The next step carried out in the bindery was the connection of the text-block to the book cover. In order to accomplish this task the text-block was inserted into the space between the cover's binder boards and then the entire outside surfaces of the endsheets were glued directly to the boards.

Step 20: Decorating the Spine

The spine of the 1830 edition of the Book of Mormon was decorated with several elements. First, it was embossed with a series of gold double-line patterns. These were applied by heating a device called a "rule," placing gold foil facedown over the book spine, and then running the rule over the foil. The spine also sported a hand-painted black leather label that had the words "Book of Mormon" embossed upon it in gold lettering.

With the completion of this last step in the printing and binding processes the Book of Mormon was ready to be made available to the public.

NOTES TO APPENDIX 3

1. Lavina F. Anderson, ed., *Lucy's Book: A Critical Edition of Lucy Mack Smith's Family Memoir* (Salt Lake City: Signature Books, 2001), 459–60.
2. John H. Gilbert, "Memorandum," 8 September 1892, Palmyra, New York, 2, cited in Royal Skousen, "John Gilbert's 1892 Account of the 1830 Printing of the Book of Mormon," in Stephen D. Ricks, Donald W. Parry, and Andrew H. Hedges, eds., *The Disciple as Witness: Essays on Latter-day Saint History and Doctrine in Honor of Richard Lloyd Anderson* (Provo, Utah: FARMS, 2000), 383–405.
3. Pomeroy Tucker, *Origin, Rise, and Progress of Mormonism* (New York City: D. Appleton and Co., 1867), 53.
4. Gilbert, "Memorandum," 3.
5. Tucker, *Origin, Rise, and Progress of Mormonism*, 53.
6. Gilbert, "Memorandum," 3.
7. See ibid., 2.
8. See *Detroit Post and Tribune*, 3 December 1877.
9. Gilbert, "Memorandum," 2–3.
10. Ibid., 2.
11. John H. Gilbert to James T. Cobb, 10 February 1879, New York Public Library, New York City, New York.
12. Gilbert, "Memorandum," 3.
13. See ibid.
14. Ibid., 2.
15. Ibid., 4. David Whitmer states that "when [the Book of Mormon was] being printed, Oliver Cowdery would . . . proofread and see that the work was done properly, and continued his vigil to the end" (*Saints' Herald*, vol. 31, 21 June 1884).
16. These figures are arrived at in the following manner: 37 signatures (x) 16 pages per signature = 592 pages per book [590 printed / 2 blank]. 592 pages per book (x) 5,000 copies of the book = 2,960,000 total printed pages (32 pages per double-sided sheet (x) 92,500 sheets = 2,960,000 total printed pages). This

means that the press arm had to be pulled by the shop's workers at least 185,000 times in order to create the first edition of the Book of Mormon—not counting errors.

APPENDIX 4

THE SPALDING-RIGDON THEORY

Soon after Joseph Smith publicly announced that the Book of Mormon was an ancient and divinely-revealed scriptural text, people began to put forward a variety of theories about what they thought was its "true" origin. Alexander Campbell, for instance, wrote in February 1831: "I could swear that this book was written by one man. And as Joseph Smith is . . . called *the author* on the title page, I cannot doubt for a single moment that he is the sole author and proprietor of it. . . . [It is] certainly Smith's fabrication."[1] In the same month of the same year, however, it was reported in the *Cleveland Advertiser* that some people believed that Sidney Rigdon—a recent convert to the Church—was the person who actually wrote the Book of Mormon.[2]

By 1833 a new version of the Rigdon theory began to take shape. On 3 June of that year, a man named Philastus Hurlbut was excommunicated from the Church for "un-Christian conduct with women" while serving as a missionary.[3] He was granted an appeal on 21 June 1833, and after offering a liberal confession he was reinstated.[4] Two days later, however, he was excommunicated again because he boasted that he had "deceived Joseph Smith's God" in getting himself restored to Church membership.[5]

Sometime after his second excommunication, Philastus joined forces with an Ohio anti-Mormon committee whose stated purpose was to "ascertain the real origin of the Book of Mormon."[6] Benjamin Johnson reports that while Hurlbut was serving as a missionary around the Jacksonville, Pennsylvania, area he had "learned of Solomon Spa[lding], who once lived in that vicinity, and had written a romance called 'Manuscript Found,' and out of this [Hurlbut] hoped to gain notoriety, obtain money, and work his spite upon the Mormons. So he gave notice to [the] enemies [of the Saints] that he had struck a lead to destroy Mormonism, and if they would come together he would tell them where 'Joe Smith' got his 'Mormon Bible.'"[7] The components of Hurlbut's theory regarding the origin of the Book of Mormon were that

> the leading features of the "Gold Bible" were first conceived and concocted by one Solomon Spalding, while a resident of Conneaut, Ashtabula County, Ohio. . . .
>
> Solomon Spalding first wrote the leading incidents of the Book of Mormon [in a document called "Manuscript Found"], instead of its being found by the Smith family. . . .
>
> [T]he Book of Mormon is the joint production of Solomon Spalding and some other designing knave. . . .
>
> [M]ost of the names and leading incidents contained in the Mormon Bible, originated with Solomon Spalding. . . .
>
> [Jonathan H. Lambdin, a Pittsburg printer,] placed the "Manuscript Found," of Spalding, in the hands of [Sidney] Rigdon, to be embellished, altered, and added to, as he might think expedient. . . .
>
> When Lambdin died in 1826 Sidney Rigdon became the sole proprietor of the embellished and altered manuscript and he took it to Joseph Smith in order to "bring it before the world" because the Prophet had acquired a certain amount of "fame" and was skilled in the "arts of deception." . . .
>
> [Thus,] Sidney Rigdon . . . [was] the original "author and proprietor" of the whole Mormon conspiracy.[8]

Philastus claimed that his theory about Book of Mormon origins was supported by the written statements of people who had personally known Solomon Spalding[9] and had either heard the "Manuscript Found" document read to them by Spalding or had read it themselves about twenty years before.[10] Some of these people admitted that because of the substantial lapse in time between their acquaintance with the manuscript and their written statements their memories of the document's contents were not clear,[11] but they nevertheless recalled parallels between it and the "Gold Bible" after having *recently* read passages in the Book of Mormon.[12]

The Ohio anti-Mormon committee dispatched Hurlbut to meet with Spalding's widow, and if possible, he was to acquire "Manuscript Found" so they could publish it and expose the "true" origin of the Book of Mormon.[13] Hurlbut located the widow (Matilda Davison) in Monson, Massachusetts, and was told by her that Spalding's manuscript was kept in a trunk at the Hartwick, New York, residence of Jerome Clark. Hurlbut was given written permission to retrieve the manuscript from the trunk after he promised Spalding's widow that after it had been published he would return it to her and she would receive half of the profits generated by its publication.[14]

Spalding's daughter, Philastus Hurlbut, and a member of the Ohio anti-Mormon committee all publicly declared that the document Hurlbut retrieved from the trunk in Hartwick, New York, was Spalding's "Manuscript Found."[15] But when this document was shown to some of the people who had signed statements attesting to parallels between it and the Book of Mormon, they were unable to match their assertions with the document that was before them—the parallels simply weren't there.[16] At this point the anti-Mormon committee decided against publishing this document[17] and they then theorized that there must be another "lost" Spalding manuscript somewhere that contained parallels to the Book of Mormon.[18]

Solomon Spalding's manuscript was never returned to his widow in Monson, Massachusetts, but was stored somewhere in the Painesville, Ohio, print shop of Eber D. Howe. When Lewis L. Rice (an editor who worked with Howe in the *Painesville Telegraph* office) bought Howe's printing establishment in 1839 he unknowingly acquired the Spalding manuscript and eventually took it to Honolulu,

Hawaii, when he moved there. Rice discovered the document in 1884 while he was searching through his collection of papers at the request of Oberlin College president James H. Fairchild.[19] When Rice, Fairchild, and several other people made an initial comparison between the Spalding manuscript and the Book of Mormon they "could detect no resemblance between the two, in general or detail."[20]

LATTER-DAY SAINT REACTION
TO THE SPALDING-RIGDON THEORY

Several months after Philastus Hurlbut began to lecture on the Spalding-Rigdon theory Joseph Smith and Sidney Rigdon issued a brief, but formal response. In a First Presidency letter dated 9 January 1834 they said: "Philastus Hurlb[u]t, an apostate Elder from this Church, has been to the state of New York, and gathered up all the *ridiculous stories* that could be *invented,* and some affidavits respecting the character of Joseph [Smith] and the Smith family; and exhibited them to numerous congregations in Chagrin, Kirtland, Mentor, and Painesville; and he has fired the minds of the people with much indignation against Joseph and the Church."[21] But this was not the only time that these two men spoke out on this subject. In one Church publication, Joseph Smith made a connection between Hurlbut, *Mormonism Unvailed,* and "falsehood."[22] (*Mormonism Unvailed* [*sic*], the first anti-Mormon book, was ostensibly authored by Eber D. Howe, but much of the material for the book was provided by Hurlbut.) The Prophet also wrote in an epistle to some of the Saints in Jackson County, Missouri, that Hurlbut was "lying in a wonderful manner" in order to "spite" the Church.[23] Sidney Rigdon was less reserved. A letter that he sent to an Illinois newspaper not affiliated with the Church called the Spalding-Rigdon theory "a moonshine story" and a "batch of lies."[24] At one time Rigdon stood before a large gathering of people in Ohio and reportedly said:

> I testify in the presence of this congregation, and before God and all the holy angels up yonder, (pointing towards heaven), before whom I expect to give account at the judgment day, that I never saw a sentence of the Book of

Mormon, I never penned a sentence of the book, I never knew there was such a book in existence as the Book of Mormon, until it was presented to me by Parley P. Pratt, in the form that it is now in.[25]

Parley P. Pratt verified that he was "a personal actor in the scenes which brought S[idney] Rigdon into an acquaintance with the 'Book of Mormon.'" He relates: "About the 15th of October, 1830, I took my journey, in company with Elder O[liver] Cowdery, and Peter Whitmer, to Ohio. We called on Elder S[idney] Rigdon, and *then* for the *first* time, his eyes beheld the 'Book of Mormon'; I, myself, had the happiness to present it to him in person. He was much surprised, and it was with much persuasion and argument, that he was prevailed on to read it, and after he had read it he had a great struggle of mind before he fully believed and embraced it." Then, "early in 1831, Mr. Rigdon having been ordained, under our hands, visited Elder J[oseph] Smith, Jr. in the state of New York, for the first time."[26] Other Latter-day Saints, such as David Whitmer, Emma Smith, William Smith, Katherine Smith, and George A. Smith confirmed that Sidney Rigdon and Joseph Smith did not know each other until after the Book of Mormon had been published.[27]

The Three Witnesses of the Book of Mormon (David Whitmer, Oliver Cowdery, and Martin Harris) were each granted the privilege of receiving a sure knowledge of the divine authenticity of the Book of Mormon. Each of them had also served as scribes while the manuscript of the book was being produced. Because they had acted in this capacity each one of them was able to testify that "while [Joseph] Smith was dictating the translation he had no manuscript, notes or other means of knowledge save the seerstone and the characters as shown on the plates."[28] David Whitmer was even more specific in regard to the Spalding rumor. When he was asked, "Had Joseph Smith any manuscripts of any kind by him at the time of translating the Book of Mormon that he could read from? His answer was: 'No, sir. *We did not know anything about the Spa[l]ding manuscript at that time.*'"[29]

Oliver Cowdery didn't think that Hurlbut's "tales" were even worthy of a mention in the official Church newspaper and had "no fear" that he would "overturn the truth" regarding the origin of the

Book of Mormon.[30] Oliver knew the truth regarding this matter and he forthrightly affirmed, "I wrote, with my own pen, the entire Book of Mormon (save a few pages), as it fell from the lips of the Prophet Joseph Smith, as he translated it by the gift and power of God. . . . Sidney Rigdon did not write it. Mr. Spa[l]ding did not write it. I wrote it myself, as it fell from the lips of the Prophet."[31]

NOTES TO APPENDIX 4

1. *Millennial Harbinger,* vol. 2, no. 2, 7 February 1831, 93, 95; emphasis in original. Joseph Smith was listed on the title page of the first printing of the Book of Mormon as the "Author and Proprietor." For further reading on the reason for this designation, see Miriam A. Smith and John W. Welch, "Joseph Smith: 'Author and Proprietor,'" in John W. Welch, ed., *Reexploring the Book of Mormon* (Salt Lake City: Deseret Book; Provo, Utah: FARMS, 1992), 154–57. On the copyright document for the Book of Mormon—which refers twice in the preprinted text to "authors and proprietors"—Joseph Smith elected to claim his copyright as "author" even though in the description of the book that is also written on this document (from the Book of Mormon's title page) it clearly states that the text was derived from "an account written by the hand of Mormon upon plates" and the "interpretation" of the text was accomplished "by the gift and power of God."

2. See *Cleveland Advertiser,* vol. 1, no. 5, 15 February 1831.

3. Brigham H. Roberts, ed., *History of the Church,* rev. ed., 7 vols. (Salt Lake City: The Church of Jesus Christ of Latter-day Saints, 1932–1951), 1:352.

4. See ibid., 1:354.

5. Ibid., 1:355. Elder George A. Smith was present during Philastus Hurlbut's Church court and relates the following information about what happened. "The first Council I ever attended where the Prophet was present was at the trial of Doctor P[hilastus] Hurlb[u]t. This occurred in June, 1833. He had been cut off from the Church by the Bishop's Council, and a Council of twelve High Priests was organized to try the case on appeal. Hurlb[u]t did not deny the charge, but begged to be forgiven, made every promise that a man could make that he would from that day live a virtuous life. Finally the Council accepted of his confession, and agreed that he might on public confession be restored to the Church again. . . . As soon as this Council had made this deci-

sion upon Hurlb[u]t, Joseph arose and said to the Council, 'He is not honest, and what he has promised he will not fulfill; what he has confessed are not the thoughts and intents of his heart, and time will prove it.' Hurlb[u]t stated to the Branch in Thompson, Ohio that he had deceived Joseph Smith's God or the spirit by which he is actuated, 'I have proved that Council has no wisdom. I told them I was sorry; I confessed and they believed it to be an honest confession; I deceived the whole of them and made them restore me to the Church'" (George D. Watt, comp., *Journal of Discourses,* 26 vols. (London: F. D. and S. W. Richards and Sons, 1854–1886), 11:8).

6.   *Painesville Telegraph,* vol. 5, no. 33, 31 January 1834.

7.   Benjamin F. Johnson, *My Life's Review* (Independence, Mo.: Zion's Printing and Publishing, 1947), 24–25. Hurlbut apparently first heard about Solomon Spalding's "Manuscript Found" from the Jackson family and others who had known Spalding personally. But when Hurlbut asked Mr. Jackson to sign an affidavit stating that there were similarities between Spalding's manuscript and the Book of Mormon he refused, insisting that "there was no agreement between them" and "express[ing] his indignation and contempt" for Hurlbut's "base and wicked project to deceive the public" (Benjamin Winchester, *The Origin of the Spaulding Story* [Philadelphia: Brown, Bicking, and Guilpert, 1840], 8–9).

8.   Eber D. Howe, *Mormonism Unvailed* (Painesville, Ohio: Telegraph Press, 1834), 278, 287, 288, 289, 290. Joseph Smith stated in an 1835 newspaper article that Eber D. Howe was "the illegitimate author of 'Mormonism Unv[a]iled,'" while Philastus Hurlbut was "the legitimate author of the same." The Prophet explained that Howe was listed as the book's author "in order to give currency to the publication, as Mr. Hurlb[u]t, about [the] time [of publication], was bound over to court, for threatening life"—namely the Prophet's (*Messenger and Advocate,* vol. 2, no. 15, December 1835, 228). The Prophet wrote in another publication that Hurlbut "was author of a book which bears the name of E. D. Howe, but it was this said Hurlb[u]t that was the author of it. But after the affair of Hurlb[u]t's wife and the pious old deacon, the persecutors [i.e., the Ohio anti-Mormon committee] thought it better to put some other name as author to their book than Hurlb[u]t, so E. D. Howe substituted his name" (*Elders' Journal,* vol. 1, no. 4, August 1838, 59–60). George A. Smith tells the same story. Hurlbut "went to work and got up the 'Spaulding story'—that famous yarn about the 'Manuscript Found.' When about to publish this lying fabrication, in several of his exciting speeches

having threatened the life of Joseph Smith, he was required to give bonds, by the authorities of Ohio, to keep the peace. In consequence of this, the name of E. D. Howe was substituted as the author, who published it" (*Journal of Discourses,* 7:113; see also 11:9–10). Sidney Rigdon relates, "Before Hu[r]lb[u]t got through, his conduct became so scandalous, that the company utterly refused to let his name go out with the lies which he had collected, and he and his associates had made; and they substituted the name of E. D. Howe" (*Quincy Whig,* vol. 2, no. 6, 8 June 1839). John C. Dowen notes, "Hurlbut sta[yed] at my house every three or four days for as many months. I read all of his manuscript. . . . Hurlbut let E. D. Howe, of Painesville, have his manuscript to publish" (Sworn statement, 2 January 1885, published in A. B. Deming Society, *Naked Truths About Mormonism,* vol. 2, no. 1, December 1988, 1).

9.　There are alternate spellings for the name Spalding. This spelling has been determined to be the most accurate.

10.　"Spalding had read to me more than twenty years before" (Howe, *Mormonism Unvailed,* 282); "I read and heard read, more than 20 years ago" (ibid., 281); "I read and heard read from the writings of Spalding, more than twenty years ago" (ibid., 284); "more than twenty years before" (ibid., 285); "through the lapse of 22 years" (ibid., 287). Orson Hyde served as Philastus Hurlbut's missionary companion, and he made these insightful remarks: "In the spring of 1832 I preached in New Salem, Ohio; the place where Rev. Mr. Sp[a]lding resided at the time he wrote his romance, though he was not residing there at the time I preached there. I raised up a branch of the Church at that place, and baptized many of Mr. Sp[a]lding's old neighbors; but they never intimated to me that there was any similarity between the Book of Mormon and Mr. Sp[a]lding's romance; neither did I hear such an intimation from any quarter until the immoral Hu[r]lb[u]t, a long time after, in connection with some very pious ministers, such, perhaps, as Mr. Storrs and Mr. Austin, brought forth the idea. I then went to these neighbors of Mr. Sp[a]lding and inquired of them if they knew anything about his writing a romance; and if so, whether the romance was anything like the Book of Mormon. They said that Mr. Sp[a]lding wrote a book, and that they frequently heard him read the manuscript; but that anyone should say that it was like the Book of Mormon, was most surprising, and must be the last pitiful resort that the devil had" (Orson Hyde to George J. Adams, 7 June 1841, published in John E. Page, *The Spaulding Story* [Pittsburgh: Gospel Light Press, 1843], 11).

11. "The lapse of time which has intervened, prevents my recollecting but few of the leading incidents of [Spalding's] writings" (Howe, *Mormonism Unvailed,* 280); "the general features of the story have passed from my memory" (ibid., 287).

12. "I have recently read the Book of Mormon" (ibid., 280); "I have read the Book of Mormon, which has brought fresh to my recollection" (ibid., 281); "Some months ago I borrowed the Golden Bible" (ibid., 282); "I have recently examined the Book of Mormon" (ibid., 283); "I obtained the [Book of Mormon], and on reading it . . ." (ibid., 285); "I have lately read the Book of Mormon" (ibid., 286); "The Mormon Bible I have partially examined" (ibid., 287).

13. "Mr. Howe, did you send Hurlb[u]t to get The Manuscript Found? 'Yes, I did, and the idea was proposed to me by him'" (Ellen E. Dickinson, *New Light on Mormonism* [New York: Funk and Wagnalls, 1885], 73).

14. See the Matilda Spalding (McKinstry) statement in *Scribner's Monthly,* vol. 20, no. 4, August 1880, 615; Matilda Spalding (Davison) statement in the *Quincy Whig,* vol. 2, no. 29, 16 November 1839; John A. McKinstry to James T. Cobb, 2 June 1879, Theodore A. Schroeder Papers, Special Collections, University of Wisconsin Library, Madison.

15. • *Evidence from Spalding's daughter that Philastus Hurlbut took possession of Solomon Spalding's "Manuscript Found":*

    Matilda Spalding (McKinstry): "[A] man named Hurlb[u]t came to my house at Monson [Massachusetts] to see my mother, who told us that he had been sent by a committee to procure the 'Manuscript Found' written by the Rev. Solomon Sp[a]lding, so as to compare it with the Mormon Bible. He presented a letter to my mother from my uncle, W[illiam] H. Sabine, of Onondaga Valley, in which he requested her to loan this manuscript to Hurlb[u]t, as he (my uncle) was desirous 'to uproot' (as he expressed it) 'this Mormon fraud.' Hurlb[u]t represented that. . . through the 'Manuscript Found' [he] wished to expose [Mormonism's] wickedness. My mother . . . reluctantly consented to his request. The old trunk, containing the desired 'Manuscript Found,' she had placed in the care of Mr. Jerome Clark of Hartwicks, [New York,] when she came to Monson, [Massachusetts]— intending to send for it. On the repeated promise of Hurlb[u]t to return the manuscript to us, she gave him a letter to Mr. Clark to open the trunk and deliver it to him. We afterwards heard that he had received it from Mr. Clark at Hartwicks, [New York]" (*Scribner's Monthly,* vol. 20, no. 4, August 1880, 615).

• *Evidence from Philastus Hurlbut that he had possession of Solomon Spalding's "Manuscript Found":*

"P[hilastus] Hurlb[u]t, of Kirtland, Ohio, who has been engaged for some time in different parts of this state, but chiefly in this neighborhood, on behalf of his fellow-townsmen, in the pursuit of facts and information concerning the origin and design of the Book of Mormon, . . . requests us to say that *he has succeeded in accomplishing the object of his mission,* and that an authentic history of the whole affair will shortly be given to the public. The original manuscript of the Book [of Mormon] was written some thirty years since by a respectable clergyman, now deceased, whose name we are not permitted to give [i.e., Solomon Spalding]. It was designed to be published as a romance, but the author died soon after it was written; and hence the plan failed. The pretended religious character of the work has been superadded by some more modern hand believed to be the notorious [Sidney] Rigdon" (*Wayne Sentinel*, vol. 11, no. 14, 20 December 1833; emphasis added).

"Mr. Hurlb[u]t, did you get the manuscript from Mrs. Davison? . . . '[Y]es, I got one she gave me an order for.' . . . Did you get 'The Manuscript Found' at her order in Hartwick, New York from Jerome Clark? 'Yes, I got what they said was Spa[l]ding's manuscript'" (Dickinson, *New Light on Mormonism*, 65–66).

"In a letter written to J. E. Gaston in 1842, Mrs. Dav[i]son says that shortly after Hurlbut left Munson [Massachusetts] with the order from her to get the manuscript of the 'Manuscript Found' from the trunk at Mr. Clark's at Hartwicke, N[ew] Y[ork], she received a letter from Hurlbut, in which he told her that he had obtained from the trunk what he had come for, the manuscript of 'Manuscript Found'" (Clark Braden, *Braden-Kelley Debate* [St. Louis: Clark Braden, 1884], 95–96).

John C. Dowen: "I heard . . . P[hilastus] Hurlbut . . . deliver his first lecture . . . on the origin of the Book of Mormon. He said he had been in New York and Pennsylvania and had obtained a copy of Sp[a]lding's Manuscript Found. He read selection[s] from it. . . . Hurlbut sta[yed] at my house every three or four days for as many months. I read all of his manuscript, including Sp[a]lding's Manuscript Found" (Sworn statement, 2 January 1885, published in A. B. Deming Society, *Naked Truths About Mormonism*, vol. 2, no. 1, December 1988, 1).

V. I. Pickdew: "Hurlb[u]t . . . stated in my hearing at a public meeting . . . that he had obtained MSS [F]ound, it was in Sp[a]lding's [hand]writing" (Statement, 6 September 1884, published in the *Independent Patriot*, vol. 6, no. 31, 25 June 1891).

Alexander Phelps: "Heard Hurlb[u]t lecture on . . . [the] origin of Mormonism. He showed the audience a copy of MSS [F]ound which he obtained in New York, and read from it" (Statement, 1 November 1884, published in the *Independent Patriot,* vol. 6, no. 32, 2 July 1891).

William R. Hine: "I heard Hurlbut lecture in . . . Kirtland. He said he *would,* and *he did* prove that the 'Book of Mormon' was founded on a fiction called 'Manuscript Found,' written by Solomon Spa[l]ding. . . . Hurlbut had a copy of Spaulding's 'Manuscript Found' with him" (Undated statement, published in Arthur B. Deming, *Naked Truths About Mormonism,* vol. 1, no. 1, January 1888, 2; emphasis in original).

C. Morse: "Was present and heard Hurlb[u]t lecture in a church. He said he had obtained Mss[.] [F]ound someplace in New York. Said he held it in his hands, and held it up before the audience, and read portions of it" (Undated sworn statement, published in the *Independent Patriot,* vol. 6, no. 31, 25 June 1891).

Jacob Sherman: "Myself and wife attended Hurlbut's lecture on Mormonism. . . . He said he had been to New York and obtained a copy of the fiction written by Solomon Spa[l]ding called 'Manuscript Found.' He read from it" (Sworn statement, 24 February 1885, published in Arthur B. Deming, *Naked Truths About Mormonism,* vol. 1, no. 2, April 1888, 3).

Charles Grover: "I heard D. P. Hurlbut lecture on the origin of the 'Book of Mormon' in the Willoughby town hall in 1833 or 1834. He said that the object of his lecture was to show that the 'Book of Mormon' was founded on a fiction written by Solomon Spa[l]ding at Conneaut, O[hio], in the early part of the century, which he called 'Manuscript Found.' He said he had been to Pittsburgh, P[ennsylvania] and learned that Sidney Rigdon had stolen it from the printing office where it was left to be printed. He had obtained another copy from which he read selections" (Sworn statement, 5 March 1885, published in Arthur B. Deming, *Naked Truths About Mormonism,* vol. 1, no. 2, April 1888, 3).

• *Evidence from a member of the Ohio anti-Mormon committee that Philastus Hurlbut had possession of Solomon Spalding's "Manuscript Found":*

James A. Briggs: "In the winter of 1833–34, a self-constituted committee of citizens of Willoughby, Mentor, and Painesville met a number of times at the house of the late Mr. Warren Corning, of Mentor, to investigate the Mormon humbug. At one of the meetings we had before us the original manuscript of the Rev. Solomon Sp[a]lding. . . . It was entitled . . . 'The Manuscript

Found.' . . . From this work of the Rev. Mr. Sp[a]lding the Mormon Bible was constructed. I do not think there can be any doubt of this. It was the opinion of the committee after comparing the Mormon Bible with the manuscript. The style of composition, the names, etc., were the same" (James A. Briggs to John Codman, letter, March 1875, in *International Review,* vol. 11, no. 3, September 1881, 222).

James A. Briggs: "In the winter of 1833–34 several gentlemen in Willoughby, Painesville, and Mentor formed themselves into a committee to inquire into the origin of the Mormon Bible. Of the members of the committee in Willoughby were Judge Allen, Dr. and Samuel Wilson, Jonathon Lapham, and myself. . . . They employed a man by the name of Hu[r]lbut, who was once a Mormon, to help in the investigation. . . . We compared ['The Manuscript Found'] with the Mormon Bible, and the names and language and style of the Bible were so like the manuscript that all were convinced that the 'Mormon Bible' was made out of this manuscript of Spalding. A number of letters were received from those who had known Mr. Spalding, and from all the facts obtained tended to convince the committee that Sidney Rigdon, when he lived in Pittsburgh, copied 'The Manuscript Found' and from it made the Mormon Bible" (James A. Briggs, letter, 19 January 1884, in *Cleveland Leader,* vol. 37, January 1884).

James A. Briggs: "In the winter of 1833–34, a self-constituted committee, consisting of Judge Allen, Dr. Card, Samuel Wilson, Judge Latham, W. Corning and myself, met at Mr. Corning's house, in Mentor, now known as the Garfield Farm, to investigate Mormonism and the origin of the Mormon Bible. Dr. D. P. Hurlbut . . . was employed to look up testimony. He was present with the committee and had Sp[a]lding's original manuscript with him. We compared it, chapter by chapter, with the Mormon Bible. It was written in the same style; many of the names were the same, and we came to the conclusion, from all the testimony before us, that the Rev. Sidney Rigdon, the eloquent Mormon preacher, made the Mormon Bible from this manuscript. Of this the committee had no doubt whatever. . . . In 1879, Dr. Hurlbut was living at Gibbsonburgh, Ohio. In a letter to Mr. Patterson, of Pittsburg, he says: 'I gave the manuscript with all my other documents connected with Mormonism to Mr. Howe.' Mr. Rice was the successor of Mr. Howe in *The Telegraph* [office], and this accounts for his possession of the '[M]anuscript [F]ound' at this late day in an island in the Pacific Ocean [i.e., Hawaii]" (Letter to the editor, 29 January 1886, in *New York Tribune,* 31 January 1886).

• *Textual evidence that the Oberlin College manuscript is, in fact, Solomon Spalding's "Manuscript Found":*

There is one piece of compelling evidence that the Oberlin Manuscript discovered by Lewis L. Rice in 1884 is indeed Solomon Spalding's "Manuscript Found." Matilda Davison (Solomon Spalding's widow) and Artemas Cunningham (one of the *Mormonism Unvailed* "witnesses") report that "Manuscript Found" "purported to have been a record found buried in the earth, or in a cave" (Howe, *Mormonism Unvailed,* 286). "It claimed . . . to have been *recovered from the earth,* and, assumed the title of 'Manuscript Found'" (*Boston Recorder,* vol. 24, no. 16, 19 April 1839; emphasis in original). The Oberlin Manuscript specifically states at its outset that its contents were derived from "manuscripts" that were "found" in a "cave" (Rex C. Reeve Jr., ed., *Manuscript Found: The Complete Original "Spaulding" Manuscript* [Provo, Utah: BYU Religious Studies Center, 1996], 1).

16. See Howe, *Mormonism Unvailed,* 288.

17. Spalding's widow received a letter from a member of the anti-Mormon committee informing her that her late husband's manuscript "did not read as they expected," and they therefore had decided against publishing it (*Quincy Whig,* vol. 2, no. 29, 16 November 1839; reprinted in *Times and Seasons,* vol. 1, no. 3, January 1840, 47).

18. Howe, *Mormonism Unvailed,* 290.

19. See Ebenezer Robinson, autobiography, L. Tom Perry Special Collections Library, Harold B. Lee Library, Brigham Young University, Provo, Utah, 57.

20. *New York Observer,* 5 February 1885.

21. *History of the Church,* 1:475; emphasis added.

22. *Messenger and Advocate,* vol. 2, no. 3, December 1835, 228.

23. Dean C. Jessee, ed., *The Personal Writings of Joseph Smith,* rev. ed. (Salt Lake City: Deseret Book, 2002), 311.

24. *Quincy Whig,* vol. 2, no. 6, 8 June 1839. This lengthy letter is notable for how many times it refers to the Spalding-Rigdon theory as a lie.

25. Phineas Bronson, Hiel Bronson, and Mary Bronson to Joseph Smith III, 14 March 1872, Princeville, Illinois. In 1865 Sidney Rigdon's son, John W. Rigdon, interviewed his father in regard to the origin of the Book of Mormon. John said to his father:

> "You have been charged with writing that book and giving it to Joseph Smith to introduce to the world. You have always told me one story; that you never saw the book until it was presented to you by

Parley P. Pratt and Oliver Cowdery; and all you ever knew of the origin of that book was what they told you and what Joseph Smith and the witnesses who claimed to have seen the plates had told you. Is this true? If so, all right; if it is not, you owe it to me and to your family to tell it. You are an old man, and you will soon pass away, and I wish to know if Joseph Smith, in your intimacy with him for four-teen years, has not said something to you that led you to believe he obtained that book in some other way than what he had told you. Give me all you know about it, that I may know the truth."

My father, after I had finished saying what I have repeated above, looked at me a moment, raised his hand above his head and slowly said, with tears glistening in his eyes: "My son, I can swear before high heaven that what I have told you about the origin of that book is true. Your mother and sister, Mrs. Athalia Robinson, were present when that book was handed to me in Mentor, Ohio, and all I ever knew about the origin of that book was what Parley P. Pratt, Oliver Cowdery, Joseph Smith and the witnesses who claimed they saw the plates have told me, and in all of my intimacy with Joseph Smith he never told me but one story, and that was that he found it engraved upon gold plates in a hill near Palmyra, New York, and that an angel had appeared to him and directed him where to find it; and I have never, to you or to anyone else, told but the one story, and that I now repeat to you." I believed him, and now believe he told me the truth. He also said to me after[ward] that Mormonism was true, that Joseph Smith was a prophet, and this world would find it out some day.

After my father's death, my mother, who survived him several years was in the enjoyment of good health up to the time of her last sickness, she being eighty-six years old. A short time before her death I had a conversation with her about the origin of the Book of Mormon and wanted to know what she remembered about its being presented to my father. She said to me in that conversation that what my father had told me was true, about the book being presented to him, for she was present at the time and knew that was the first time he ever saw it, and that the stories told about my father writing the Book of Mormon were not true." (Brigham H. Roberts, *A Comprehensive History of The Church of Jesus Christ of Latter-day Saints,* 6 vols. [Salt Lake City: Deseret News Press, 1930], 1:233–35.)

David Whitmer emphatically affirmed that he "heard [Sidney] Rigdon, in the pulpit and in private conversations, declare that the Sp[a]lding story—that he had used a book called 'The Manuscript Found' for the purpose of preparing the 'Book of Mormon'—was as false as were many other charges that were then being made against the infant Church, and [Whitmer] assures [his interviewer] that the story is as untruthful as it is ridiculous" (*Chicago Times,* 17 October 1881).

26. Parley P. Pratt, *Mormonism Unveiled,* 2nd ed. (New York: Orson Pratt and Elijah Fordham, 1838), 40, 41, 42; emphasis in original. In an interview with Elmira College President A. W. Cowles, Sidney Rigdon "solemnly affirm[ed]" that when he received a copy of the Book of Mormon from Oliver Cowdery and his missionary companions in late 1830, it "was his *first* personal knowledge of Joe Smith and the Mormons" (*Moore's Rural New Yorker,* vol. 20, no. 4, 23 January 1869; emphasis added). An article in the Church's official newspaper states that when Parley P. Pratt, Ziba Peterson, Oliver Cowdery, and Peter Whitmer Jr. presented Sidney Rigdon with a copy of the Book of Mormon, it was "*the first time* he had ever heard of or seen" it. The missionaries told him that "it was a revelation from God," but Sydney "felt very much prejudiced at the assertion" and said that he had "considerable doubt" with regard to their claim. Rigdon declined to debate the missionaries about the divine origin of the Book of Mormon but promised to read it and give it "a full investigation." Rigdon pondered on the things that he had heard from the missionaries and the things that he had read in the book and prayed to God for direction. After two weeks he became "fully convinced of the truth of the work" because he received "a revelation from Jesus Christ, which was made known to him in a remarkable manner" (*Times and Seasons,* vol. 4, no. 19, 15 August 1843, 289–90; emphasis added). This particular revelation is described in an early newspaper account. Sidney, it is said, decided that "he must 'receive a testimony from God.' In order to [obtain] this, he labored as he was directed by his Preceptor [teacher, instructor, tutor], almost incessantly and earnestly in praying, till at length, his mind was wrapped up in a vision; and to use his own language, 'to my astonishment I saw the different orders of professing Christians passing before my eyes, with their hearts exposed to view, and they were as corrupt as corruption itself. That society to which I belonged also passed before my eyes, and to my astonishment, it was as corrupt as the others. Last of all that little man [Parley P. Pratt] who brought me the Book of Mormon, passed before my eyes with his heart open, and it was as pure as an

angel: and this was a testimony from God, that the Book of Mormon was a divine revelation'" (*Ohio Star*, vol. 2, no. 49, 8 December 1831).

27. David Whitmer: "Neither Joseph Smith, Oliver Cowdery, Martin Harris or myself ever met Sidney Rigdon until after the Book of Mormon was in print. I know this of my own personal knowledge, being with Joseph Smith, in Seneca County, N[ew] Y[ork], in the winter of 1830, when Sidney Rigdon and Edward Partridge came from Kirtland, Ohio, to see Joseph Smith, and where Rigdon and Partridge saw Joseph Smith *for the first time* in their lives. The Sp[a]lding manuscript story is a myth" (David Whitmer, *An Address to All Believers in Christ* [Richmond, Mo.: David Whitmer, 1887], 11; emphasis added).

Joseph Smith III: Emma Smith "informs me that . . . she never saw, or knew any Sidney Rigdon until long after the Book of Mormon was translated, and she thinks, published. . . . [She] further states that she knew the Pratts before she knew Rigdon, and it is quite positive that Joseph Smith became acquainted with him through the Pratts, one or both [i.e., Parley and Orson]. . . . [She] is certain of the fact, that acquaintance with them preceded acquaintance . . . with S[idney] Rigdon" (Joseph Smith III to James T. Cobb, 14 February 1879, Joseph Smith III Letterbook, no. 2, p. 6, Community of Christ Archives, Independence, Mo.).

William Smith: The Book of Mormon "was not written from the Sp[a]lding romance. That story is false. Some say this romance was stolen by Sidney Rigdon while at Pittsburg. This is false. Sidney Rigdon knew nothing about it. He never saw or heard tell of the Book of Mormon until it was presented to him by P[arley] P. Pratt and others. He was never at my father's house to see my brother until after the book was published" (*Saints' Herald*, vol. 31, no. 40, 4 October 1884, 643–44).

Katherine Smith: "[P]rior to the latter part of the year A.D. 1830, there was no person who visited with, or was an acquaintance of, or called upon the [Smith] family, or any member thereof to my knowledge, by the name of Sidney Rigdon; nor was such person known to the family, or any member thereof, to my knowledge, until the last part of the year A.D. 1830, or the first part of the year 1831, and some time after the organization of the Church of Jesus Christ, by Joseph Smith, Jr., and several months after the publication of the Book of Mormon" (Sworn statement, 15 April 1881, published in Francis W. Kirkham, *A New Witness for Christ in America* [Independence, Mo.: Zion's Printing and Publishing, 1942], 1:315–16).

George A. Smith: "[I]t is very well known that there had no connection ever existed between these parties" (*Journal of Discourses*, 11:9).

28. *Chicago Times,* 17 October 1881. This source specifically states that each of the Three Witnesses made this declaration. In connection with this statement is one made by Emma Smith to her son. She said, "the larger part of [the translation] was done in her presence, and where she could see and know what was being done; that during no part of it . . . did Joseph Smith have any [manuscripts] or book of any kind from which to read, or dictate, except the metallic plates" (Joseph Smith III to James T. Cobb, 14 February 1879).

29. *Saints' Herald,* vol. 29, no. 12, 15 June 1882; emphasis added. David Whitmer also "states that Elder Sidney Rigdon was not known to the Elders of the Church until long after the Book of Mormon was issued; and that of his knowledge Elder Rigdon had nothing to do with the manuscript of the Book of Mormon; that he was familiar with Joseph Smith, the methods of translation, and the circumstances connected with it and the publishing of the book, and from this acquaintance knows that the Spa[l]ding manuscript story is false and without a shadow of truth in it" (*Saints' Herald,* vol. 29, no. 9, 1 May 1882). "In regard to the statement that Sidney Rigdon had purloined the work of one Spa[l]ding, a Presbyterian preacher, who had written a romance entitled 'The Manuscript Found,' Mr. Whitmer says there is no foundation for such an assertion. The 'Book of Mormon' was translated in the summer of 1829, and printed that winter at Palmyra, N[ew] Y[ork] and was in circulation before Sidney Rigdon knew anything concerning the Church of Christ, as it was known then. His attention was especially brought to it by the appearance at his church, near Kirtland, O[hio], in the fall of 1830, of Parley Pratt and Oliver Cowdery, he being at the time a Reformed or Christian preacher, they having been sent west by the Church in New York during that summer as evangelists, and they carried with them the printed book, *the first time* that he knew such a thing was in existence" (*Chicago Times,* 17 October 1881; emphasis added). "Father Whitmer, who was present very frequently during the writing of [the Book of Mormon] manuscript, affirms that Joseph Smith had no book or manuscript before him from which he could have read as is asserted by some that he did, he (Whitmer) having every opportunity to know whether Smith had Solomon Spa[l]ding's or any other person's romance to read from. . . . [T]he supposition that the Rev. Solomon Spa[l]ding wrote the Book of Mormon is absurd and 'a weak invention of the enemy'" (*St. Louis Republican,* 16 July 1884).

30. *Evening and Morning Star,* vol. 2, no. 19, April 1834, 150.

31. Reuben Miller Journal, 21 October 1848, Historical Department Archives, The Church of Jesus Christ of Latter-day Saints, Salt Lake City, Utah, published in *Deseret News,* 13 April 1859.

SELECTED BIBLIOGRAPHY

SOURCES CITED

Books

Anderson, Lavina F., ed. *Lucy's Book: A Critical Edition of Lucy Mack Smith's Family Memoir*. Salt Lake City: Signature Books, 2001.

Backman, Milton V. Jr. *Eyewitness Accounts of the Restoration*. Orem, Utah: Grandin Book, 1983.

Braden, Clark. *Braden-Kelley Debate*. St. Louis: Clark Braden, 1884.

Cannon, Abraham H., ed. *Scraps of Biography*. Salt Lake City: Juvenile Instructor Office, 1883.

Cannon, George Q. *Young People's History of Joseph Smith*. Salt Lake City: George Q. Cannon and Sons, 1912.

Clark, John A. *Gleanings by the Way*. Philadelphia: W. J. and J. K. Simon, 1842.

Cook, Lyndon W. *The Revelations of the Prophet Joseph Smith*. Salt Lake City: Deseret Book, 1985.

Cowley, Matthias F. *Wilford Woodruff: His Life and Labors*. Salt Lake City: Deseret News Press, 1916.

Gates, Susa Young. *The Life Story of Brigham Young*. New York: Macmillan, 1930.

Howe, Eber D. *Mormonism Unvailed*. Painesville, Ohio: Telegraph Press, 1834.

Jessee, Dean C., ed. *The Personal Writings of Joseph Smith*. Rev. ed. Salt Lake City: Deseret Book, 2002.

Jenson, Andrew. *LDS Biographical Encyclopedia.* 4 vols. Salt Lake City: Andrew Jenson History Company, 1901–1936.

Johnson, Benjamin F. *My Life's Review.* Independence, Mo.: Zion's Printing and Publishing, 1947.

Kirkham, Francis W. *A New Witness for Christ in America.* 2 vols. Independence, Mo.: Zion's Printing and Publishing, 1942.

Ludlow, Daniel H., ed. *Encyclopedia of Mormonism.* 4 vols. New York: Macmillan, 1992.

Metcalf, Anthony. *Ten Years before the Mast.* Malad, Idaho: n.p., 1888.

Page, John E. *The Spaulding Story.* Pittsburgh: Gospel Light Press, 1843.

Pratt, Orson. *An Interesting Account of Several Remarkable Visions.* Edinburgh, Scotland: Ballantyne and Hughes, 1840.

———. *Divine Authority or the Question "Was Joseph Smith Sent of God?"* Liverpool, England: R. James, 1848.

Pratt, Parley P. *Mormonism Unveiled.* 2nd ed. New York: Orson Pratt and Elijah Fordham, 1838.

———. *Key to the Science of Theology.* Liverpool: F. D. Richards, 1855. Reprint, Salt Lake City: Deseret Book, 2002.

Proctor, Scot F., and Maurine J. Proctor, eds. *Autobiography of Parley P. Pratt.* Rev. ed. Salt Lake City: Deseret Book, 2000.

Reeve, Rex C., Jr., ed. *Manuscript Found: The Complete Original "Spaulding" Manuscript.* Provo, Utah: BYU Religious Studies Center, 1996.

Ricks, Eldin. *The Case of the Book of Mormon Witnesses.* Salt Lake City: Deseret News Press, 1971.

Roberts, Brigham H. *Life of John Taylor.* Salt Lake City: George Q. Cannon and Sons, 1892.

———, ed. *A Comprehensive History of The Church of Jesus Christ of Latter-day Saints.* 6 vols. Salt Lake City: Deseret News Press, 1930.

———, ed. *History of The Church of Jesus Christ of Latter-day Saints.* Rev. ed. 7 vols. Salt Lake City: The Church of Jesus Christ of Latter-day Saints, 1932–1951.

Shipps, Jan, and John W. Welch, eds. *The Journals of William E. McLellin: 1831–1836.* Provo, Utah: BYU Studies; Urbana: University of Illinois Press, 1994.

Smith, William B. *William Smith on Mormonism.* Lamoni, Iowa: Herald Steam Book and Job Office, 1883.

Tucker, Pomeroy. *Origin, Rise, and Progress of Mormonism.* New York: D. Appleton and Co., 1867.

Watt, George D., comp. *Journal of Discourses.* 26 vols. London: F. D. and S. W. Richards and Sons, 1854–1886.

Weed, Thurlow. *Autobiography of Thurlow Weed.* 2 vols. Boston: Houghton, Mifflin and Co., 1884.

Whitmer, David. *An Address to All Believers in Christ.* Richmond, Mo.: David Whitmer, 1887.

Winchester, Benjamin. *The Origin of the Spaulding Story.* Philadelphia: Brown, Bicking, and Guilpert, 1840.

Wymetal, Wilhelm R. von. *Joseph Smith the Prophet, His Family and His Friends.* Salt Lake City: Tribune Printing and Publishing, 1886.

Articles

Anderson, Richard L. "The Reliability of the Early History of Lucy and Joseph Smith." *Dialogue* 4, no. 2 (summer 1969): 13–28.

———. "The Organization Revelations." In Robert L. Millet and Kent P. Jackson, eds., *Studies in Scripture, Volume 1: The Doctrine and Covenants,* 109–18. Salt Lake City: Deseret Book, 1989.

Arts, Valentin. "A Third Jaredite Record: The Sealed Portion of the Gold Plates." *Journal of Book of Mormon Studies* 11, no. 1 (2002): 50–59.

Enders, Donald L. "The Joseph Smith, Sr., Family: Farmers of the Genesee." In Susan Easton Black and Charles D. Tate, Jr., eds., *Joseph Smith: The Prophet, The Man,* 213–25. Provo, Utah: BYU Religious Studies Center, 1993.

Faulring, Scott H. "The Book of Mormon: A Blueprint for Organizing the Church." *Journal of Book of Mormon Studies* 7, no. 1 (1998): 60–69, 71.

Hill, Marvin S. "Joseph Smith and the 1826 Trial: New Evidence and New Difficulties." *BYU Studies* 12, no. 2 (winter 1972): 223–33.

Jessee, Dean C. "Joseph Knight's Recollection of Early Mormon History." *BYU Studies* 17, no. 1 (fall 1976): 29–39.

Madsen, Gordon A. "Joseph Smith's 1826 Trial: The Legal Setting." *BYU Studies* 30, no. 2 (spring 1990): 91–107.

Porter, Larry C. "The Colesville Branch and the Coming Forth of the Book of Mormon." *BYU Studies* 10, no. 3 (spring 1970): 365–85.

———. "The Priesthood Restored." In Robert L. Millet and Kent P. Jackson, eds., *Studies in Scripture, Volume 2: The Pearl of Great Price*, 389–407. Salt Lake City: Randall Book, 1985.

Read, Lenet H. "Joseph Smith's Receipt of the Plates and the Israelite Feast of Trumpets." *Journal of Book of Mormon Studies* 2, no. 2 (fall 1993): 110–20.

Rich, Russell R. "The Dogberry Papers and the Book of Mormon." *BYU Studies* 10, no. 3 (spring 1970): 315–20.

Smith, Miriam A., and John W. Welch. "Joseph Smith: 'Author and Proprietor.'" In John W. Welch, ed., *Reexploring the Book of Mormon*, 154–56. Salt Lake City: Deseret Book; Provo, Utah: FARMS, 1992.

Tvedtnes, John A. "The Role of the Book of Mormon in the Restoration of the Church." Transcript. Provo, Utah: FARMS, 1997.

Woodford, Robert J. "The Articles and Covenants of the Church of Christ and the Book of Mormon." In H. Dean Garrett and Rex C. Reeve Jr., eds., *Doctrines for Exaltation*, 262–73. Salt Lake City: Deseret Book, 1989.

Periodicals

Boston Recorder
Catholic Telegraph
Chenango Union
Chicago Inter-Ocean
Chicago Times
Chicago Tribune
Cleveland Advertiser
Cleveland Leader

Contributor
Daily Iowa State Register
Deseret Evening News
Deseret News
Detroit Post and Tribune
Elders' Journal
Evangelical Magazine and Gospel Advocate
Evangelist
Evening and Morning Star
Fall River Herald
Fredonia Censor
Illinois Patriot
Improvement Era
Independent Patriot
International Review
Kansas City Journal
Kansas City Times
Le Roy Gazette
Messenger and Advocate
Millennial Harbinger
Millennial Star
Moore's Rural New Yorker
Morning Courier: New York Enquirer
New Hampshire Gazette
New York Observer
Observer and Telegraph
Ohio Observer
Ohio Star
Omaha Herald
Painesville Telegraph
Peoria Register and North-Western Gazetteer
Quincy Whig
Reflector
Republican Advocate
Saints' Herald
Salt Lake Herald
St. Louis Republican

Susquehanna Register
Tiffany's Monthly
Times and Seasons
Wayne Sentinel
Zion's Ensign

SOURCES CONSULTED

Books

Adams, George J. *Plain Facts Showing the Origin of the Spaulding Story.* Bedford, England: C. B. Merry, 1841.

Anderson, Richard L. *Investigating the Book of Mormon Witnesses.* Salt Lake City: Deseret Book, 1981.

Bradford, M. Gerald, and Alison V. P. Coutts, eds. *Uncovering the Original Text of the Book of Mormon: History and Findings of the Critical Text Project.* Provo, Utah: FARMS, 2002.

Brown, S. Kent, Donald Q. Cannon, and Richard H. Jackson, eds. *Historical Atlas of Mormonism.* New York: Simon and Schuster, 1994.

Bushman, Richard L. *Joseph Smith and the Beginnings of Mormonism.* Urbana: University of Illinois Press, 1984.

Conkling, J. Christopher. *A Joseph Smith Chronology.* Salt Lake City: Deseret Book, 1979.

Cook, Lyndon W., ed. *David Whitmer Interviews: A Restoration Witness.* Orem, Utah: Grandin Book, 1991.

McConkie, Mark L. *The Father of the Prophet: Stories and Insights from the Life of Joseph Smith, Sr.* Salt Lake City: Bookcraft, 1993.

Reynolds, George. *The Myth of the Manuscript Found or the Absurdities of the "Spaulding Story."* Salt Lake City: Juvenile Instructor Office, 1888.

Reynolds, Noel B., ed. *Book of Mormon Authorship Revisited: The Evidence for Ancient Origins.* Provo, Utah: FARMS, 1997.

Welch, John W., ed. *Reexploring the Book of Mormon: The FARMS Updates.* Salt Lake City: Deseret Book; Provo, Utah: FARMS, 1992.

Articles

Anderson, Richard L. "Reuben Miller, Recorder of Oliver Cowdery's Reaffirmations." *BYU Studies* 8, no. 3 (spring 1968): 277–93.

———. "The Impact of the First Preaching in Ohio." *BYU Studies* 11, no. 4 (summer 1971): 474–96.

———. "Gold Plates and Printer's Ink." *Ensign,* September 1976, 71–76.

———. "By the Gift and Power of God." *Ensign,* September 1977, 79–85.

———. "The Credibility of the Book of Mormon Translators." In Noel B. Reynolds, ed., *Book of Mormon Authorship: New Light on Ancient Origins,* 213–32. Provo, Utah: BYU Religious Studies Center, 1982.

———. "Did Oliver Cowdery, One of the Three Special Book of Mormon Witnesses, Express Doubt about His Testimony?" *Ensign,* April 1987, 23–25.

———. "Personal Writings of the Book of Mormon Witnesses." In Noel B. Reynolds, ed., *Book of Mormon Authorship Revisited: The Evidence for Ancient Origins,* 39–60. Provo, Utah: FARMS, 1997.

Arrington, Leonard J. "James Gordon Bennett's 1831 Report on 'The Mormonites.'" *BYU Studies* 10, no. 3 (spring 1970): 353–64.

Ashurst-McGee, Mark. "Moroni: Angel or Treasure Guardian?" *Mormon Historical Studies* 2, no. 2 (fall 2001): 39–75.

Black, Susan Easton. "Isaac Hale: Antagonist of Joseph Smith." In Larry C. Porter, Milton V. Backman Jr., and Susan Easton Black, eds., *Regional Studies in Latter-day Saint History: New York,* 92–108. Provo, Utah: BYU Department of Church History and Doctrine, 1992.

Bushman, Richard L. "The Recovery of the Book of Mormon." In Noel B. Reynolds, ed., *Book of Mormon Authorship Revisited: The Evidence for Ancient Origins,* 21–38. Provo, Utah: FARMS, 1997.

Carmack, John K. "Fayette: The Place the Church Was Organized." *Ensign,* February 1989, 14–19.

Enders, Donald L. "Two Significant Sites of the Restoration." *Ensign,* September 1998, 30–37.

Godfrey, Kenneth W. "'By the Gift and Power of God': The Remarkable Story of the Coming Forth of the Book of Mormon." In *A Symposium on the Book of Mormon.* Salt Lake City: The Church of Jesus Christ of Latter-day Saints, 1986, 57–65.

———. "A New Prophet and a New Scripture: The Coming Forth of the Book of Mormon." *Ensign,* January 1988, 6–13.

Hartley, William G. "The Knight Family: Ever Faithful to the Prophet." *Ensign,* January 1989, 43–49.

Hedges, Andrew H. "'All My Endeavors to Preserve Them': Protecting the Plates in Palmyra, 22 September–December 1827." *Journal of Book of Mormon Studies* 8, no. 2 (1999): 14–23, 84–85.

Horton, George A., Jr. "Book of Mormon—Transmission from Translator to Printed Text." In Paul R. Cheesman, ed., *The Book of Mormon: The Keystone Scripture,* 237–52. Provo, Utah: BYU Religious Studies Center 1988.

Jackson, Kent P. "The Appearance of Moroni to Joseph Smith." In Robert L. Millet and Kent P. Jackson, eds., *Studies in Scripture, Vol. 2: The Pearl of Great Price,* 336–63. Salt Lake City: Randall Book, 1985.

———. "Moroni's Message to Joseph Smith." *Ensign,* August 1990, 13–16.

Jenson, Janet. "Variations Between Copies of the First Edition of the Book of Mormon." *BYU Studies* 13, no. 2 (winter 1973): 214–22.

Jessee, Dean C. "The Original Book of Mormon Manuscripts." *BYU Studies* 10, no. 3 (spring 1970): 259–78.

Ord, Gayle G. "The Book of Mormon Goes to Press." *Ensign,* December 1972, 66–70.

Perkins, Keith W. "Thou Art Chosen Still." *Ensign,* January 1993, 15–19.

Peterson, H. Donl. "Moroni: Joseph Smith's Teacher." In Larry C. Porter, Milton V. Backman Jr., and Susan Easton Black, eds., *Regional Studies in Latter-day Saint History: New York,* 49–69. Provo, Utah: BYU Department of Church History and Doctrine, 1992.

Porter, Larry C. "William E. McLellin's Testimony of the Book of Mormon." *BYU Studies* 10, no. 4 (summer 1970): 485–87.

———. "Solomon Chamberlain—Early Missionary." *BYU Studies* 12, no. 3 (spring 1972): 314–18.

———. "From a Book Coming Forth." *Ensign,* July 1988, 42–46.

———. "The Book of Mormon: Historical Setting for Its Translation and Publication." In Susan Easton Black and Charles D. Tate Jr., eds., *Joseph Smith: The Prophet, the Man,* 49–64. Provo, Utah: BYU Religious Studies Center, 1993.

Reeve, Rex C., Jr. "The Book of Mormon Plates." In Monte S. Nyman and Charles D. Tate Jr., eds., *First Nephi: The Doctrinal Foundation.* Provo, Utah: BYU Religious Studies Center, 1988, 99–111.

Reeve, Rex C., Jr., and Richard O. Cowan. "The Hill Called Cumorah." In Larry C. Porter, Milton V. Backman Jr., and Susan Easton Black, eds., *Regional Studies in Latter-day Saint History: New York,* 71–89. Provo, Utah: BYU Department of Church History and Doctrine, 1992.

Rich, Russell R. "Where Were the Moroni Visits?" *BYU Studies* 10, no. 3 (spring 1970): 255–58.

Ricks, Stephen D. "Translation of the Book of Mormon: Interpreting the Evidence." *Journal of Book of Mormon Studies* 2, no. 2 (fall 1993): 201–206.

Roper, Matthew. "Comments on the Book of Mormon Witnesses." *Journal of Book of Mormon Studies* 2, no. 2 (fall 1993): 164–93.

Skousen, Royal. "How Joseph Smith Translated the Book of Mormon: Evidence from the Original Manuscript." *Journal of Book of Mormon Studies* 7, no. 1 (1998): 22–31.

———. "John Gilbert's 1892 Account of the 1830 Printing of the Book of Mormon." In Stephen D. Ricks, Donald W. Parry, and Andrew H. Hedges, eds., *The Disciple as Witness: Essays on Latter-day Saint History and Doctrine in Honor of Richard Lloyd Anderson,* 383–405. Provo, Utah: FARMS, 2000.

Tate, Charles D., Jr. "John H. Gilbert's Work on the Book of Mormon." In Larry C. Porter, Milton V. Backman Jr., and Susan Easton Black, eds., *Regional Studies in Latter-day Saint*

History: New York, 112–27. Provo, Utah: BYU Department of Church History and Doctrine, 1992.

Walker, Kyle R. "Katherine Smith Salisbury's Recollections of Joseph's Meeting with Moroni." *BYU Studies* 41, no. 3 (2002): 5–17.

INDEX